TANTRIC TRADITIONS

Gods, Rituals, & Esoteric Teachings in the Kali Yuga

MANTICORE PRESS

GWENDOLYN TAUNTON

·TANTRIC TRADITIONS:
Gods, Rituals, & Esoteric Teachings in the Kali Yuga
Gwendolyn Taunton

THEMA Classification:
QRBD (*Hinduism: Tantra*), QRDP (*Hindu Practice*), QRDF (*Hindu Sacred Texts*), QRYX2 (*Magic & Alchemy*), VXWM (*Magic & Alchemy*).
978-0-6482996-0-8

MANTICORE PRESS
WWW.MANTICOREPRESS.NET

Knowledge imparted to untrue disciples lacking devotion becomes impure like cow's milk mixed with dog's fat. If one initiates—out of fear, greed, or for monetary considerations—someone who is unfit, one invites the curses of deities and the act is futile.

Kulārṇava Tantra (14.17-18)

CONTENTS

PREFACE

Initially conceptualized in 2012, the creation of *Tantric Traditions* has been a long and laborious task, not only due to the nature of the research itself, but also due to the imposition of extraordinarily rare events. Due to these extreme circumstances I have been on a prolonged hiatus from writing. Perhaps these are karmic events, or perhaps not—but nonetheless the experience of unusual events is a factor which shapes our perception of the world, and when it is an extreme experience, the effect is much more pronounced than it is with normal experiences—birth, education, employment, and death etc. This is what the Tantric Traditions themselves teach us...that widening the range of experience can lead an individual towards greater wisdom.

Now that this process is finally over, I would like to thank Alexander Jacob for the editing and Mother Kālī's favorite son William Clark for kindly granting permission to use his artwork on the cover.

INTRODUCTION

Those who have lost the sense of *śruti* must run back to the Tantra to rediscover the path of the Vedas.

Louis Renou, *Destiny of the Veda in India.*

T*antra.* The word conjures a myriad images to mind—secrecy, magic, power, sex—the forbidden and the occult. The popular image of Tantra appears to many as simultaneously both sacred and profane, but is this conception of Tantra truly representative of its inner teachings, or is this a purely fabricated image of Tantra, concealing what is, in essence, a much more conventional core? Very few people take the time to look beyond their own imagination to discover Tantra for what it is—a Tradition hundreds of years old which, despite its colorful reputation, has far more in common with mainstream Hinduism than the average person is prepared to admit. What is even more interesting about the nature of Tantra is the radically different reputation of Tantra in Western countries (particularly the 'Pop' or 'Californian' Tantra currently in vogue in the United States) compared to its reputation within India. In the West, it is connected with the totally occidental phenomenon of 'sacred sex' and is more a by-product of the New Age movement which entered American culture in the 1970s. In India Tantra is more closely identified with esoteric practices. It is, therefore, the task of any reputable scholar to unravel these threads which have been spun by members outside of the Tradition and place together the different facets in order to see how the range of practices all combine together to create the complex teachings popularly known as Tantra. There are a number of issues posed by differing representations of Tantra, even without considering those of people whose only encounters with Tantra have emerged from Western pop culture. Besides which, there are still very fundamental problems with the basic definition of what Tantra actually is.

The first issue we encounter when attempting to describe the essence of the Tantric Traditions is that Tantra cannot technically be classified as a singular, unified Tradition. Rather, it is best described as a cluster of schools, which practice different techniques and worship different deities, within a loosely defined framework. Every school and every Guru provides their own unique perspective and teaching for Tantra, which makes providing a concrete definition of 'what is' or 'what is not' Traditional Tantra difficult, because Tantra itself is continuously in flux. Accordingly, the term 'Tantrism' itself can be seen as an artificial construct of the academic mind. In this regard, David Gordon White raises an important question: "If then, the Western scholarship that has purportedly focused on "Tantra" has in fact been a study of "Tantrism", what is this thing called "Tantra" that has been left relatively unexplored?"[1] The answer can only be that the term itself has been misused to designate a broad variety of teachings, outside of their actual semantic context. Suffice to say that this grouping together of different factions to create the illusion of unity as a 'Tradition' is not unique and it can be argued that the word 'Hinduism' also is a construct of the Western imagination and that it might be more appropriately referred to (when discussing Indian religions as a unified group) as *Sanātana Dharma*. Tantra is more correctly thought of as an esoteric technique applied in multiple instances, each of which teaches a unique application and

[1] WHITE, D. G., *Kiss of the Yogini: "Tantric Sex" its South Asian Contexts* (USA: The University of Chicago Press, 2006), 16.

which is an expansion of existing teachings. It is entirely incorrect to approach the subject as a unified 'movement'.

The task of definition is complicated further by the fact that Tantra is primarily esoteric in nature, meaning that its teachings are not intended to be understood by those outside of Tantric circles. This makes it an onerous task for scholars to decipher texts, as the majority of authors are writing from a perspective in which they have no personal experience of authentic Tantric practice and, as such, their view is often an entirely etic entity, constructed on the basis of either what is currently in vogue in academia, or a personal exegesis of texts. For these reasons, a substantial amount of literature on Tantra should be viewed as nothing more than a construct of scholarship and the Western imagination. As André Padoux says it is "An etic not an emic entity."

Secondly, there are a number of problems concerning the term Tantra itself. Tantra has been defined numerous times, and yet a satisfactory and accurate "textbook" definition of what Tantra is eludes us, and definitions of Tantra remain vague to this day. There are a number of reasons for this, part of which is the aforementioned esoteric nature of Tantra itself, and another reason is that the nature of Tantra is often misunderstood by those who seek to catalog and define it. This problem with the interpretation of Tantrism undoubtedly results from the number of contradictory stances in relation to Vedic and/or Orthodox Hinduism. In particular, Tantra appears to partake of an oppositional role in regard to Vedic teachings. This antagonism reaches its apex in the more infamous Tantric rites, which seem to be antinomian in character, and at times even a direct inversion of Vedic ritual. Examples such as the *Pañcamakāra* (5 M's)—which in addition to the use of forbidden substances can also involve the violation of caste restrictions—transgress not only the boundaries of purity and impurity but also the boundaries of Indian social structure itself, as has been observed by Louis Dumont. These rites, and in particular the now notorious '5 M's' are often viewed as mere transgression, in which the practitioner derives spiritual and temporal power from the violation of the sacred. This, however, is based on nothing more than an oversimplification of what is, in fact, a much more complex system of ritual practice. In stark contrast to these and other Tantric teachings, there are also elements in Tantrism that strive to reinforce their links and heritage with the Vedas. Vaidika Tāntrikas, by way of example, identify themselves as a part of the continuous legacy of the Vedic Tradition.

In some regards, this problem of diverse and seemingly irreconcilable Tantric teachings is a reflection of what was discussed previously—inaccurate definitions of the term Tantra—and more importantly, the labeling of different teachings as a singular body of texts. This difficulty in creating a standardized definition of Tantra has also been addressed by Teun Goudriaan.

> Tantric texts ... develop an identity by elaborating a complex and diffuse mosaic of concepts, doctrines, and ritual practices. These Catholic and denominational "Tantric elements" evidenced in texts are manifest in the different religions, sects, and schools that represent Tantrism's various forms of spiritual discipline (*sādhanā*). Thus, speaking of the "Tantras" as if they represent a homologous body of thought can be extremely misleading.[2]

Goudriaan here adopts the modern view of Tantrism, that it employs radically different methodologies in its approach to the divine and cannot be correctly classified as a singular tradition. These differing factions have been grouped together under the overarching umbrella term 'Tantrism' in order to assist in the Western systematic cataloging of the Hindu belief system. As H. V. Guenther remarks, Tantrism is "probably one of the haziest notions and misconceptions the Western mind has ever evolved." In sum, the currently accepted definition of Tantrism is, like Hinduism, an artificially constructed term which has been superimposed on a number of entirely separate teachings.

---

[2] BROOKS, D. R., *The Secret of the Three Cities: An Introduction to Hindu Sakta Tantrism* (USA: University of Chicago Press, 1990), 4.

The wide range of contrast between different Tantric Sects is at its most apparent when we examine the practices of so-called *Vāmācāra* Tantra which involve antinomian or 'transgressive' ritual acts, with those of *Dakṣiṇācāra* which elects to reject elements of alcohol, sex, meat, and in some instances even the external act of ritual itself. Broadly speaking, these two terms only vaguely correspond to what is popularly referred to in Western Esotericism as the Left-Hand Path (Vāmācāra) and the Right-Hand Path (Dakṣiṇācāra). The socio-cultural elements are different, since the definition from Western Esotericism is formed on a Judeo-Christian social model, which is obviously different to its manifestation in Hinduism. Vāmācāra takes it's name from an emphasis on the role of the female in practice (because traditionally the female is seated to the left of her husband in Hinduism), whereas the European Left Hand Path focuses on deities which oppose the Semitic Yahweh.

Based on the similarities between Dakṣiṇācāra and Vāmācāra, however, it is reasonably safe to discard the common assertion that part of the definition of Tantra involves the violation of social norms and transgressive behavior. Nonetheless, the fact that an older definition has failed does not bring one closer to replacing it with an adequate definition. In order to do so, one must rediscover the relationship between the Tantras and the Vedic past.

According to Hugh Urban, Tantra has a very mundane meaning: "typically it means any rite or form of worship of a particular deity, such as worship of the Goddess Kāmākhyā or Vaiṣṇavī (Kāmākhyā Tantra, Vaiṣṇavī Tantra)."[3] This, however, is not specific enough to explain Tantra. The word Tantra originates from the Sanskrit root *Tan-* (to stretch, to expand), and *tra-* (to save). Douglas Renfrew Brooks implies that this means the Tantras expand the possibilities of human liberation and empowerment in the increasingly degenerate Kali Yuga. Gavin Flood also makes a similar statement when he says that "*tan-tra* might literally be taken to mean 'method or instrument of extension', perhaps with the implication that it is

[3] URBAN, H., *The Power of Tantra: Religion, Sexuality, and the Politics of South Asian Studies* (USA: I. B. Tauris & CO Ltd, 2010), 5.

the self or body that is extended to become coterminous with the divine body."[4] David Gordon White reinforces these theories by placing them within the historical framework when he states that the textual pedigree of the term "goes back to the pre-fifth-century BCE *Śrauta Sūtras*, a corpus of ritual instructions for Vedic specialists ... the opening verses of the Āśvalayana Śrauta Sūtra employ the term "tantra" to mean "ritual framework," or "interweaving of rites," and such is precisely the subject matter of the Tantras."[5] The development of Tantra to expand on pre-existent spiritual teachings seems to be the most feasible interpretation. In the context of religious practice, this would mean utilizing different techniques to obtain salvation. This interpretation of the term would be in keeping with other forms of Tantra—Buddhist Tantra, for example, refers to its Tantric teachings as a method for accelerated enlightenment by which the practitioner gains liberation within a single lifetime. The difficulty of Tantric practice for both internalized and externalized modes of delivery gives credence to the Tibetan Buddhist definition. Given the nature of many Tantric rites, it seems likely that the root 'Tan' was indeed utilized in this sense.

Another insight into an acceptable definition of Tantrism can be found within the *paribhāṣās*, which makes a distinction between Tantra as the "woof" or texture, and the main ritual component, the *pradhāna*. Tantra here comprises the auxiliary acts or *aṅga* (member) of the ritual complex of a given sacrifice. This serves to illustrate the fact that Tantrism is not entirely a Tradition in its own right, but rather an esoteric technique within the larger corpus of Hindu Tradition. The depiction of Tantrism as a methodological or philosophical path within other traditions serves to explain the wide contrast between different branches of Tantrism—the Tantra, or texture of the teachings, has been applied differently within multiple organizations. This definition would also help to explain the central and pivotal role of the Guru within Tantric circles, as it would be

4 FLOOD, G., *The Tantric Body: The Secret Tradition of Hindu Religion* (USA: I. B. Tauris & Co. Ltd, 2006), 12.

5 WHITE, D. G., *Kiss of the Yogini: "Tantric Sex" its South Asian Context*, 16.

the role of the Guru to apply the teachings in accordance within his own particular branch of Tantra—hence, each Guru teaches his own individual interpretation of Tantra. If such an interpretation of the role of the Tantric Guru is correct, then each Guru would be akin to a Master painter who is applying his own unique style within the wider context. The methodological technique of Tantra, is as the word implies, intended to 'stretch' the boundaries of spiritual possibility. In its most extreme forms, Tantra will surpass all social barriers, whilst other forms of Tantrism will remain extremely conventional.

A *tāntrika* would then be defined as one who believes in the primacy of a specific methodology of spiritual practice. This methodology originates from a specific Guru lineage, each of which has established its own style and mode of delivery for the teachings. Moreover, the *Rauravāgama* explicitly states that rites being performed prescribed by one Tantra should not be mixed with rites from another.

Tantric teachings, whether internalized or externalized, all involve a significant degree of complexity in order to produce an accelerated mode of spiritual learning, with the goal of liberation. All of these differing branches will stress the importance of *sādhanā*. The techniques taught are largely esoteric and taught in full only to initiates. What distinguishes Tantric thought from other Hindu teachings is its systematic emphasis on the identity of the highest truth (*paramārtha*) and the phenomenal (*vyavahāradaśā*) world when filtered through the experience of sādhanā. A practitioner of Tantra is called a *sādhaka* (if male) or a *sādhikā* (if female). Other terms are tāntrika, or *tantra-yogīn* (if male) and *tantra-yoginī* (if female). An adept of the Tantric path is typically known as a *siddha* ("accomplished one," from *sidh*, meaning "to be accomplished" or "to attain") or *mahā-siddha* ("greatly accomplished one," that is, a great adept).[6] A female adept is called *siddha-anganā*. The keyword here is *experience*, *direct experience* that is the result of Tantric sādhanā. The significance of this will be explained later, after an

[6] FEUERSTEIN, G., *Tantra: The Path of Ecstasy* (USA: Shambala, 1998), 2.

examination of the Vedic material and how it sowed the seeds for the later development of what we have come to refer to as Tantrism.

As Robert Mayer has also shown, there is no evidence for a non-Āryan substratum for Tantrism, and it must be understood as a predominantly Brāhmanical, Sanskritic tradition with its roots in the Vedas.[7] Though, as the nature of Hindu society shifted and underwent change, other elements were absorbed into Tantrism—and, despite the denunciation of *varṇa,* to a certain extent the system reinforces it within a new esoteric hierarchy—not via birthright or entitlements, but by nature and temperament, sometimes dividing practitioners into a clear stratification of *pashu*, *vīra*, and *divya*. Though these do not correlate directly to varṇa, they are an obvious cognate to the Samkhya classification of the *guṇas*, based on the qualities of *tamas*, *rajas*, and *sattva*. In this classification of the three types of tāntrika, the divya or god-like mode is the highest, but also the rarest. The vast majority of practitioners, will, in fact, be classified as 'pashu' or possessed of the tamas elements until they demonstrate to their Guru that they are capable of practicing in the vīra mode without endangering either themselves or others. Though many Western practitioners seem to imagine themselves in the vīra role, in reality the vast majority of Tantrics do not engage in sexual practices, and indeed, proclaiming one's self to be a vīra is very probably a strong contradiction of the ability to actually be one. This is why traditional Tantra places emphasis on the role of the Guru. Without a qualified instructor, the practices can be psychologically or physically dangerous. It is for this reason that such great emphasis is placed on initiation; unlike the majority of esoteric Traditions in the West, the Tantric Traditions remain largely taught as an oral tradition from Guru to disciple. Although we shall relate a number of techniques in this book, they remain only theoretical. Expecting them to work without any practical experience would be like attempting to fly a plane based on what you read in a book—and therefore not a wise idea. In addition to this, the importance of initiation is reiterated in the *Kulārṇava Tantra,*

---

[7] FLOOD, G., *The Tantric Body: The Secret Tradition of Hindu Religion,* 14.

> O beloved! Just as iron turns to gold when penetrated by mercury, so the self-attains Śiva-hood when it is penetrated by initiation.
>
> When *karmas* are burned by the fire of initiation, the fetters of *māyā* are severed. One who is without [karmic] seed and has attained the supreme condition of wisdom becomes Śiva.
>
> The initiate does not need to accomplish anything through asceticism, rules, or vows, nor by going to sacred places or by controlling the body.
>
> But, O Beloved, the recitation, worship, and other rituals of those who are not initiated bear no fruit and are like seed sown on [a] rock.[8]

Initiation, however, is the primary reason for much of the misunderstanding that surrounds Tantrism both in the West and India, because the secrecy and esotericism of the Tantric Traditions makes them difficult to study from an etic perspective. Unlike other Traditions, Tantra is one that has managed to maintain a sense of dignity and has not released all its secrets to the general public. The fact that the real Tradition remains in the hands of the Gurus and is accessible only to adepts also means that the majority of books published on the subject will either be erroneous or completely fraudulent. Those that do maintain the genuine Traditions of Tantrism will also take great care not to reveal all its secrets; the teachings are not revealed in full because initiation into the Tantric Tradition is a desired prerequisite. Therefore, those who know the secrets of Tantrism do not speak, and those who do not know speak. Accordingly, this book shall only reveal some things, but not all.

[8] FEUERSTEIN, G., *Tantra: The Path of Ecstasy*, 108.

PART I

GODS, SACRED SITES, & THE KALI YUGA

ŚIVA

Naṭarāja, Śankara, & Higher Consciousness

When one contemplates the Gods of India, ancient or modern, it is impossible to bypass the figure of Śiva, who has retained a position of prominence in Indian thought throughout the ages. Yet, despite Śiva's importance in the social and religious life of India, Śiva remains a complex God whose iconography and descriptions are often ambiguous and seemingly contradictory. At times the very essence of Śiva is paradoxical, and his different aspects are harshly contrasting. Thus, to the observer, Śiva defies a concrete description, his true nature remaining deeply shrouded in mystery and known only to a few individuals. On this level Śiva is the personification of the Divine itself, forever distant yet always in proximity, known and yet unknown, consisting of *sat-cit-ānanda* (Being (*sat*), consciousness (*cit*), and Bliss (*ānanda*)).[1] However, Śiva is more than a figure who transcends duality, for each of his aspects is distinctive and must be analyzed individually to assess the characteristic components which are aspects of the God. As Śiva transcends duality, his characteristics become singular, until they reach one defining unity. In order to explain how this process works, two images of Śiva will be compared—namely Naṭarāja and Śankara.

---

[1] FEUERSTEIN G., *Tantra, The Path of Ecstasy* (USA: Shambala, 1998), 74.

One of the most well-known portrayals of Śiva is that of Naṭarāja, the King of the Dance where Śiva is seen dancing furiously, oblivious to the external world. In his frenzied dance, Śiva is framed by a blazing aura of flame and heat; this is his *tapas* that surrounds him, the power generated by the dance. Symbolically crushed underfoot by his dance lies the dwarf of ignorance. Fierce and active, this image of the triumphant dancing Śiva is in stark contrast to another of the God's popular aspects, namely that of Śankara the Beneficent. The figure of Śankara sits calm, tranquil, immersed in quiet contemplation—this is the personification of Śiva as an ascetic or yogīn. Amongst the animals of the forest he sits totally absorbed in thought, in a classic yoga pose. Compared with his activity as Naṭarāja, there can be no clearer diametric opposition, for one appears to be an active image, the other passive. The opposition between the two images of Śiva, is, however, not as clear-cut, for what looks like a dichotomy between the images is, in reality, a continuum. The two aspects of Śiva, Naṭarāja and Śankara, contain elements of each other. The same element is at play in the depiction of both these aspects, namely the induction of a transcendental state of consciousness. The outward appearance of contrast between the two aspects of Śiva is not due to the polarity of the images but rather a projection of two different modes for achieving this altered state of consciousness. These two methods, as we shall see, are not mutually exclusive, but rather two different methods for obtaining the same result. Prior to explaining these techniques, though, it is necessary to explore the history of the God Śiva himself, for only by illustrating a common origin in the development of Śiva can we begin to understand the implications of the continuum formed by the depictions of Naṭarāja and Śankara.

It is commonly accepted today that the figure of Śiva partially originates in that of the Vedic deity Rudra as the result of a gradual syncretism of Vedic thought with other traditions of India. From this point of origin Śiva began to rise in prominence, gradually replacing the Vedic Gods. This process is recorded in the Purāṇas which place emphasis on Śiva above the Vedic Gods. Śiva's at times seemingly paradoxical nature can be traced back to the legacy he inherited from the superficially ambiguous nature of Rudra as creator and destroyer, the God with a shining exterior and a dark interior, God of storms and healing herbs.[2] From the beginning of creation itself, Rudra is portrayed as an enigmatic and at times disturbing God. From his first appearance as Paśupati, the Lord of the Animals, the God's behavior can be seen as threatening to creation, as is illustrated from the following myth recounted by Kramrisch.

> The primordial, paradigmatic myth of Rudra is told in the Maitrāyaṇī Saṃhitā of the *Black Yajurveda*. Father Heaven, henceforth acting under the name of Prajāpati, Lord of Generation, desired his daughter Uṣas, the Dawn. She became a female antelope, he became an antelope and pursued her. While he was taking his perverse pleasure in her, he suddenly turned around toward one who was aiming his arrow at him. Addressing the Archer, Prajāpati in fear exclaimed: "I make you Lord of the Animals (*paśūnāṃ pati*)." "Leave me." Thus his name is Paśupati, Lord of the Animals. The first seed that fell was surrounded by fire produced by Agni (MS.4.2.12)[3]

Not only can this action be interpreted as a threat to Prajāpati, it also shows Rudra as a figure who protects the social order against disruptive behavior, for Prajāpati's desire for his daughter Uṣas is incestuous, and thus a violation of what is permissible within social norms. By necessity, in order to protect a society, one must be, to a certain extent, beyond its influence. Thus, from the moment of his first appearance, Paśupati-Rudra is cast into the role of the 'outsider'; he is one who is both threatening and protective, hence the ambiguous nature of his auspicious and inauspicious aspects. This is reinforced by his appearance also, for Kramrisch describes Paśupati-Rudra as one whose "guise and appearance were those of an outsider, come from the north ... He was clad in black and was

[2] DONIGER O'FLAHERTY, W., *Śiva: The Erotic Ascetic* (UK: Oxford University Press, 1981), 83.

[3] KRAMRISCH, S., *The Presence of Śiva* (USA: Princeton University Press, 1981), 6.

uncanny."[4] Furthermore, not only does Paśupati-Rudra possess an appearance dissimilar to the other Vedic Gods, he also does not share their origin nor direction; a fact which again indicates his separation from the Vedic social structure.

> He seemed a stranger. He had come from the north, which is Rudra's direction (SB.1.7.3.3, 30; TS.2.6.6.5-6). He came from beyond his Himālayan mountain residence beyond Mount Mūjavat. That was his dwelling in the wilderness on earth. But the north is also the cosmic north, the zenith. The other Gods have east as their direction.[5]

The threatening nature of Rudra arises from this source; by necessity his role as a social enforcer is as an outsider. As an outsider he is unknown, his very essence is that of ambiguity, which is part of the legacy that Śiva has inherited from Rudra. Both Gods are able to move freely outside permissible social norms.

Another common factor which is shared by Rudra and Śiva is their association with fire, heat, and tapas. Tapas, the generation of the mystical heat that is so characteristic of yoga and ascetic practices in India, is akin to a spiritual fire. It is also associated with the raising of Kuṇḍalinī in Tantric practice, therefore, its esoteric significance is tied to Śiva, who is sometimes referred to as the Master Yogīn. The fire which burns within Rudra is also said to be his tapas, the ardor of the ascetic discipline of yoga, of which he is to be Lord.[6] Likewise, Rudra is also associated with the guṇa of tamas, as is Śiva, for, of the three guṇas, tamas is said to be that which is Śiva's nature, hence his depiction as 'white'. His skin color is opposite to the guṇa with which he is associated with, for black is the color of tamas, just as Viṣṇu, whose skin color is black, is associated with white, the color of the sattva guṇa. Viṣṇu and Śiva (with whom there is a significant dichotomy/rivalry) both contain elements of their opposites, hence, the color of their skin holds polarity with the respective guṇas.

---

[4] KRAMRISCH, S., *The Presence of Śiva*, 63.

[5] Ibid.

[6] Ibid., 21.

Like Śiva, Rudra is associated with tamas, and thus is portrayed not only as a destroyer, but also as an outsider. When tamas accelerates and dissolves the cosmos into darkness and density, the fivefold categories of existence and the three guṇas are dissolved together with their numbers, five and three, which are Śiva's sacred numbers.[7] A similar sentiment is expressed by Daniélou, who states that this concept of Rudra being the embodiment of tamas was entrenched at the time of the composition of the Upaniṣads.

Rudra, the Vedic equivalent of Śiva, begins to take his place clearly as the deity of transcendent darkness, embodiment of the disintegrating tendency (tamas), only in the Upaniṣads, which are the expression of an age when Vedic thought had abandoned much of its primeval naturalistic vision to become impregnated with other conceptions borrowed from the ancient culture of the land.[8]

Rudra then, as the principle of tamas, like his successor Śiva, is the destroyer, time, and the principle of death, and as such he is subsequently identified with Śiva.[9] It would be naïve, however, to perpetuate the conception that this is merely destruction on the physical plane—Śiva can also be seen as being destructive of mental processes that hinder spiritual development and, in his aspect as Bhairava, he is the Devourer of Sin. Hence, even in this role, he is ambiguous, for his acts of destruction as Bhairava are positive acts. The name Śiva is even first applied as an alternative to Rudra, thus illustrating the apparent dichotomy at work, for when the God is cruel and wild he is named Rudra, whilst when he is at peace with himself and kind he is Śiva, and within his being are fierceness and grace at opposite ends of one diameter.[10]

> In the *Yajur Veda Śrī Rudram*, an ancient account in which the Āryans stored their memories, Śiva-Rudra is called the lord of fire and water, of trees and herbs (life), of waking and sleeping (states of consciousness), and of the high and low (spirits). He

[7] KRAMRISCH, S., *The Presence of Śiva*, 81.
[8] DANIÉLOU, A., *Hindu Polytheism* (UK: Routledge & Kegan Paul Ltd, 1964), 188.
[9] DANIÉLOU, A., *Gods of Love and Ecstasy* (USA: Inner Traditions International, 1992), 28.
[10] KRAMRISCH, S., *The Presence of Śiva*, 21.

> is addressed as the wanderer, hunter, healer, holy man, dweller-in-caves, master thief, and smith ... The image of the tribal shaman, as it appeared in early humanity, shines through most of these appellations.[11]

In addition to Śiva's heritage from Rudra though, there is also a link to another Vedic deity, Soma, the Moon God, which Kramrisch describes as follows:

> The moon is a mystic container, a vessel from which gods and the dead, the ancestors drink Soma, the ever-refilling water of life, of immortality (SB.2.4.4.15, CHUP.5.10.4). On his head, Śiva carries the crescent moon, symbol of the renewal of vegetative life, of recurrent time, and the abode of the dead. Thus, the moon is the Lord of the Plants (MBH.12.52.33), [a] luminous vessel of Soma and one with Soma, who himself from ancient times is their king.[12]

As with Rudra, Soma can be seen to have a link to altered states of mind, not via *tapas*, but through the mysterious substance known as *soma*.

As the syncretism of thought continued to alter Śiva's form, new roles began to consolidate in the minds of the population. He absorbed many different aspects of the Vedic deities—among them Agni, Soma, and even Sūrya—but principally it is the form of Rudra which has contributed the most to the concept of Śiva in India, as we understand it today. This tendency of Śiva to absorb the qualities of other deities into his own is one of the factors that contribute to the God's complexity and seemingly polarized qualities. Today, Śiva has a multitude of names and titles, of which Zimmer provides a brief list here.

> The plenitude of Śiva's mutually antagonistic functions and aspects is made evident by the fact that his worshipers invoke him by a hundred names. He is described also

[11] STORL, W. D., *Siva: the Wild God of Power and Ecstasy* (USA: Inner Traditions, 2004), 35.
[12] KRAMRISCH, S., *The Presence of Śiva*, 38.

> under twenty-five "playful manifestations" (*līlāmūrti*), or according to another tradition, sixteen. Occasionally we find the multitude of expressive aspects reduced to five: (1) The Beneficent Manifestation (Anugrahamūrti), (2) the Destructive Manifestation (Saṃhāramūrti), (3) The Vagrant Mendicant (Bhikṣāṭanamūrti), (4) The Lord of Dancers (Nṛttamūrti), (5) The Great Lord (Maheśamūrti). Among the titles included in the longer lists are The God with the Moon in his Hair (Candraśekhara), The Supporter of the Ganges (Aṅgādhara), The Slayer of the Elephant-Demon (Gajasaṁhāra), Consort of the Goddess Uma and Father of Skanda, the War God (Somāskanda), The Lord who is Half Woman (Ardhanārīśvara), The Destroyer of Time (Kālasaṁhāra), Lord of Cattle (Paśupati), The Beneficent (Śankara), The Propitious (Śiva), The Howler (Rudra).[13]

Whilst it would be a vast undertaking to examine all the aspects of the God in order the truly understand the nature of Śiva, an important part of his being, namely the power to transcend opposites, can be illustrated by examining two well-known manifestations of Śiva; namely that of Śankara (The Beneficent) and Naṭarāja (The King of Dancers).

As Śankara, the God sits completely still, eyes closed, immersed in contemplation. Śankara is the living definition of peace and tranquility—his entire being is passive—he sits in classic yoga pose atop the skin of a tiger, symbolizing his triumph over the forces of nature; not only does he wear the sacred thread, he is also adorned with a serpent for a garland, and in his hands the God is equipped with the trident, symbolizing his power over the three guṇas, and a drum; the Ganges flows down from his hair, which is also lit by a silver crescent moon. This is the figure of Śiva as Śankara, also known as the Lord of the Mountains (Girīsha).[14] Śankara emphasizes Śiva as the Master Yogīn—his quality of stillness, comparable with

[13] ZIMMER, H., *Myths and Symbols in Indian Art and Civilization* (USA: Princeton University Press, 1972), 126.

[14] STORL, W. D., *Shiva: the Wild God of Power and Ecstasy*, 75.

the *rasa* of *śānta* advocated by Abhinavagupta, is the outward echo of his ascetic discipline. Storl reads a similar meaning into the God's adornments, in addition to his overall appearance and mood.

> Śankara's other bodily decorations can be understood in a similar way. The poisonous cobras he wears as armbands, rings, necklaces, and hair decoration, signify that he has overcome the cold-blooded reptilian nature inside of himself. He does not fear their power. They do not crawl, stealthily hidden, through the darkest recesses of his psyche, as they do in so many people who seem, externally seen, to be so proper and decent. Much like the shaman with his badges and pendants, or the sailor or warrior with tattoos signaling having left fear behind, these vipers are the external insignia of inner self-mastery.[15]

It is by virtue of his discipline that Śiva, a God paradoxically also known for his wildness, is known as the Lord of Yoga. What, though, is this discipline of yoga that is so intrinsically wed to the imagery of Śankara? More than any other elements illustrated in the iconography of Śankara, it is the God's yogīc power which is emphasized. The practitioner of yoga is by definition a yogīn and has always been considered a *mahāsiddha*, a possessor of occult powers, which could be broadly defined as a "magician."[16] By itself, magic, however, is far from being an adequate description of the process involved in yoga—the attainment of *siddhi* (which could be thought as a type of magic or psychic powers) is not a necessary condition to the practice of yoga, nor is it the desired result of yogīc practice; any attainment of the siddhi is merely a byproduct of yogīc practice—it neither describes the condition itself nor the goal of the practice. Yoga would be better defined as a state of consciousness brought about by a controlled and restrained use of breathing techniques that is self-contained and deeply introspective. This is a key element in the depiction of Śankara—

[15] STORL, W. D., *Shiva: the Wild God of Power and Ecstasy*, 76.

[16] ELIADE, M., *Yoga: Immortality and Freedom* (USA: Princeton University Press, 1990), 88.

the peace he radiates is that of one who has looked inwards, and knows their depths—only in this manner can one be truly at one with the cosmos for, until there is unity within the self, there will be conflict on external levels. Thus, the meditative state of Śankara is a depiction of the body as a microcosm of the cosmos itself; when one comes to understand their internal nature it will be reflected on an external level and the microcosm of the body will come to reflect the macrocosm of the universe. Yoga is also thought to generate tapas, and by the use of yoga, Śiva is thought to generate his tapas. By virtue of renunciation, of asceticism (tapas), men, demons, or Gods can become powerful to the point of threatening the economy of the entire universe.[17] Daniélou defines the mental state of a yogīc practitioner thus:

> The state attained by the yogīn who has silenced his mind is the root of knowledge. It is there that he can grasp the unmanifest source of manifestation. All teachings of yoga and the process of liberation are witnessed by the yogīn in the cavern of his heart as the form of Maheśvara. Maheśvara is thus the great Yogī, the teacher of all that is beyond the reach of sensorial experiment. To him is attributed the revelation to mankind of the technique of yoga. Śiva is himself represented as the perfect ascetic (Mahā Yogī), in who has centered the perfection of austerity, penance, and meditation, through which unlimited powers are attained. He is shown naked, "clad in space" (*digambara*), "loaded with matted hair" (*dhūr-jaṭi*), his body smeared with ashes.[18]

Again, the strong link betwixt Śiva and yogīc technique is emphasized in the above passage. The defining essence of the God Śiva lies in his relationship to yoga, and in no aspect of Śiva is this more aptly illustrated or exemplified than in the calm meditative state of Śankara. The link between Śiva and yoga should be immediately apparent. However, what the link actually is constructed of remains vague and ambiguous, for the mental

[17] ELIADE, M., *Yoga: Immortality and Freedom*, 89.
[18] DANIÉLOU, A., *Hindu Polytheism*, 202.

state attributed to the practice of yoga needs to be elucidated. With regard to the actual practice of yoga, Daniélou defines it as the stage of higher consciousness, outside of the scope of everyday existence. In the extract quoted below, he makes it very clear that it is not a mode of thought that is to be encountered in the regime of mundane thought and existence—like Śiva, the yogīn is a type of 'outsider', for yoga places the mind on the very fringe of normalcy. It is a mental state which is not comparable to normal mundane thought.

> One essential fact must always be borne in mind: the yogīn works on all levels of consciousness and of the subconscious, for the purpose of opening the way to trans-consciousness (knowledge-possession of the Self, the puruṣa). He enters into "deep sleep" and into the "fourth state" (*turīya*, the cataleptic state) with the utmost lucidity; he does not sink into hypnosis.[19]

What is being described here is an induced alteration of the mental state, with the goal of obtaining a higher consciousness. Though the techniques differ from those employed in other parts of the globe, an induced state of altered consciousness is easily identifiable with the image of the shaman, yet the shaman's hallmark is another equally ambiguous term, that of 'ecstasy'. Ecstasy, in varying forms is employed by shaman to enter into these altered states of consciousness. The issue of contention here is that, although the methods utilized by the yogīn and the shaman differ, the goal is the same—communication with a higher authority (spirits in the case of shaman) or with a higher self (in the case of a yogī).

The case for similarity between altered states of consciousness found in yoga and in shamanism can also be seen in the following quotation from the *Nāda Bindu Upaniṣad*.

> This state of meditation probably resembles a state of catalepsy, for the text says that "the yogīn will remain like a dead man. He is liberated [*mukta*]." In this *unmanī* state (realized at the moment

[19] ELIADE, M., *Yoga: Immortality and Freedom*, 99.

> that the yogīn has passed beyond even mystical hearing), his body is "as a piece of wood, he has no cognizance of neither cold nor heat nor pain nor pleasure." He no longer hears any sound. This Upaniṣad, too, evinces its "experimental" origin; it was certainly composed in a yogīc circle that specialized in "mystical auditions"—that is, in obtaining "ecstasy" through concentration on sounds.[20]

This state describes a deep mental introversion, which Eliade finds comparable with the shamanic element, for it refers to the obtainment of ecstasy via aural means. The problem in drawing a direct comparison between yoga and shamanism lies not only in tenuous definitions of both techniques but also in cross-cultural relationships; to say that one is the same as the other is too broad in scope to be effective as a relationship, however, to say that both have the same goal provides a solid basis on which to provide a workable premise. Whilst it can now be seen that yoga and shamanism share a common goal, it should be pointed out that, although the trances employed by shamans may produce a similar effect to yoga, the techniques employed in yoga (rigid asceticism, advanced breathing techniques, *mantra*, etc.) are particularities of yoga, which are not applicable to the methods employed by shamans in achieving an altered mind state. Thus, it should be remembered that, although the goal is the same, the techniques employed to reach it differ. In sharp contrast to the yogīn and the figure of Śankara, the trance techniques employed by the shaman are often extroverted and involve a sense of wild abandon to invoke the feeling of ecstasy which is the defining point of the shamanic path. This aspect, though, whilst not seen in the depiction of Śankara, does appear in another portrayal of Śiva; namely that of Naṭarāja, the King of Dancers.

In his role as Naṭarāja, Śiva is seen harshly contrasted with his other aspect of Śankara. Here, the God is now active, awake, and in ceaseless motion. Śiva dances in a flurry of activity, his

[20] ELIADE, M., *Yoga: Immortality and Freedom*, pp. 132-33.

hair cascading wildly behind him. He is encircled by a ring of flame and he stands upon a dwarf, representing his transcendent consciousness and conquest of ignorance. Here Śiva is seen as a wild God, an extrovert who teaches the dance and the music which leads to ecstasy, "the intoxication which takes [a] man out of himself ... He is Melpomenos (the Singer) or Naṭarāja, the King of Dance and of the Theatre."[21] The image of Naṭarāja as described by Zimmer is as follows:

> Śiva-Naṭarāja is represented in a beautiful series of South Indian bronzes dating from tenth and twelfth centuries AD. The details of these figures are to be read, according to the Hindu tradition, in terms of a complex pictorial allegory. The upper right hand, it will be observed, carries a little drum, shaped like an hour-glass, for the beating of the rhythm. This connotes Sound, the vehicle of speech, the conveyor of revelation, tradition, incantation, magic and divine truth. Furthermore, Sound is associated in India with Ether, the first of the five elements. Ether is the primary and most subtlety persuasive manifestation of the divine Substance. Out of it unfold, in the evolution of the universe, all the other elements, Air, Fire, Water, and Earth. Together, therefore, Sound and Ether signify the first, truth-pregnant moment of creation, the productive energy of the Absolute, in its pristine, cosmogenetic strength.[22]
>
> Śiva as the Cosmic Dancer is the embodiment and manifestation of eternal energy in its "five activities" (*paňca-kriya*): (1) Creation (*sṛiṣṭi*), the pouring forth or unfolding, (2) Maintenance (*sthiti*), the duration, (3) Destruction (*saṁhāra*), the taking back or reabsorption, (4) Concealment (*tiro-bhāva*), the veiling of True Being behind the masks and garbs of apparitions, aloofness, display of māyā, and (5) Favor (*anugraha*) acceptance of the devotee, acknowledgment of the pious endeavor of the yogīn, bestowal of peace through

[21] DANIÉLOU, A., *Gods of Love and Ecstasy*, 51.

[22] ZIMMER, H., *Myths and Symbols in Indian Art and Civilization*, 152.

> a revelatory manifestation. The first three and the last two are matched, as groups of cooperative mutual antagonisms; the God displays them all. And he displays them, not only simultaneously, but in sequence. They are symbolized in the positions of his hands and his feet—the upper three hands being respectively, "creation," "maintenance," and "destruction"; the foot planted in Forgetfulness is "concealment," and the foot uplifted, "favor"; the "elephant hand" indicates the linkage of the three to the two, and promises peace to the soul that experiences the relationship. All five activities are made manifest, simultaneously with the pulse of every moment, and in sequence through the changes of time.[23]

Once again, there is a much more esoteric level to this aspect of Śiva than simply a description, for, just as the defining element of Śankara's iconography is the practice of yoga, the defining element of Naṭarāja's iconography is the dance itself. Śiva's dance is cosmogonic, replicating the interaction of the three guṇas and the creation and destruction of the universe itself.

> "The Dance of Śiva," or *tāṇḍava*, is famous and is depicted by Naṭarāja, the cosmic dancer. In one hand (he is allegorically given two pairs of arms) he holds the cosmic drum of creation, which is a symbol of creation and produces the primordial sound (*śabda*). This is the sound expressed through mantra, which provides the vehicle of expression for the creative power of sound. In one left hand is held a ball of flame, which is the symbol of destruction, transmutation, and, ultimately, also of regeneration. An outer circle of fire is normally described around the perimeter of the icon, and Naṭarāja is seen standing on an evil spirit, which symbolizes the conquest of good over evil. There are variations to this imagery, and just as there are many names for Śiva, so there are many different dances.[24]

[23] ZIMMER, H., *Myths and Symbols in Indian Art and Civilization*, 155.
[24] Ibid., 150.

Zimmer continues with his description, referring to dancing as a type of magic.

> The dancer becomes amplified into a being endowed with supra-normal powers. His personality is transformed. Like yoga, the dance induces trance, ecstasy, the experience of the divine, the realization of one's own secret nature, and, finally, emergence into the divine essence. In India consequently, the dance has flourished side by side with the terrific austerities of the meditation grove—fasting, breathing exercises, absolute introversion. To work magic, to put enchantments upon others, one has to first put enchantments on one's self. And this is affected as well by dance as by prayer, fasting, and meditation. Śiva therefore, the arch-yogīn of the Gods, is necessarily also the master of the dance.[25]

As can be seen in the above quote, Zimmer is stating that the dance has many qualities in common with yoga and that the two methods of inducing an altered state are not necessarily mutually exclusive. The use of dance to bring about a type of altered consciousness is equally as viable as that of yoga. What differs here is not the goal but the method. With Śankara the mental stage reached was one of contemplative calm and introspection; what is exhibited in the dance of Naṭarāja is a wild abandonment, and a frenzy of activity that is externalized in the world and not in the self; thus, the images of Śankara and Naṭarāja appear on the surface to be polar opposites that are irreconcilable.

From the comparison of these two identities of Śiva, namely Śankara and Naṭarāja, an apparent dichotomy emerges. At one end sits Śankara, passive, peaceful, and inactive. At the other end Naṭarāja dances; wild, active and alive with motion. So strong is the contrast between these two portrayals of Śiva that one must constantly remind oneself that they are indeed the same entity. Here, when faced with what seems to be a starkly drawn boundary separating the twin aspects of Śiva and drawing them as polar opposites, the two images

[25] ZIMMER, H., *Myths and Symbols in Indian Art and Civilization*, 151.

force one to a sudden realization of Śiva's divine nature—Śiva, as a God, can be described as a God that transcends opposites and the limitations of the human condition. In the context of Hinduism, Śiva is the God of ascension, *par excellence*. Bearing this in mind, what at first appears to be a mutually antagonistic polarization of images, is in fact, a continuum—one aspect moves and shifts to another through varying degrees of activity. Action and passivity are not opposed in the same sense as 'black and white', nor are mutually exclusive either. An object or subject in the principles of 'action' and 'non-action' can vary in quantity by degrees or shades, and this is the central issue of the comparison of the two images. They represent two different 'degrees' or 'shades' of the same principle; both Śankara and Naṭarāja depict Śiva in a trance or state of altered consciousness. The only difference between the two images is in one the state is reached by an active route to the divine consciousness (Naṭarāja) and the other a passive route to the divine consciousness (Śankara). This notion of active and passive routes correspond to the principles of *nivṛtti* (drawing in, contraction, introspection), and *pravṛtti*, (drawing out, expansion, losing the sense of self). To a certain extent these qualities are also expressed directly within the frame of Rudra and Śiva, for, as Daniélou expresses, "the two names, Rudra and Śiva, are now used as equivalents, yet theoretically Rudra represents the fearful, manifest aspect, Śiva the peaceful aspect of the tamas tendency, that which alone remains when the two other tendencies come to rest."[26] In support of this theory of illusory duality, it is also worthwhile to examine the following portion of the *Bhāgavata Purāṇa* (IV, chap. 2-7).

> Dakṣa says, " Against my own will, at the instigation of Brahmā, I gave my daughter to this unclean being, the destroyer of rites and social barriers, who teaches the texts to men of low birth, to the Śūdras."[27]

[26] DANIÉLOU, A., *Hindu Polytheism*, 197.

[27] DANIÉLOU, A., *Gods of Love and Ecstasy*, 47.

What is notable here is the distinction that Śiva is a destroyer of social barriers, for barriers are themselves a form of separation and distinction, just as is the illusory drawing of opposites, for to define an opposition one must define the middle or meridian of the continuum. This meridian is another type of barrier that separates one form of acceptable behavior from another. Hence, just as the barriers erected by society are in truth illusory, so too are the illusions of logic that cause us to separate one descriptive quality from another—in the case of Śankara and Naṭarāja, that descriptive quality is the dichotomy of activity/stillness. The principles of Śankara and Naṭarāja also bear similarities to the apparent dichotomy between *prakṛti* and *puruṣa*.

> It explains the universe as consisting of two and only two principles, i.e. inert nature (prakṛti) and the pure, conscious principle (puruṣa). Whatever happens in the universe, happens in and through prakṛti; puruṣa does not act—it is the pure witness.[28]

Śiva, as a God who transcends opposites, absorbs these polarized definitions into his own being, thus destroying the barriers which were in essence, only illusory anyway. In this manner, the one which transcends all the illusory barriers, Śiva is also depicted as the hermaphrodite Ardhanarīshvara.[29]

By accepting that the contrast between Śankara and Naṭarāja is not an opposition but instead a continuum, involving the principles of action and non-action, it then becomes necessary to examine further what the two images are expressing that is not contradictory, in order to understand the essence of the continuum formed by the two images. The difference between them is the degree of movement, but what is the quality by which they can be defined as similar—what ties these two images together as aspects of the God Śiva? To phrase it simply, both portray a state of altered consciousness. In the case of Śankara, the Lord of Yoga, the technique utilized to reach this

[28] BHARATI, A., *The Tantric Tradition* (UK: Rider & Company, 1965), 204.
[29] DANIÉLOU, A., *Gods of Love and Ecstasy*, 63.

stage is obviously yoga. In the case of Naṭarāja however, this is not so apparent, and in order to see the state of consciousness symbolized by Naṭarāja, one must step outside of the orthodox framework of India, and compare the techniques used in yoga with other techniques to communicate with the sacred. To achieve this one first needs to look at the possible origins of yogīc technique. The problem with this approach is that only rudimentary forms of yoga can be traced back to the Vedas; however, those ancient texts refer to ascetic disciplines and "ecstatic" ideologies that, if they are not always directly related to yoga properly speaking, finally found a place in the yogīc tradition.[30] One type of individual described in the *Rig Veda* appears to form of 'prototype' for the yogīn or ascetic. This type of person, known as the *vrātya*, is described by Eliade as follows:

> Thus, a hymn of the *Rig Veda* (X, 136) tells of the muni, long-haired (*keśin*), clad in "soiled yellow," "girdled with wind," and into whom "the Gods enter" (2). He proclaims: "In the intoxication of ecstasy we are mounted on the winds. You, mortals, can perceive only our body." (3) The muni flies through the air (4), he is the steed of the wind (*Vāta*), the friend of Vāyu, "impelled by the Gods"; he inhabits the two seas, that of the rising and that of the setting sun (5); "he travels by the road of the *Apsarases*, the *Gandharvas*, and wild beasts, he knows thoughts" (6) and "drinks with Rudra from the cup of poison."[31]

This passage raises a number of interesting points about the vrātya; firstly the phrase proclaimed by the vrātya mentions the use of 'intoxication of ecstasy' in a context which obviously pertains to ritual or magical practice. This is of relevance as the use of a mysterious state of consciousness known as ecstasy is one of the hallmarks of shamanic practice. Secondly, the references to winds here may imply a connection with Tantrism as the term winds are often used in connection with the currents of energy or nāḍī which flow through the body in Tantric meditation. Thirdly, these

[30] ELIADE, M., *Yoga: Immortality and Freedom*, 102.
[31] Ibid.

mysterious vrātya are mentioned explicitly in connection with Rudra in the last sentence. Rudra, as has already been pointed out, is the Vedic god from whom the figure of Śiva later emerged. The drinking of poison here should also be noted, for the throat of Śiva is colored blue from an occasion when he also had to drink poison. In this circumstance involving the vrātya, it could also be possible that the poison being ingested is a beverage or intoxicant of some variety, of which the consumption induces shamanic ecstasy. Eliade, furthering describing the vrātya, goes on to describe their appearance and role in Vedic society.

> This mystic fellowship was, in any case, important, for a special sacrifice, *vrātyastoma,* had been organized to restore its members to Brāhmanic society. The texts treating of the *vrātyastoma* and the *mahāvrata* (solstitial rite in which a number of archaic elements survive) give us a glimpse of these mysterious personages; they wore turbans, dressed in black, and had ram skins, one white, one black, slung over their shoulders; as insignia, they had a sharp-pointed stick, an ornament worn around the neck (*niṣka*), and an unstrung bow (*jyāhroḍa*). The stick-lance (proto-type of the Śivaistic śula?) and the bow, recur in certain Asiatic shamanisms.[32]

As was mentioned earlier, Rudra too is described as being clad in black, which further strengthens the case for Rudra and the vrātya being connected. This connection can also be seen in some of the commentaries in which Rudra is called *vrātya-pati*, and the *Mahābhārata* still uses the term vrātya to designate the Śivaistic bacchantes.[33] In Chakravati's work *The Concept of Rudra-Śiva*, another image of the vrātya is described.

> The vrātyas were an obscure non-sacrificing ethnic group of people—whether Āryan, either fallen or uninitiated, or non-Āryan—belonging to a roving band (*vrāta*) and were swallowers

[32] ELIADE, M., *Yoga: Immortality and Freedom*, pp. 103-104.
[33] Ibid., 105.

> of poison. Roth considers the praise of the vrātya in the *Atharva Veda* as an idealizing of the devout vagrant or mendicant (*parivrājaka*) who is the benefactor of human society. The extravagant respect paid to the *vrātyas* in this Veda either shows that they themselves, through their representatives, compiled the hymns after gaining victory over the Āryan, or it indicates "the lofty spirituality of the Āryan culture which sublimated the lewd and repulsive features of the vrātya cult before it was absorbed into Brāhmanism and developed into Śaivism."[34]

This description of the vrātya seems to portray them as a type of ascetic that existed on the fringes of Vedic society, who were respected but were also outcasts. From all three of these descriptions, the vrātya seem very similar to being a type of proto-ascetic or proto-tantric. The description of their practices, in so far as they can be interpreted from the Vedas, seems to bear connections with both Tantrism and Shamanism, thus suggesting that there may also be a more direct connection between the two forms of practice. The theory of shamanism having its origins in India or the Orient is by no means a new idea and has been expressed, dissented, argued with, and at times risen to popularity on many an occasion. Eliade comments on the possible linguistic origins of the word 'shaman' in the following paragraph.

> The word "shaman," we saw, comes to us through Russian from the Tungusic *šaman*. The derivation of this term from the Pali *samaṇa* (Sanskrit *śramaṇa*) through the Chinese *sha-men* (a mere transcription of the Pali word), which was accepted by the majority of nineteenth-century Orientalists, was nonetheless questioned quite early ... but G. J. Ramstedt has shown that Németh's phonetic law is invalid. Then too, the discovery of similar words in Tokharian (*ṣamāne* "Buddhist monk") and in Sogdian (šmṇ = šaman) revived the theory of Indian origin.[35]

---

[34] CHAKRAVATI, M., *The Concept of Rudra-Śiva* (India: Motilal Banarsidass, 1986), 12.

[35] ELIADE, M., trans. Trask, W. R., *Shamanism: Archaic Techniques of Ecstasy* (New York: Bollingen Foundation, 1964), 496.

The linguistic evidence for an Indian origin of the word shaman has also been examined by Gibson, who shares Eliade's suspicion that the similarity between the words śramaṇa and shaman is too great to be thought of as purely coincidental.

> First and most basically, the parallels in the Turkic languages add weight to the case for a derivation of the Tunguz shaman from śramaṇa. Secondly, that several different Buddhist words are used to refer to the shaman (śramaṇa-shaman, *vira-dpa', bo, burxan*, and *bakshi*) indicates that Buddhism's effects cannot be explained by positing a single wave but must be seen as a process that was repeated several times.[36]

However, even if one can provide a concrete linguistic link between the two cultures, there are factors to consider concerning the logic of such connection. Firstly, given the geographic distance between the Tunguz and India, some method of travel and communication between the people involved needs to be speculated upon. Secondly, there are problems in defining the meaning of the word shaman itself, for, as Reinhard has remarked, "The situation is, in brief, that there is a Tungusic word, its ultimate origin and meaning uncertain, associated with a Tungusic phenomenon, its ultimate origin, and original form unknown."[37] Gibson outlines the problems involving a cross-cultural definition of the shaman in the following paragraph, in which he mentions assumptions that have been made about the role of the shaman:

> 1) "Shamanism" is a word that can be legitimately applied to, and adequately accounts for, a wide variety of non-literate religious complexes, which may or may not be historically related, 2) Shamanism being non-literate, it is, therefore, pre-literate. 3) Being pre-literate, it is, therefore, ahistorical, existing unchanged from the dawn of human existence (or at least from the beginnings of a given society). 4) Any element of a

[36] GIBSON, T., Notes on the History of the Shamanic in Tibet and Inner Asia in *Numen*, Vol.44 (Netherlands: Koninklijke Brill NV, 1997), 51.
[37] Ibid., 40.

> culture's religious landscape which cannot be accounted for by its prevailing scriptural tradition can be explained as a "vestige" of a primordial shamanistic substrate.[38]

What Gibson considers a shaman to be is far less complex than the previously perceived definition, for Gibson states that a working definition of shamanism can be reached by the recognition of a single fact—"a person is recognized by his own society as being in direct contact with the divine or extra human (however that society defines it) by virtue of concrete demonstrations of unusual capabilities, then he or she is a shaman."[39] This definition, though simple, is extremely workable, and does not preclude other religious types of esoteric practitioners from now entering into the definition of the shaman. By adopting this new, more simplistic terminology, one can view other traditions in a different light, and cease to perceive shamanism as a primitive technique employed by less literate societies. Shamanism, in some form, has been employed on an almost universal scale if Gibson's definition is to be accepted.

If the definition of the shaman is now 'a person recognized by his own society as being in direct contact with the divine or extra human (however that society defines it) by virtue of concrete demonstrations of unusual capabilities' then to complete the conundrum related to the imagery of Śiva, this definition of the shaman must be brought into the Indian context. Within the Tantric traditions, the definition becomes an exact description of how a Tantric is perceived. The practice of Tantra is alleged to provide those who practice the path with mystic endowments or siddhi. Numerous texts at least from the thirteenth century on mention the very same prodigies performed by sorcerers and magicians, who also possessed the power to fly and to make themselves invisible, exactly like the shamans and yogīns.[40] Whilst the linkage betwixt shamanism in India has not yet been directly established, it has been done so in Tibet, for

---

[38] GIBSON, T., Notes on the History of the Shamanic in Tibet and Inner Asia in *Numen*, Vol.44, 40.

[39] Ibid., 44.

[40] ELIADE, M., *Shamanism: Archaic Techniques of Ecstasy*, pp. 429-430.

Tantric Buddhism is a syncretism of Buddhism, Tantric technique and an indigenous form of shamanism known as Bon. Within Tantric Buddhism, there are also rituals which are clearly derived from shamanic sources. Eliade cites one example of a rite named *chöd* (*gchod*), which is clearly shamanic in structure; it consists of offering one's own flesh to be eaten by demons—which is curiously reminiscent of the future shaman's initiatory dismemberment by "demons" and ancestral souls.[41] Eliade also speculates that the origins of such rites found in Tantric Buddhism primarily arose in the shamanic sphere, and after time developed in a highly complex teaching that gradually merged with Buddhism. Citing an example of a meditative practice found in Tibetan Tantra, Eliade describes the process involved and concludes that the shamanic element was altered once incorporated in Tantrism, and thus transformed, which illustrates that the two forms developed side by side in Tibet, even if Tantrism is not a progressive development on Shamanism.

> We cite some Tantric meditations whose object is the practitioner's stripping his own body of flesh and contemplating his skeleton. The yogīn is asked to imagine his body as a corpse and his mind as an angry goddess, with a face and two hands holding a knife and a skull. "Think that she severeth the head from the corpse … and cutteth the corpse into bits and flingeth them inside the skull as offerings to deities." Another exercise consists in his seeing himself as "a radiant white skeleton of enormous size, whence issueth flames, so great that they fill the voidness of the Universe." Finally, a third meditation sets the yogīn the task of contemplating himself as transformed into the raging *dākinī*, stripping the skin from his own body … These few extracts suffice to show the transformation that a shamanic schema can undergo when it is incorporated into a complex philosophical system, such as Tantrism.[42]

---

[41] ELIADE, M., *Shamanism: Archaic Techniques of Ecstasy*, 436.

[42] Ibid., 437.

There are also connections between shamanism and yoga to be found in India. One such common concept that pervades most Hindu traditions is the idea of tapas or 'mystical heat.'[43] As Eliade explains, tapas is a concept that is documented in Vedic texts, and also holds a considerable place in yogīc-tantric techniques. This "heat" is induced by holding the breath and especially by the "transmutation" of sexual energy, a yogīc-tantric practice which, although quite obscure, is based on *prāṇāyāma* and various "visualizations."[44] Tapas is clearly documented in the *Rig Veda*, and its powers are creative on both the cosmic and spiritual planes; through tapas, the ascetic becomes clairvoyant and even incarnates the Gods.[45] Comparing the magical increase of the temperature within the body, which Eliade goes on to describe as a universal feat amongst medicine men, shamans, and *fakirs*, he describes tapas as being one of the most typical yogīc-tantric techniques for producing 'mystic heat.' He then continues on to say that the continuity between the oldest known magical technique and Tantric Yoga, is in this particular, undeniable.[46] The idea of mystic heat is not unknown outside of India, for as Georges Dumézil has shown, several terms in the Indo-European "heroic" vocabulary—*furor*, *ferg*, *wut*, *ménos*—express precisely this "extreme heat" and "rage" which, on other levels of sacrality, characterize the incarnation of power.[47] In their own linguistic context, most of the words here have a connection with altered mental states that could be linked to shamanism also, which would identify the induction of a state of 'mystical heat' as a prerequisite for traditions which revolve around shamanism.

Thus working on the definitions of tapas and shamanism provided by such authors as Eliade, Dumézil, and Gibson, the shamanic elements found in the imagery of Śankara and Naṭarāja now need to be scrutinized. In the figure of Naṭarāja, the Lord

[43] ELIADE, M., *Shamanism: Archaic Techniques of Ecstasy*, 437.
[44] Ibid.
[45] ELIADE, M., *Yoga: Immortality and Freedom*, 106.
[46] Ibid.
[47] Ibid.

of the Dance, a number of shamanic elements are immediately obvious. Firstly his dance is surrounded by a halo of flame that symbolizes the great tapas he generates as he dances, and secondly, there is the dance itself, for dancing is universally recognized as a technique utilized in shamanism to induce a trance or communicate with spirits. Such trance states are not merely the product of the repetitive physical motions found in dancing—the music involved in the dance also plays an important role in achieving this new state of mind. More than any instrument, it is the drum which is used as the musical instrument employed by the shaman.

> The shamanic drum is distinguished from all other instruments of the "magic of noise" precisely by the fact that it makes possible an ecstatic experience. Either this experience was prepared, in the beginning, by the charm of the sounds of the drum, a charm that was evaluated as "voices of the spirits," or an ecstatic experience was attained through the extreme concentration provoked by a long period of drumming.[48]

Such a drum is held in the hands of Naṭarāja as he dances. For the dancer, the drum is the instrument of choice to open the higher realms of consciousness, for its repetitive rhythms enables one to lose one's sense of self and abandon oneself to the music, or to the dance. The drum can produce what psychologists call "hypnotic regression" and touch the deeper, archetypal self that is still one with the cosmos, open to all other forms of being and connected with the most distant stars.[49]

In the figure of Śankara, the connection with shamanism is less direct, in contrast to the connection with altered mental states, which is more apparent in the figure of the Lord of Yoga. Seated serene and calm in his classic yogīn poise, Śankara is deeply engrossed in yoga. In order to connect this image with shamanism, it is necessary to establish that what is involved in the practice of yoga is an altered state of consciousness. Such a definition is immediately apparent

[48] ELIADE, M., *Shamanism: Archaic Techniques of Ecstasy*, 175.
[49] STORL, W. D., *Shiva: the Wild God of Power and Ecstasy*, 143.

in the passages of the *Śiva Sūtras*. For example, the Śāmbhavopāya 1.7 states that the "fourth state of consciousness is experienced by piercing through the states of waking consciousness, the dream state and the state of dreamless sleep, in blissful awareness of the true nature of reality."[50] The fourth state of mind is furthermore defined within the *Śiva Sūtras* as being a state of mind which is not normally entered into. In the *Śiva Sūtras* (Āṇavopāya, 3.9), it is even said that "One who has realized his spiritual nature is like a dancer, dancing to the rhythm of the universe."[51] This again adds further evidence that the dance of Naṭarāja is not merely dancing, but an allegory for a being that is spiritually awakened, and a higher level of consciousness. Similarly, for a definition of yoga, there is one in the first chapter of the *Yoga Sūtra*.

> Concentration ... Yoga is contemplation (*samādhi*), and it is a characteristic of the mind pervading all its planes ... the commentator now removes the doubt as to the meaning of the word "yoga," which arises from its ordinary connotation. Thus says he, "Yoga is contemplation."[52]

Yoga should be seen not just a form of meditation, but as a type of higher thought which differs from the normal perception of reality. It is a higher state of awareness, which allows the mind to contemplate subjects and objects from a different level or plane of operation than that found in everyday existence. The fact that this type of deep contemplation is also comparable with a trance state is also seen in the *Yoga Sūtras*, which states that "the cognitive trance (samādhi) is accompanied by the appearances of philosophical curiosity, meditation, elation, and egoism."[53] This statement describes a similar state of mind as is found in the shamanic descriptions of ecstasy.

---

[50] WORTHINGTON, R., *Finding the Hidden Self: a Study of the Siva Sutras* (USA: The Himalayan Institute Press, 2002), 15.

[51] Ibid., 72.

[52] MOORE, C., & RADHAKRISHNAN, S., *A Sourcebook in Indian Philosophy* (USA: Princeton University Press, 1989), 454.

[53] Ibid., 457.

Abhinavagupta in his poem on śāmbhavī mudrā, or the '*Seal of Śambhu*' also offers a description of the Śaivite yogīn's state of consciousness.

> "Even though gazing outside, the eyes neither opening nor closing, one should direct one's attention within. This is the seal (*mudrā*) of Bhairava, concealed as the best secret of all the Tantras." Curiously, this verse begins with the same term in Sanskrit that begins Abhinavagupta's poem: *antar-laksya*, literally, that which is to be perceived within, referring to the innermost object of perception. This is Śiva, the highest consciousness to be recognized or perceived inwardly by the yogīn and the true and deepest nature of both the inner Self and the outer world.[54]

This adds the final piece of evidence to the apparent polarity between Naṭarāja and Śankara; they are both forms of Śiva, and Śiva himself is represented as the highest state of consciousness experienced by the yogīn. Śiva is not just linked via the practice of Tantra or yoga to the practitioner's mental state; Śiva is described here as the mental state itself. Such a description of Śiva is also found in the *Vijñāna-Bhairava-Tantra*, which describes this form of meditative practice as follows (verse 80): "Fixing the gaze on some outer object and yet at the same time making his mind free of the prop of all thought constructs, the yogīn acquires the state of Śiva without delay."[55]

This is why the figure of Śiva is so complex and at times defies all descriptions, absorbing opposite ideas and thoughts into his own beings—he is a purely cerebral deity that presides over human mental states and a higher form of consciousness. This is not just evident in the roles of Naṭarāja and Śankara, but in all of his imagery. In his role as the loving spouse of Pārvatī, he transcends the normal mental state through the principle of eros. As the wild God who haunts burial grounds and forests, he dwells on the fringes of society, where

[54] WHITE, D. G., ed., *Tantra in Practice*, (USA: Princeton University Press, 2000), 576.
[55] Ibid., 579.

mental barriers to thought and action are no longer applicable—he transcends the barriers of social rules and violates boundaries through the use of the impure, thus transporting his consciousness to a higher level by the removal of artificial social barriers and destroying māyā. As the divine hermaphrodite, the union of Śiva and Śakti, Śiva again transcends the realm of normal consciousness, for he experiences the totality of human existence, transcending even the boundaries of the sexes and sexual experience. As Naṭarāja, he transcends to a higher level of consciousness through wild action and the dance of the universal, cosmic drumbeat, and as Śankara, his consciousness is elevated via intense meditation.

Seen in this light Naṭarāja and Śankara are by no means representational of opposing polarities in the behavior of Śiva—the polarity that is at first apparent in their imagery is illusory, for it is not representative of a dichotomy, but instead is a continuum. This can be seen clearly from the following extract.

> In Śankara, resting motionless in meditation, the three principles, the red, white, and black guṇas, are in harmonious, undisturbed balance, but when Śiva becomes Naṭarāja, these elements are swirled into motion, churned and infinitely mixed and remixed. When he starts the drumbeat, the oneness of Śankara's silence is shattered.[56]

This continuum is evidenced profoundly by the fact that Śiva can move from one form to the other, transported by the shamanic beating of the drum. What separates the images of Naṭarāja and Śankara is the level of activity portrayed; one is dancing, the other engrossed in yoga. Both are generating extreme mystical heat or tapas, and both are representational of a higher state of consciousness. The only difference between the two images is how this higher state is reached, and how the consequential release of tapas is generated. In the case of Naṭarāja this is produced by an active route to the divine consciousness, and in the case of Śankara, it is produced by a passive route to the divine consciousness. To

[56] STORL, W. D., *Shiva: the Wild God of Power and Ecstasy*, 138.

a certain extent, the parables seen here in Naṭarāja and Śankara are also found in earlier portrayals of the Vedic God Rudra, whom when fierce was referred as Rudra, and when benevolent carried the title of Śiva. Given that Rudra appears to have been an earlier form of Śiva, it is not surprising that this dualistic split in Rudra's personality was inherited by Śiva, albeit in the form of Naṭarāja and Śankara.

Rudra's connections to the vrātya, who may have been shamanic practitioners also provides a link between the shamanic use of ecstasy and the yogīc production of tapas, which may be cross-cultural terms for the same phenomena, for as we have seen the production of mystical heat is utilized in both yoga, shamanism, and certain magical acts. Tapas, whether it is generated by dancing (which is a common technique in shamanism) or by yoga, is the byproduct of the achievement of an altered state of consciousness. This higher state can be achieved either through an active route (dancing, music, ecstasy) or by a passive route (yoga, trance, bliss). Not only is the production of tapas very similar to the shamanic phenomenon, as was mentioned by Eliade, Tantra also shares a number of similarities with shamanism to such an extent that in Tibet shamanism and Tantrism have merged into a single tradition. The possibility of an Asiatic origin for shamanism, as is seen in the linguistic roots of the word 'shaman', also has a number of implications for the identification of Śiva, for if it can be proven that the word does have its origin in India, then it seems that the aforementioned vrātya, may have been a class of Vedic shaman, or at the very least a type of proto-shaman, for from the descriptions of them provided it seems clear that their practices were on the borderline between shamanism and yoga. If Rudra was connected with shamanism, then so was Śiva, for his character is partially based on that of Rudra. Furthermore, it seems possible that if the vrātya were Āryan, then as the Āryans continued their migration, knowledge of the vrātya, if not the vrātya themselves, would have been carried with them. This could account for the occurrence of similarities in the languages for the word 'shaman' being found in geographical regions that are separated from one another. This would not necessarily imply that yoga is shamanism; rather it would imply that yoga is based on a form of shamanism, which over time developed a highly advanced system of philosophy and esoteric technique. In the case of India, shamanism could perhaps be described as a form of proto-yoga or an earlier and more primitive technique on which yoga came to be based.

To conclude, it seems that Naṭarāja and Śankara are both representative of a form of higher consciousness and that this is not restricted to these two forms of Śiva. This higher consciousness can be reached by many different techniques—in Śankara the passive introspective technique known as yoga is utilized. In the image of Naṭarāja, the wilder, shamanic aspect of the God is dominant. Yet neither of these images is an opposite or mutually exclusive of the other; they are purely representative of the transportation of human consciousness to a higher plane. Śiva is not simply a being that is representative of higher consciousness and ascension, he is that ascension—by connecting him to the higher consciousness experienced in humans via acts of Tantra, yoga or shamanism, one transcends duality just as Śiva himself does. Śiva, as Naṭarāja and Śankara, represents a bridge between man and God; they are the representation of the road to higher consciousness or ascension of the human condition. By means of achieving this state of higher consciousness, the practitioners achieve a form of divine mortality.

THE DEVĪ

From Satī to Kālī

The Devī is best conceived of as a multi-faceted Goddess who has numerous aspects, all of which encapsulate different aspects of her infinite form. Because the infinite is incomprehensible to the finite mind, these different aspects of the Devī manifest under many different names and forms. The complexity and multiplicity of forms overlaying the Devī tend to obscure her nature, but just as oil clings to and obscures the nature of water, it is only a layer of superficial covering, and underneath the clarity is perfect. This is also true with regard to nature of the Goddess.

Tantra operates from a non-dualistic polar reality wherein the opposites merge and disappear into a singular totality. The imagery tends to be composed of dyads, with 'consort pairings'. Śiva's first bride, the original incarnation of the Devī, is the primordial Satī, after whom the practice of immolation is named (*suttee/sati*). Śiva, in his role as an outcast God dwelling in cremation grounds, spent most of his time devoted to asceticism with no interest in taking a consort. But one day,

> Brahmā said: Who should be the wife of Śambhu? Who shall be able to enchant him? I have given my thought to this question

> but am unable to find out a lovely woman. O Dakṣ! Except for illusion of Viṣṇu (Viṣṇumāyā) known also as Mahāmāyā, who is omnipresent, Sāvitrī, Sandhyā, and Umā (or, worshiped by Sāvitrī, Sandhyā, and Umā), none shall be able to enchant him.[1]

Ironically, Śiva's consort Satī is the daughter of Dakṣa, the law-giver, whose rituals are necessary for the maintenance of both human and cosmic order. Naturally, as the personification of cosmic order, Dakṣa is not pleased by his daughter's marriage to Śiva, who is, in essence, his opposite. Śiva, therefore, represents to Dakṣa a most troublesome son-in-law, and Dakṣa bans Śiva from attending festivities at his domicile. This simple event leads to one of the most important incidents for the representation of the Devī.

In her role as Dakṣa's daughter, the Devī is also quite obviously connected with Āryan/Vedic Tradition. Satī, like her husband Śiva, is a master of yoga, and being deeply annoyed with her father's behavior, she decides to punish him for the dishonorable treatment of her husband. Satī then uses yoga to immolate herself in flame and releases her soul from its body. Her physical body becomes empty and Satī appears to be dead. It is commonly thought to be from this incident that the rite of suttee originates. However, it seems more likely that the myth of Satī was corrupted for political purposes at a later time due to society no longer wanting to provide for widows. Earlier in India's history, suttee was unheard of and men simply married their brother's widow, incorporating her into his own family. The burning of widows was enforced at a political level and there is nothing in the Hindu religion that supports the practice.

Dakṣa and Śiva believe Satī to be dead. Śiva, when he finds out what occurred, is none too pleased and attacks Dakṣa, decapitating him (this part also corresponds to the decapitation of Brahmā which will be discussed in a later chapter). Other deities are also seriously assaulted in the attack, losing eyes and teeth. However, the important aspect here is the symbolic one. By decapitating Dakṣa Śiva emphasizes his destructive role, not just because of assaulting

1 SHASTRI, B. N., *The Kālikā Purāna,* Part I (India: Nag Publishers, 1992), 40.

Dakṣa, but because of what the attack represents. Dakṣa maintains the cosmic order—he performs the cosmic sacrifice which assures the existence of the world and the cosmos—Śiva, therefore, violates the nature of the cosmic order itself, thus demonstrating his ability to transgress even the cosmic law.

Śiva, mourning for Satī, flies away carrying her corpse. Viṣṇu, taking pity on him, dissects the body of Satī into parts, each of which falls to the earth to become the major *Seats of Power* or *Śakta Pīṭhas* in the Tantric Traditions where the Goddess is worshiped, and through these different locations she manifests in different aspects which reflect the different parts of the Devī's body. The Devī possesses an ability to divide herself into different aspects of divinity and in her totality (when the parts are 'rejoined') she is the equivalent of Kṛṣṇa's 'universal form'. The Devī is a composite entity that, at times of extreme plight or dismay, divides herself into other Goddesses or 'Śakti clusters'. This seems to be a feature shared by other manifestations of the Devī, as one can instantly recall the ability of Durgā to call Kālī into being in the *Devī Māhātmyam*. Similarly, this trait of the Devī's can also be seen in the group of Goddesses known as the Mātṛs or Mothers.

> In Purāṇic literature, there seems to be a more or less standard form of myth for Mātṛs: They are conceived of as personified energies of seven (or eight) Brāhmanical gods and as appearing to aid Śiva or the Devī in destroying Asura(s). They fight ferociously and often become drunk with blood. A few more examples may be given. An account similar to the DM version is given in the *Vāmana Purāṇa* (30). An interesting deviation here is that though the Mātṛs are named after the male deities, as usual, they issue from different parts of the Devī's body (30.3-9).[2]

The Mātṛs, like the Tantric Pīṭhas, arise from the body parts of the Devī who is Satī. The fact that Satī is the Devī is revealed in an extract from the *Kālikā Purāṇa*, where it is explicitly stated that only the Devī herself is suitable to be the consort of Śiva.

[2] ONISHI, Y., *Feminine Multiplicity* (India: Sri Satguru Publications, 1997), 65.

There is another group of Goddesses connected to the Devī that are known as the Mahāvidyā. They are depicted in many temples throughout India and seem to be regarded as an expression of the way in which the Goddess assumes many different forms.[3] The Mahāvidyās play a particularly significant role within Śakta Tantra. According to textual references, the Mahāvidyās came into existence in the *Mahābhāgavata Purāṇa*. They are explicitly linked to the death of Satī and the origin of the Śakta Pīṭhas. This is clearly a variant of the previously cited version in which Satī dies and her body is dismembered. Onishi, in his book entitled *Feminine Multiplicity*, recounts the birth of the Mahāvidyās as follows,

> When Dakṣa, Satī's father, decided to perform a great sacrifice, he invited everyone residing in the heaven to attend it, except for Śiva and Satī because he did not like Śiva's uncivilized habits and appearance. Satī, greatly insulted (though Śiva was not), intended to go to disrupt the sacrifice but was forbidden by Śiva to attend the sacrifice. Unable to change her husband's mind, Satī eventually lost her temper, assuming a dreadful form. She then went on to multiply herself into ten different forms which are Mahāvidyās—Kālī, Tārā, Chinnamastā, Bhuvaneśvarī, Bagalā, Dhūmāvatī, Kamalā, Mātaṅgī, Soḍaśī, and Bhairavī.[4]

This origination of the Mahāvidyās in the body of Satī illustrates the fact that her ability to render herself into different parts, or aspects, also happens when she is alive. The sanctity that is derived from the falling of her limbs on various parts of the earth is a reflection of the ability of the Devī to break herself down into smaller entities, highlighting her composite nature. It is not just her limbs that fall to the earth but the various esoteric aspects of her being that endow the ground on which they fall with her power.

Regarding Satī's gift to render her body and spirit into other female entities, it is also important to consider the number of the Mahāvidyās, for Kumar suggests that the number ten was chosen to

[3] ONISHI, Y., *Feminine Multiplicity*, 104.
[4] Ibid.

match the ten primary incarnations of Viṣṇu.[5] Another significant point regarding the multiplicity found in the Mahāvidyās is that, in terms of myth, the Ten Goddesses are not entirely separate or different from one another; they are in fact different forms assumed by one Goddess—not only does Satī manifest herself in these ten forms, she also withdraws them back into herself.[6]

Satī, however, was a skilled yoginī. Even Śiva did not realize that only her physical body perished. His second wife/consort Pārvatī is in fact just the reincarnation of Satī, her soul transferred from one body to another via the yogīc teaching of 'consciousness transference'. The method of yoga she employed to immolate herself is similar to another teaching known as the 'Razor of the Night which is Death', and the means by which to transfer the consciousness from the body during death is one of the highest yogīc teachings, passed only from master to disciple by oral means. A similar process is found in the Tibetan *Vajrayāna* and is linked to the process of reincarnation in Tibet.

Pārvatī, Śiva's second consort, plays a dual role. Firstly, she is a companion in her asceticism, and it is only through her fierce devotion to asceticism that she manages to seduce him. Secondly, following this, Pārvatī provides a second function and essentially domesticates Śiva, toning down his antisocial behavior. Once her role as an ascetic is fulfilled, Pārvatī transforms herself into the paradigm of the Hindu wife. Though Pārvatī is one of the popularized forms of Śiva's consorts, she is not the only one—Śiva, in many different forms is paired with the Devī in many different forms. Just as Pārvatī sits at one polarity as the 'good girl', Śiva's other consort, Kālī is the 'bad girl'. They are, however, in essence both forms of the Devī, as is seen in the following passage:

> In the *Vāmana Purāṇa* Pārvatī is called Kālī because of her dark complexion. When Pārvatī hears Śiva use this name, she takes offense and does austerities to rid herself of her dark skin. After

[5] ONISHI, Y., *Feminine Multiplicity*, 106.
[6] Ibid.

> she succeeds, she is renamed Gaurī, the golden one. Her dark sheath, however, is transformed into the furious battle queen Kauśikī, who subsequently creates Kālī herself in her fury. So again, although there is an intermediary Goddess, Kauśikī, Kālī is shown to play the role of Pārvatī's dark, negative, violent nature.[7]

In her relation to Śiva, Kālī appears to play the opposite role from that of Pārvatī. Pārvatī calms Śiva, counterbalancing his antisocial or destructive tendencies. It is she who brings Śiva within the sphere of domesticity and who, with her soft glances, urges him to soften the destructive aspects of his tāṇḍava dance. Kālī is Śiva's 'other' wife, as it were, provoking him and encouraging him in his mad, antisocial, or often destructive habits. It is never Kālī who calms Śiva, but Śiva who must calm Kālī. Her association with criminals also reinforces her dangerous role *vis-a-vis* society. She is at home outside the moral order and is unbound by that order.[8]

Within the Tantric Traditions, however, it is not always the peaceful and benign Pārvatī who is held as the supreme deity, often it is the dark and outwardly menacing Kālī who holds dominance. It is Kālī who is the supreme power of Tantrism and the mother deity of the Tāntrikas. She exists outside the moral confines of the social order, because her power transgresses it—Kālī, quite simply is so powerful that she has no use for it, and thus is free to act as she wishes. As the personification of time, transgression, and impurity there is quite simply nothing for Kālī to fear, thus her retinue of ghosts, criminals, magicians, and the undead can do her no harm. She is Time, and will be the last entity to perish at the end of the cosmic cycle. Śiva, in his destructive aspect, retains his connections to time and death, and for this reason is her consort as Mahākāla.

Kālī is also closely associated with the Goddess Durgā, who also transforms herself into Kālī during battle, and the most famous

[7] KINGSLEY, D. R., Blood and Death Out of Place: Reflections on the Goddess Kālī in eds., Hawley, J. S., & Wulff D. M., *The Divine Consort: Rādhā and the Goddess of India* (USA: Beacon Press, 1986), 146.

[8] Ibid., 148.

myth featuring Kālī is that of the Goddess Durgā's destruction of the demons Śumbha and Niśumbha. In the *Devī Māhātmyam* version of this myth, Kālī is born when two demon generals, Caṇḍa and Muṇḍa, are sent to taunt and attack Durgā. Durgā loses her composure, grows furious, and from her darkened brow springs Kālī. She howls loudly, wades into the demon army crushing and devoring her enemies, until she finally decapitates Caṇḍa and Muṇḍa. Later in the battle, she is summoned by Durgā to kill the demon Raktabīja. This demon has the magical ability to recreate himself every time a drop of his blood touches the ground. When Durgā wounds him she only makes her situation more desperate, and soon the battlefield is filled with Raktabījas. Kālī rescues Durgā by swallowing the swarm of blood-borne demons and sucking the blood from the original Raktabīja until he falls lifeless. In these myths Kālī seems to be Durgā's embodied fury, appearing when Durgā loses control or is confronted with a formidable task.[9] As with Pārvatī, the Devī in her more dangerous aspect, Durgā can be transformed into Kālī. This violence which is found in only certain manifestations of the Devī remains unsurpassed by that of the male Gods who cannot defeat the demon Raktabīja. Ultimately, this is not linked to a sex-based dichotomy of power, but the model of Hindu transgression. The rise of Kālī and Tantrism to prominence in the Hindu Tradition comes from the harnessing of the terrible chthonic power of the Devī. As Biardeau writes,

> When we pass from *bhakti* to śaktism ... she becomes the preeminent divinity, the Śakti who is superior to Śiva, and this reversal of the hierarchy is accompanied ... by a reversal of dharma: what was prohibited becomes permitted, the impure becomes pure. She is closer to earthly values ... but she is also more apt to make use of the violence without which the earth could not live.[10]

---

[9] KINGSLEY, D. R., Blood and Death Out of Place: Reflections on the Goddess Kālī in eds., Hawley, J. S., & Wulff D. M., *The Divine Consort: Rādhā and the Goddess of India*, 145.

[10] URBAN, H., *The Power of Tantra: Religion, Sexuality, and the Politics of South Asian Studies* (USA: I. B. Tauris & CO Ltd, 2010), 95.

Kālī is strongly associated with the colors red and black. Knipe suggests that when red and black are found together they are symbolic of inauspicious, uncontrolled power, akin to that found in witchcraft or warfare.[11] Part of Kālī's iconography is strongly linked to blood—not because of violence, fetishism, or even the act of bloodletting itself—but because of the symbolic impurity of blood *out of place*. So strong is Kālī's association with blood it is said that even a single drop of blood and a prayer from her faithful is enough to attract her attention. Blood in Hinduism is highly impure; it is a polluting substance that must be avoided. Throughout the classical Hindu law books, the *Dharma Sūtras*, menstrual blood, and menstruating women, are surrounded with all manner of taboos. Touching a menstruating woman is said to be equal to touching an outcast or corpse; food touched by a menstruating woman is as impure as food into which hair or an insect has fallen, food touched by someone's foot, or food given by a harlot or a heinous sinner. As Madhu Khanna notes, "A woman during menstruation is compared to a fallen woman [the] temporary untouchability attributed to women and the overwhelming number of menstrual taboos imposed on them go to show that the first three days of menstruation were looked upon as dangerous and frightening."[12]

Menstrual blood is believed to be so polluting that during menstruation even the husband is sometimes held to be of an impure status. In North India, there is also a belief that every time a female menstruates an embryo, or potential child, perishes. The sin of the unborn child's death lies with the husband or father, depending on whether or not the woman is wed. Prepubescent girls, however, are regarded as being especially pure and are often worshiped by high caste men as an incarnation of Durgā. This is known as *kumāri pūjā* (worship of the virgin), and the young girl is held to be pure because she is regarded as being possessed of a non-sexual nature. The idea of women being regarded as sexually dangerous beings

[11] KNIPE, D. M., *In The Image of Fire* (India: Motilal Banarsidass, 1975), pp. 74-75.

[12] URBAN, H., *The Power of Tantra: Religion, Sexuality, and the Politics of South Asian Studies*, 55.

originates from the concept of worldly renunciation, which entails celibacy. Sex was also thought of as a far more risky activity for the male than the female, as it is believed that a man's vitality is stored within his semen, hence the power of the God Śiva, who remains celibate (despite being ithyphallic, Śiva does not ejaculate). Blood, as symbolic of both sex and death is twice as polluting as a substance, and hence it comes under Kālī's dominion, as only the Devī in her most fearsome aspect can handle such a substance and remain uncontaminated, and because Kālī is so distant from the moral and natural order, nothing can harm her. Unlike the other female deities, Kālī is pure unrestrained śakti, her power needs no external trappings of social adornments.

The female principle of śakti is also deemed to both destructive and dangerous if uncontrolled by a male, a fact which is illustrated by the inauspicious forms of the Goddess, all of whom remain unwed, whilst the benevolent forms of the Goddess are all married. Kālī is the Goddess at her most inauspicious and uncaring—naked, blood-drinking, and impure. Although she is paired with Śiva the two are not married, representing the lack of interest in social order and convention. In terms of iconography, both Durgā and Pārvatī represent śakti under control—their power is bound, they wear jewelry, bracelets and restrain their hair. Kālī, however, does not. Nonetheless, Kālī is a Goddess and not a demon. To mistake her for a demonic force would be a grievous error, for she serves the cosmic order and guards it, but her protection is fierce, and it is for this reason that she is regarded as attentive to her devotees.

Despite the time-honored denial from the puritanical European Right that Kālī cannot possibly be an Āryan or Indo-European Goddess, evidence actually points to the opposite. She is the Left-Hand Path current of the Indo-Āryan Tradition. Part of this confusion arises from the erroneous correlation of Gods skin colors with mortal racial features when, in fact, there is no correlation. It is also worth noting that a number of deities also appear as green, yellow, and bright red, all of which are purely symbolic on the esoteric level. On the contrary, to add to the confusion, the physical skin color is often the reverse of the guṇa they embody. Śiva, for example, is portrayed as white because he is possessed of the tamasic or physical guṇa, whereas Viṣṇu and Kṛṣṇa are both black because they are both pure sattva. The same applies to Kālī. She is black because she is of the sattva current. There is absolutely no evidence that Kālī holds her origins in any tradition which is not Vedic in origin. She first appears within the last great Āryan epic, the *Mahābhārata*. In the *Mahābhārata* we also see Arjuna, one of the leading characters within the Bhagavad Gītā addressing a hymn to Kālī:

> Arjuna said, "I bow to thee, O leader of Yogīns, O thou that art identical with Brahman, O thou that dwellest in the forest of Mandara, O thou that art freed from decrepitude and decay, O Kālī, O wife of Kapala, O thou that art of a black and tawny hue, I bow to thee. O bringer of benefits to thy devotees, I bow to thee, O Mahākālī, O wife of the universal destroyer, I bow to thee. O proud one, O thou that rescuest from dangers, O thou that art endued with every auspicious attribute. O thou that art sprung from the Kata race, O thou that deservest the most regardful worship, O fierce one, O giver of victory, O victory's self, O thou that bearest a banner of peacock plumes, O thou that art decked with every ornament, O thou that bearest an awful spear, O thou that holdest a sword and shield, O thou that art the younger sister of the chief of cowherds, O eldest one, O thou that wert born in the race of the cowherd Nanda! O thou that art always fond of Buffalo's blood, O thou that wert born in the race of Kusika, O thou that art dressed in yellow robes, O thou that hadst devoured Asuras assuming the face of a wolf 1, I bow to thee that art fond of battle! O Uma, Sakambhari, O thou that art white in hue, O thou that art black in hue, O thou that hast slain the Asura Kaitabha, O thou that art yellow-eyed, O thou that art diverse-eyed, O thou of eyes that have the color of smoke, I bow to thee. O thou that art the Vedas, the Śrūtis, and the highest virtue, O thou that art propitious to Brāhmaṇa engaged in sacrifice, O thou that hast a knowledge

> of the past, thou that art ever present in the sacred abodes erected to thee in cities of Jamvudwipa, I bow to thee. Thou art the science of Brahmā among sciences, and thou that art that sleep of creatures from which there is no waking. O mother of Skanda, O thou that possessest the six (highest) attributes, O Durgā, O thou that dwellest in inaccessible regions, thou art described as Swaha, and Swadha, as Kāla, as Kashta, and as Sarasvatī, as Savitra the mother of the Vedas, and as the science of Vedānta. With inner soul cleansed, I praise thee. O great Goddess, let victory always attend me through thy grace on the field of battle. In inaccessible regions, where there is fear, in places of difficulty, in the abodes of thy worshipers and in the nether regions (Pātāla), thou always dwellest. Thou always defeatest the Danavas. Thou art the unconsciousness, the sleep, the illusion, the modesty, the beauty of (all creatures). Thou art the twilight, thou art the day, thou art Sāvitrī, and thou art the mother. Thou art contentment, thou art growth, thou art light. It is thou that supportest the Sun and the Moon and that makes them shine. Thou art the prosperity of those that are prosperous. The Siddhas and the Charanas behold thee in contemplation."[13]

The *Mahābhārata* is the last of the great epic Indian texts from the Vedic period. The fact that Arjuna, the warrior Prince of the Bhagavad Gītā, is addressing a hymn to the Devī for victory in battle should be sufficient to prevent any further discourse into the ethnic origins of non-biological entities in Vedic texts. The earliest ninth-century telling, by the Pallava poet Peruntevanar, also repeats he basic story, "Aravan agrees to sacrifice himself on the new moon night to Kālī, Goddess of the battlefield, so that, with her blessing, the Pāṇḍavas will win."[14]

---

[13] VYĀSA, K. D., trans. Ganguli, K. M., *The Mahabharata of Krishna-Dwaipayana Vyāsa*, Bhagavat-Gita Parva, section XXIII.

[14] HILTEBEITEL, A., Rethinking India's Oral and Classical epics: Draupadī among Rajputs, Muslims, and Dalits in *Criminal Gods and Demon Devotees: Essays On the Guardians of Popular Hinduism* (USA: State University of New York, 1998), 55.

The role of the Devī is not restricted to the above passage either. Her presence subsists on an esoteric level throughout the *Mahābhārata*. Early in the *Mahābhārata*, the Vedic model of the Goddess appears in the figure of Kuntī, wife of Pāṇḍu. He is prevented by a curse from having intercourse with her, and she begs five Vedic Gods to impregnate her (producing the five Pāṇḍavas, who all marry Draupadī, a multiform of Kuntī herself).[15] The Pāṇḍavas are of course the heroes of the epic, and it is quite revealing that all five heroes are married to one woman. Draupadī is also regarded as a Goddess in Gingee (northern Tamilnadu), and although regarded there as an incarnation of Śri, she is more similar to a multiform of Durgā or Kālī, and the "Village Goddesses" of rural South India.

When one first encounters the character of Draupadī, her connection with the Goddess is not immediately apparent. Without an understanding of the rituals and complexities surrounding the figure of Draupadī, or indeed, the subtle iconography of the Goddess herself, it is easy to perceive Draupadī as being little more than the main female character within the context of the *Mahābhārata*. Yet, even without such specialized knowledge, there are within the *Mahābhārata*, certain passages which allude to the important role of the Goddess in the epic. Misra, for example, states that one hundred and eight names of Goddesses can be found in the *Mahābhārata*.[16] This is, of course, a sacred Hindu number and highly unlikely to be coincidental. The fact that Draupadī is more than the Pāṇḍavas common wife is clear even before the exile begins, for, in the *Sabha Parva*, Draupadī is the last to be gambled by Yudhiṣṭhira, a fact which appears to indicate that Yudhiṣṭhira places a higher value on Draupadī than upon his possessions, his brothers, and even his own freedom. The fact that the Goddess plays a part within the *Mahābhārata* is evident; it is her connection with the enigmatic figure of Draupadī which must be examined.

---

[15] DONIGER O'FLAHERTY, W., The Shifting Balance of Power in the Marriage of Śiva and Pārvatī in eds., Hawley, J. S., & Wulff D. M., *The Divine Consort: Rādhā and the Goddess of India* (USA: Beacon Press, 1986), 129.

[16] MISRA, O. P., *Mother Goddess in Central India* (India: Agam Kala Prakashan, 1985), 75.

Of the Goddesses who appear in the *Mahābhārata*, the most obvious one to connect Draupadī with is Durgā, as she plays a role in the epic as the protectress of the Pāṇḍavas. The *Mahābhārata* relates that Durgā dwelt in the Vindhya Mountains, rode atop a lion, and was offered oblations of meat and wine.[17] Durgā is also worshiped twice in the *Mahābhārata*, once in the Virata Parva by Yudhiṣṭhira, and once in the Bhisma Parva by Arjuna. The hymn sung by Yudhiṣṭhira to Durgā portrays the Goddess as the Supreme Deity, calling her by the name Tribhuvaneśvari, and stating that she is prayed to by the Gods for the protection of the three worlds.[18] The *stotra* sung to Durgā by Arjuna contains the statement that the Goddess abides eternally in her various shrines and sacred places throughout Jambu-dvīpa.[19]

The importance of the Goddess in these hymns is also implied by the names and epithets which are applied to her, such as Ārya, Kālī, Bhadra-Kālī, Mahākālī, Karali, Candi, Canda, Kapāli, Kauśikī, Uma, Sakambhari, and Virupaksi.[20] It is also Kṛṣṇa himself who instructs Arjuna to worship Durgā, saying, "O one having many arms, standing in the face of battles, say a hymn to Durgā for the purpose of defeating your enemies."[21] These hymns, however, are found in the apocrypha and may not have been part of the original tradition. As such, they are not found in the critical edition of the *Mahābhārata*, and it is believed that these hymns to Durgā might have been added to the *Mahābhārata* at a later date.[22] However, in another version of the *Mahābhārata* studied by Alf Hiltebeitel, Draupadī has a guardian named Pottu Raja whose names means "Buffalo King." This can be traced back to South Indian buffalo rituals, and make it clear that Pottu Raja is a manifestation on Mahisasura, the "Buffalo Demon" who is both the foe and victim of the Goddess Durgā.[23]

[17] BHATTACHARJI, S., *Legends of Devi* (India: Orient Longman Ltd, 1995), 30.
[18] TIWARI, J. N., *Goddess Cults in Ancient India* (India: Sundeep Prakashan, 1985), 61.
[19] Ibid., 18.
[20] Ibid., 62.
[21] KINGSLEY, D., Blood and Death Out of Place: Reflections on the Goddess Kālī in eds. Hawley, J. S., & Wulff D. M., *The Divine Consort: Rādhā and the Goddess of India*, 107.
[22] TIWARI, J. N., *Goddess Cults in Ancient India*, 75.
[23] HILTEBEITEL, A., Draupadī's Two Guardians: The Buffalo King and the Muslim Devotee

Furthermore,

> While the Gingee myths retain the name, Pottu Raja, with its unrecognized and apparently forgotten meaning of "Buffalo King", the Pormannan myth has as its unmistakable subtext the myth of the mahisasuramardana: the "Killing of the Buffalo Demon" (Mahisasura) by the Goddess Durgā. For not only is [he] a Durgā multiform. He himself is Draupadī's surrogate on the mission to Pormannan's kingdom, a mission which reanimates one of the perennial themes in the mythology of the Goddess and the Buffalo Demon: the Goddess' seduction of the demon to draw him into battle. If, as Biardeau has so persuasively and insightfully argued, Pottu Raja is ultimately "identical with Mahisasura, but with a Mahisasura who has been converted" by his death at Durgā's hands, one can see how both of his myths develop from such a premise. Indeed, among guardian deities, Pottu Raja is the perfect type of the "demon devotee."[24]

One of the clearest illustrations of Draupadī's connection with the Goddess is found in the performance of the *Pandāv Līlā* in Gharwal. In the *Pandāv Līlā*, and indeed throughout Gharwal itself, Draupadī is identified with Kālī, a Goddess who also has prominent links to Durgā. This identification of Draupadī with Kālī is so complete in Gharwal that there is a common saying that, "Draupadī incarnated eight times; the Kālī of Kailash did Kurukshetra (i.e. caused the war)."[25] Another example of the identification of Draupadī with Kālī can be found in a chant recorded by William Sax in Sutol village.

> Woman of five brothers:
> In Satyayuga you stayed with Rāma, incarnate as Sita

---

in *Criminal Gods and Demon Devotees: Essays On the Guardians of Popular Hinduism* (USA: State University of New York Press), 339.

[24] Ibid., pp. 354-355.

[25] SAX, W., Draupadī and Kuntī in the Pandāv Lila in eds., Micheals, A., Vogelslanger C., & Wilke, A., *The Wild Goddess in South Asia* (Switzerland: Peter Lang, 1996), 358.

In Tretāyuga with Śiva, your name was Pārvatī
In Dwaparyuga, you incarnated as Draupadī
In the home of Drupad Raja.
You were born from the fire pit
And you wear a burning headcloth
And in Kaliyuga you are incarnate as Kālī.
The mother of four yugas and
The dangerous woman of (duranari) of five brothers—
I have sent my bumblebee messengers,
O drummer, and a pair of escorts.[26]

Not only is Draupadī seen is this passage to be connected with the Goddess, she is also mentioned in the same context as Sīta and Pārvatī, who occupy very different roles in Hinduism. It could be said that not only is Kālī identified with Draupadī in Gharwal, but that Kālī is also thought of as an incarnation of the Mahā-Devī. Although Kālī and Draupadī are clearly linked in Gharwal, in this chant Draupadī and Kālī are stated as being existent in two different Yugas, the Dvāpara Yuga, and the Kali Yuga. This is not to say that they cannot be the same aspect of the Indian Pan-Goddess, only that at some stage a transformational process occurs, similar to those in Hindu mythology when Kālī is born from the fury of another Goddess. The requirement then, becomes to find a catalyst which causes the process to occur, and the best place to look for this is in the symbolism of the Goddess herself.

An identification of Draupadī with Kālī can also be found in the *Terukkūtta* plays of the cult of Draupadī in Tamil Nadu. Although Kālī is not mentioned by name, the use of imagery in extracts from the *Terukkūtta* plays also portray Draupadī as a dangerous woman who could lapse into moments of great blood-lust which threaten to engulf even her husbands, the Pāṇḍavas, as seen the following extract.

Kṛṣṇa tells Bhima of Draupadī's outings and informs him that they represent a grave danger to the Pāṇḍavas. She will devour

[26] SAX, W., Draupadī and Kuntī in the Pandāv Lila in *The Wild Goddess in South Asia*, 359.

> them too if they try to stop her. But worse, should she merely return home unsatiated, she will do the same. At Kṛṣṇa's advice, the Pāṇḍavas thus close her up at midnight in their palm leaf hut [*pannaka calai*]and refuse to let her out until she promises not to harm them ... But that very night Draupadī comes back tired, thirsty, very hungry, and ferocious, and ready to eat her husbands. She bangs on the door. Bhima stands there holding it shut, and refuses to open it unless she promises not to eat them or harm the Pāṇḍavas in any way. At last, she assents. Bhima then lets the door slightly ajar so as to let her touch her fingers to his hand in the gesture of taking an oath [*cattiyam panni ceyy*]. But Draupadī grips him so hard that her five fingernails pierce his hand. Five drops of blood thus fall to the ground and immediately turn into five children who rise up shouting, "Amma!" "Mother!" The sight of the five children calling her "Mother" then pacifies Draupadī, and she returns her Viśvarūpa back to her normal form.[27]

To Hiltebeitel, the Dakṣiṇakālī position is comparable also to Draupadī's posture of standing on the bodies of her demon foes (Acalammacuran and Duryodhana).[28] Of Draupadī standing on the body of Duryodhana Hiltebeitel says the following; "Draupadī's stance as Goddess of Victory atop Duryodhana's body not only reveals her in a pose of Durgā but with the re-braiding of her hair, brings to an end the period in which she has assumed the disheveled 'form of Kālī' in the forests and in Kurukṣetra."[29] Here, in this quote, it is again seen that not only can Draupadī be identified with Kālī, there is also a connection with the Goddess Durgā. Once more, a transformational process is hinted at, which changes Draupadī into an incarnation of Kālī, and ends when she re-braids her hair. Before discussing the significance of Draupadī's hair, the symbolism of another organic substance which figures

[27] HILTEBEITEL, A., *The Cult of Draupadī* (USA: University of Chicago Press, 1988), pp. 292-293.
[28] Ibid., 294.
[29] Ibid., 292.

predominantly in the analysis of Draupadī/Kālī and is related to the symbolism of Draupadī's hair—blood—must be discussed.

One of the most prominent features which link Draupadī to Kālī is the symbolism of blood and her unquenchable thirst for it. The inauspicious forms of the Goddess, such as Kālī, are principally associated with blood, as well as with war, death, and hunger. When the Goddess is found in her inauspicious forms, she does not destroy her enemies by means of military strategy or martial skill; rather she exhibits a type of blood lust, ripping and tearing into her opponents with tooth and claw instead of weapons. This same bloodthirstiness which is apparent in the inauspicious forms of the Goddess is also apparent in Draupadī, as seen in the *Terukkūtta* plays. Another example of this is described by Sax in the following passage.

> Draupadī five sons were killed by Duryodhana. She said, "The fire in my heart will be quenched only by blood." Bhimsen said, "A second Mahābhārata can't be fought, where will the blood come from?" So he threw his club up into the sky and it landed on his chest. Blood rushed from his mouth and fell on the fire pit from which Draupadī had been born, which had burned continuously until that moment, and extinguished it.[30]

Not only is Draupadī's lust for revenge exemplified here, the imagery of blood is also linked to the 'heat' of rage. It is the blood of Bhimsen that puts out Draupadī's fire/anger, thus serving to quench her thirst for blood. The symbolism of fire and heat is also reminiscent to that of Kālī, for, as Weber pointed out, Kālī is given as a name of one of the seven flames or tongues of the Fire-God in the *Muṇḍaka Upaniṣad*.[31] In addition to this, Weber also stated that names of the Goddess such as Durgā, Kātyāyanī, and Kumari, may also point to the same source.[32] In connection with this, it is important to note

[30] SAX, W., Gender and the Representation of Violence in ed. Leslie, I. J., *Gender and Social Position in South Asian Religions*, 12-13.

[31] TIWARI, J. N., *Goddess Cults in Ancient India*, 69.

[32] Ibid., 81.

that Draupadī is born from a fire-pit. Fire, as well as blood, serves to strengthen the connection between Draupadī and Kālī. Draupadī is born of fire and that fire can only be extinguished by blood. If the word 'fire' is replaced by the wrath and anger which it symbolizes here the connection between Draupadī and Kālī becomes even more apparent. Kālī takes her origins in fire (anger/wrath) as part of the destructive nature of Agni and is often portrayed as being born in the heat of rage of another Goddess, such as Durgā in the *Devī Māhātmyam*. Draupadī is likewise born of fire, and in the end, it is only the sacrifice of Bhimsen which extinguishes this wrath. Of further significance to the symbolism of fire in the portrayal of Draupadī is that the fact that women who enact the part of Draupadī in the *Pandāv Līlā* are Rajputs.[33] Draupadī is also identified with Kālī in Gharwal and Rajasthan.

This is important to note because the Kṣatriya varṇa, as well as that of the Brahmin, is linked to the imagery of fire. On the subject, Knipe says that the,

> Kṣatriya varṇa, according to the puruṣa sūkta cosmogony, proceeded from the arms of the dismembered sacrificial person, just as the Brahmana derived from his mouth. In the ritual reconstitutions of that person, the *mahavedi* understands the two "arms" of the sacrifice to be the *marjaliya* fire (the projection of the *daksinagni*) and its symmetrical correspondent on the northern border, the *agnidhriya*. Thus, the *yajamana* and divine cosmic being have not only fire for a mouth, out of which proceeds Brahmin, but also two fires for the force (*kṣatrá*) of his arms.[34]

In this sense, the symbolism of fire (rage/anger) is connected with the violence of the warrior caste, both of which are apparent in Draupadī and Kālī. Though this serves to strengthen the growing number of linkages that Kālī and Draupadī possess, it does not fully explain the

[33] SAX, W., Gender and the Representation of Violence in Pandāv Lila in ed. Leslie, I. J., *Gender and Social Position in South Asian Religions*, 13.

[34] KNIPE, D. M., *In the Image of Fire*, 98.

transitive process by which the Goddess is incarnated as Draupadī, and who then is further transformed into the figure of Kālī. The hypothesis requires another ingredient, for although blood can be linked to rage, it can also be connected to female fertility.

At the time of Draupadī's dishonor at the hands of Duḥśāsana, Draupadī is menstruating, thus explaining why she is wearing a single garment and wearing her hair unbound, as these are signs that a woman is menstruating. If these symbols are correct, not only is Draupadī menstruating then, she is also menstruating through most of the *Mahābhārata*, as she keeps her hair unbound for fourteen years. Loose hair or dishevelment is for widows and menstruating women; the triple braid (*triveṇī*) and chignon (Tamil *kuntal* or *kontai*) are for auspicious married women; the "single braid" (*ekaveni*), a kind of ponytail, is for women separated from their husbands (*virahinis*).[35]

Draupadī does not re-braid her hair until she has first washed it in the blood of Duryodhana. This is also compatible with the iconography of Kālī, who is always portrayed with her hair unbound, symbolizing the fact that Kālī is unrestrained; unlike the bound Goddesses, her śakti is free, and thus dangerous. The hair of Draupadī also is a sign of her fertility, her śakti. Marglin (1985:54) observes: "The single Goddesses are often represented iconographically with loose flowing hair, which signals their celibate state."[36] An early medieval ascetic text, for example, warns mendicants not to beg from a *muktakesini* ("a woman with loose hair"), a term which could indicate either that there is sexual intimacy or, as we shall presently see, that she is having her monthly period.[37]

As she (Kālī/Draupadī) uses this power/śakti (as Draupadī does for fourteen years), it becomes an immense strain. The blood that the Goddess gives must be replenished, so in her inauspicious forms the Goddess takes the life back into her, via her terrible hunger and

[35] HILTEBEITEL, A., Rethinking India's Oral and Classical Epics: Draupadī Among Rajputs, Muslims, and Dalits in *Criminal Gods and Demon Devotees: Essays On the Guardians of Popular Hinduism*, 144.

[36] Ibid., 67.

[37] Ibid.

blood lust. This is why the inauspicious forms of the Goddess accept blood sacrifices; their śakti is not controlled or pacified by a husband. They are free to use their śakti at will, and it must continuously be replenished with blood. The connection of menstrual blood to śakti can be seen in the fact that before the Bhils begin sowing a field, they set a stone in the field and smear it with vermilion. This vermilion stands for menstrual blood, and the act of smearing it upon the stone implies the infusion of productive energy into the earth.[38] In addition to representing menstrual blood, vermilion is also used in the worship of Kālī. For example, in the Bagdi community of Shibpur village, Kālī receives offerings of vermilion, and at Metala village skulls are smeared with vermilion markings and placed before a special seat.[39] Kāmākhyā is also another location which links menstruation to the Devī. Kāmākhyā holds Ambuvācī Melā in Āṣāḍha (June-July), which celebrates the return of the her life giving blood to the earth.[40]

> Kāmākhyā, the place of the yoni maṇḍala, the place of the beautiful [Goddess] Tripurā Bhairavī, is the best of all places and the original home of [the Goddess] Mahāmāyā. There is no better place on earth. The Goddess appears there every month during her menstrual period.[41]

Both Draupadī's menstruation and unbound hair symbolize her sexuality and unrestrained śakti, serving to connect her with Kālī. At the time of her dishonor, Draupadī is menstruating; hence, she is at a time when her śakti is at a low ebb. As an incarnation of Durgā (for both Durgā and Draupadī are said to be the protectors of the Pāṇḍavas), this is a serious insult to the Goddess, for which she will demand vengeance. Just as Draupadī was born in fire originally, she undergoes a second birth in the heat of fury. Therefore, with the dishonor of the Durgā, Draupadī is recreated as Durgā's personified

[38] MISRA, O. P., *Mother Goddess in Central India*, 8.
[39] SAKAR, R. M., *Regional Cults and Rural Traditions* (India: Inter-India Publications, 1986), 201-203.
[40] URBAN, H. B., *The Power of Tantra: Religion, Sexuality and the Politics Asian Studies*, 53.
[41] Ibid.

wrath, Kālī. Only with the sacrifice of Bhimsen does her need to replenish her śakti dissipate, thus quenching the fire-pit from which she was born. Similarly, Draupadī does not re-braid her hair (thus symbolizing the Goddess reclaiming her power and fertility) until she has washed it in Duryodhana's blood.

> Most centrally, she vows to wear her hair disheveled (an image of Kālī) through her years of exile, and not to re-braid it until she can "oil" it with the sacrificial blood of her chief Kaurava tormentor. Here there is no question of her remaining pure while her guardians handle the sacrificial impurity on her behalf. Defiled, she will remain defiled until she can purify herself.[42]

During this process, Draupadī, by no coincidence, bathes in blood the very part of her body which was used to insult the Goddess, her hair, which is the symbol of her sexuality and female power. This blood revitalizes the power the Goddess has lost and, thus satiated, Draupadī no longer wears the form of Kālī. The insult to the Goddess, for which the *Mahābhārata* was fought, is finally forgiven. Her wrath finally appeased, the Goddess transforms back into her normal form at the end of the Great War which also marks the beginning of the Kali Yuga.

Kālī, Durgā, and Pārvatī together form a trinity. However, we would like to stress that there is no correlation between this and the Tripartite Goddess theory invented by the Wiccan movement, which attempts to draw other Goddesses into its narrative to construct a new form of Euro-centric cultural hegemony. There is little lunar symbolism to be found in these three deities, as occurs with Wicca. Though these are some of the main forms of the Devī, there are countless others, and many villages will have different names for their own local version of the Devī. Of the other main forms of the Devī to consider in Tantrism, the Mahāvidyās of Śakta Tantrism are the most important. This group of Goddesses represents different

[42] HILTEBEITEL, A., Draupadī's Two Guardians: The Buffalo King and the Muslim Devotee in *Criminal Gods and Demon Devotees: Essays On the Guardians of Popular Hinduism*, 367.

emanations of the Devī, all of whom are worshiped for different reasons. They number ten as a counterpart to the incarnations of Viṣṇu, and are also a representation of the ten directions (based on a spherical compass model). This group of ten deities is a notable difference which separates Śakta Tantrism from other schools.

***

When considering how the Pīṭhas may have originated, one of the central issues that needs to be addressed is the role of Satī herself, for the Goddess herself seems to have an ambiguous and complex nature which at times seems singular, and at other times, she manifests as a composite entity. She is simultaneously the bride of the God Śiva and the daughter of Dakṣa. As such her role within the tale seems to be predestined for tragedy, for there is considerable tension already present between Dakṣa and her husband. This tension escalates dramatically as the marriage between Satī and Śiva is formalized.

An outline of the tale of Satī's death and subsequent dismemberment is outlined as follows:

> Meanwhile, Dakṣa commences performing a great sacrifice to which except Śiva and Satī everyone is invited by him … Satī, hearing about the performance of the large-scale sacrifice by Dakṣa to which herself and Śiva are not invited, takes it as an act of deliberate insult. Satī becomes highly enraged at this wanton insult and remembers her previous terms to Dakṣa that she would cease to be his daughter the moment Dakṣa showed indifference to her. Accordingly, Satī gives up her life through the process of yoga (*prāṇashoṭa*). Before Satī sits in yoga for giving up her life she resolves to be born as the daughter of Menakā, who treated her as her daughter when she was with Śambhu on the slopes of the Himālayas.[43]

> Bhaga seeing Śiva destroying the sacrifice stops him by extending both hands; Śiva plucks out Bhaga's eyes. Then

[43] SHASTRI, B. N., *The Kālikā Purāna*, Part I, 79.

> Mātaṇda challenges Śiva; Śiva shatters his teeth and rushes to the sacrifice. All Gods having seen Bhaga blind and Mihira without teeth fled away. The sacrifice assuming the shape of a deer runs towards the realm of Brahmā. Śiva pursues the sacrifice. Ultimately the sacrifice enters into the corpse of Satī. On approaching Satī's corpse Śiva forgets the sacrifice, overcome by grief. He weeps over the dead body of Satī.[44]
>
> Śiva in his uncontrollable grief picks up the dead body of Satī on his shoulder and proceeds to the eastern region (*prācya deśa*). The Gods having seen Śiva moving like a madman thinks about how the corpse should be removed. It will not rot because it is in contact with Śiva's body. Brahmā, Viṣṇu, and Śanaiśvara enter into the dead body of Satī and render it to pieces and make pieces fall on certain parts of the earth for the welfare of the world. The different limbs of the body of Satī fell at the following places: (1) At Devikūṭa the feet, (2) at Uḍḍīyāna the thighs, (3) on Kāmagiri in Kāmarūpa the vagina (yoni) and on a mountain there the navel, (4) at Jālandhara the pair of breasts, 95) on Pūrṇagiri beyond Kāmarūpa the shoulder and neck. The region in the east traversed by Śiva bearing Satī's corpse on his shoulder earns merit to be known as the region suitable for performing a sacrifice (*yājñikadeśa*).[45]

This legend of the tragic demise of Satī and consequent dismemberment of her corpse serves to provide a mythological foundation for the origination and location of the various Pīṭhas. According to Sircar however, this legend of Satī and the disruption of Dakṣa's sacrifice by Śiva originates in an even earlier form, for Sircar traces its origin to the *Rig Veda* (X,61,5-7), paralleling the tale of Śiva and Dakṣa with a prior form of the story which depicts a similarity between the actions of Rudra/Śiva and those of Dakṣa/Prajāpati. Sircar renders this portion of the *Rig Veda* as follows:

---

[44] SHASTRI, B. N., *The Kālikā Purāna,* Part I, 80.

[45] Ibid., pp. 81-82

> Once Prajāpati, identified with Yajña or sacrifice, committed incest with his own daughter Dyaus or Ūṣas. Disgusted at this vile act of their father, the Gods approached Rudra and requested him to pierce Prajāpati with his arrow. Rudra discharged an arrow at Prajāpati whereupon the latter's *retas* (seminal fluid) fell upon the ground. As Prajāpati represents sacrifice itself and as no part of his body could be thrown away without being utilized in the performance of sacrifice, the Gods took Prajāpati's retas to Bhaga who sits on the southern side of the sacrificial ground. Bhaga looks at the thing and at once his eyes burned. The Gods then took it to Pūṣan who, on tasting it, lost his teeth ... the first portion of the legend is found a little developed in the *Gopatha Brāhmaṇa*, according to which Prajāpati, while performing a sacrifice, did not offer the requisite share of offerings to Rudra who thereupon 'seizing and piercing it (*Yajña* or *Yajñāṅga*) cut off a portion from it'. A look is said to have made Bhaga blind and Pūṣan toothless.[46]

It is clear that in both versions of this tale, Dakṣa/Prajāpati first commits an act which is construed as dishonorable. Likewise, in both formats, Prajāpati/Dakṣa also omits Rudra/Śiva from partaking in a sacrifice. An obvious continuity between the twin myths is illustrated by the fact that in both renditions Bhaga is left blind and Pūṣan is left toothless. It is also significant that in the version provided by the *Kālikā Purāṇa*, the sacrifice fled Śiva's wrath in the form of a deer and enters into the corpse of Satī; this can be compared with Prajāpati's act of incest with Ūṣas, for she is reputed to be in the form of a deer at the time of the act, thus serving to tie the figure of Satī to the earlier Vedic myth of Ūṣas. Over a period of time, this tale developed into the Dakṣa-yajña story and was popularized via the *Kālikā Purāṇa*.

Thus, not only is the power or the Pīṭhas gained from the links with the body of Satī, other Goddesses also emanate from Satī, and it is her adroitness at rendering herself into different aspects that

46 SIRCAR, D. C., *The Śakta Pīṭhas* (India: Motilal Banarsidass, 1998), 5.

grants power to either another Goddess or to the land itself. In either dimension of this ability it is clear that the physical body of Satī also plays a role. It is possible, as is elucidated by Bagchi, that this connection of Satī's multiplicity being linked to the physical body of her corpse, could have arisen as an influence from Buddhism, which may have begun to become more prevalent at the time of the composition of the Purāṇas. This idea is explained below.

> The idea of the distribution of Devī's parts bears a strong similarity with an important concept in Buddhism. After Buddha died, his hair, nail etc. were distributed in different parts of India upon which relics or '*Caityas*' were formed. In the Great Epic, we find the Mother-Goddess associated with the *Caityas*, which shows that the Śakta cult was gradually absorbing ideas from the religion of Śākyamuni.[47]

The connection between the body of Satī and the geographic locations of the Śakta Pīṭhas is thus a complex one, with multiple problems to consider. Firstly, there has been a certain degree of fusion between Satī and the incorporation of various tribal deities, to the extent that the traditions have been overlapped, making it at times impossible to determine the original locales of the Śakta Pīṭhas. This is also likely to be the cause of the wide textual discrepancies between the numbers of Śakta Pīṭhas, as it is reasonable to conclude that, if the tradition had become localized in some cases, the number of sites themselves would differ. From the prevalence of Śakta Pīṭhas in the eastern parts of India, it is also reasonable to draw the conclusion that worship of the Goddess was stronger in this region, and that the original Śakta Pīṭha sites were to be found in this locale, with other sites probably being added at a later date. The reasons that these sites were chosen to be reflections of the nature of Satī may also be due to the geographic features found at the sites themselves, as is the case with a significant number of Tīrthas. Sircar, in *The Śakta Pīṭhas,* describes

[47] BAGCHI, S., *Eminent Indian Śakta Centres in Eastern India* (India: Orient Blackswan, 1988), 2.

how particular features of the landscape could have come to be identified with the physical body of Satī:

> It should also be pointed out that hills or mountain-peaks roughly resembling a human phallus were regarded in ancient times as the śvayambhū (natural) Liṅga of Śiva. Śiva's ancient link with the autochthonous deities of India is sometimes manifested in the snake which swims up the channel of the pīṭha or coils around the shaft of the liṅga. Wherever the liṅga is, there is a Tīrtha, because the liṅga is a "crossing place" where the worlds are knit together by the shaft of Śiva. There is a reason to believe that tanks or pools of a particular shape were often conceived as the yoni of the mother-goddess. A pair of hills or peaks of the shape and position of female breasts appear sometimes to have been likewise regarded as the *stana* of the Goddess; cf. Kālidāsa's description (*Raghuvaṃśa*, IV, 51) of the Malaya and Dardura mountains in the Pāṇḍya country as the two breasts of the lady that is the southern quarter.[48]

The proposition elucidated here by Sircar is that, if parts of the earth that were seen to be protruding and bore a certain resemblance to a liṅga were identified with Śiva, a similar process may have been utilized to identify natural geographical features of the earth with his consort Satī. This would also entail that the sites were sacred prior to the death and dismemberment of Satī, and that the myth is a subtle metaphor for the body of Satī being the earth itself. If this is a correct interpretation then it also entails that the reason these sites are sacred compared to others is due primarily to their possession of unusual geographical features.

Sircar also draws to the attention another problem with regard to the study of the Śakta Pīṭhas.

> We have seen that the lists of the Pīṭhas and those of the Devīs and Bhairavas connected with each of them are variously prepared by different authors and have a great deal of

[48] SIRCAR, D. C., *The Śakta Pīṭhas*, 8.

> discrepancy among them. There was apparently little influence on these writers of something like a recognized tradition about the number of Pīṭhas, the names of the deities worshiped at them, and their association with particular limbs of the Mother-Goddess. Names of the Tīrtha, Devī, and Bhairava were often fabricated by the writers and the association of a Tīrtha with one of Satī's limbs was also determined usually by their individual imagination. The fact that in many cases entire countries are mentioned as Pīṭhas suggests that the writers had only vague ideas about some of the Tīrthas and often took resort to imagination.[49]

Thus, there is not only a vast discrepancy between the texts as to the number of Pīṭhas, there is conflict in regard to their locations, the associations of limbs at the sites, and differences between the names of the Goddesses mentioned. This reinforces the opinion that the Śakta Pīṭhas began as localized traditions that were distinct from each other, and that individual sites were chosen because of unusual geographical features of the landscape. Over a period of time, these individual Goddesses probably drifted from a polytheistic basis towards a more monotheistic outlook—hence, the different aspects became identified with the one Goddess, Devī or Satī. This also explains the ability of Devī and Satī to break down their aspects into 'multi-forms'. They were originally composite deities, and as such can project themselves into multiple female forms at will. The origin of the Śakta Pīṭhas and their relationship with the body of Satī are thus both connected to the land in which her worship originated, and the land itself is seen to embody the physical aspects of Satī, as well as the spiritual, for, as the localized village deities become solidified into Tantric Traditions, they became identified with the figure of Satī, who came to embody their being and nature. Thus, Satī can break her body down into multiple Goddesses because she originally absorbed them into her being. The tradition of the Śakta Pīṭhas is based on multiple

[49] SIRCAR, D. C., *The Śakta Pīṭhas*, 32.

figures of the Goddess, each of which is worshiped at a point of the landscape where her presence is felt to be closer because her 'body' is represented in the landscape itself. Her chthonic power and śakti is the ultimate affirming power of the earth itself, which sustains all life on the planet.

TOPOGRAPHICAL RELIGIOSITY

Śiva also has many holy sites and centers of pilgrimage in India, many of which are connected with the liṅgaṃ just as the Śakti Pīṭhas are connected with the body of the Devī. Amongst Śiva's pilgrimage sites we find the five *bhūtalingas* or natural representations of Śiva—consisting of the fire-liṅgaṃ at Arunācala, the earth liṅgaṃ at Conjeeveram, the wind-liṅgaṃ at Kalahasti, the water-liṅgaṃ at Jambunath, and the (invisible) ether-liṅgaṃ at Chidambaram.[1] One of his most interesting sites, however, is unique in that is a city—the holy city of Kāśī.

Kāśī occupies a unique role in the landscape of India, not just as a place of pilgrimage, but as a city that has become a legend itself. Existing in both history and myth alike, Kāśī is also known as Banaras and Vārāṇasī, and it is the sacred city of Śiva, where the God is said to be forever present. Indeed, the imagery of Śiva is so strongly associated with that of Kāśī it is said that merely to die in Kāśī is enough to win liberation from the cycle of death and rebirth, and it is mentioned in the *Skanda-Purāṇa* as being one of the seven cities that bestow salvation, along with Ayodhyā, Kānti, and Māyā.[2] It is within the Purāṇas that we find descriptions of the meritorious city of Kāśī and a record of traditions that were current in Indian thought at the time of the composition of the Purāṇas.

---

[1] BHARATI, A., *The Tantric Tradition* (UK: Rider & Company, 1965), 151.

[2] BHATT, G. P., *Ancient Indian Tradition & Mythology, The Skanda-Purāṇa*, Vol. 58, Part x (India: Motilal Banarsidass, 1996), 59.

Śiva, both in the Purāṇas and in other texts, is portrayed as a complex God who transcends opposites—as such, it is difficult to pinpoint just one aspect of his divinity which can be paralleled with Kāśī, the city to which he is explicitly connected to in the *Skanda Purāṇa*. So strong is Śiva's association with Kāśī that sixty-eight Śaiva shrines have been built in the Mahākṣetra of Kāśī representing their original shrines and sacred spots.[3] This connection had become so firm by the time of the composition of the Kāshī Khanda that this city was said to have been the "original ground" created by Śiva and Pārvatī.[4] It seems Kāśī was held in high regard prior to its occupation by Śiva, for it is Śiva who desires to live in Kāśī—Śiva, the great ascetic renowned for his great self-control and mastery of yoga, burns with desire to live in Kāśī. Despite eventually becoming the God who is ever present in the city, Śiva, although yearning to live in Kāśī, could not do so immediately, for his entry was forbidden by the current King of Kāśī. This is outlined in the *Vāyu Purāṇa* as follows:

> Śiva could not immediately bring his bride to Vārāṇasī because the city was already occupied by King Divodāsa. "Śiva summoned one of his attendants named Nikumbha and told him to go to Vārāṇasī and to empty out the city. Nikumbha went and appeared in a dream to a barber, telling him to establish and worship the image of Nikumbha Gana at the edge of the city. The barber did this, and Nikhumba was worshiped as the "Lord of Ganas" [Gaṇeśa] at the city gate. He was honored with incense, flowers and food offerings, and he became popular with the citizens by granting boons to those who propitiated him there. He granted all earthly desires. The Kings wife, Suyashā, who was childless, came repeatedly and worshiped Nikhumba to get a son, but Nikhumba did not answer her prayers. At length, King Divodāsa became angry and ordered the shrine of Nikhumba Gaṇeśa destroyed. Then Nikhumba

[3] AWASTHI, A. B. L., *Studies in Skanda Purana Part Three - Vol. I* (India: Navrang, 1992), 114.
[4] ECK, D., *Benares: City of Light* (USA: Princeton University Press, 1982), 94.

> pronounced a curse upon the King and his city: "Because my sacred place has been destroyed, this city shall be empty of all its inhabitants."[5]

This story is also encountered in an alternative version involving Śiva's mother-in-law, but the main point of the story still relies on Śiva manipulating the evacuation of King Divodāsa out of Kāśī so that he may move in:

> Śiva's mother-in-law, Menā, criticizes her son-in-law, whose poor-man's (*daridra*) lifestyle on the Himālaya amidst ascetics who assume all kinds of forms (*viśvarūpa*) she finds less suitable for her daughter. Pārvatī, therefore, asks Śiva to find another place to live. Śiva sets his mind on Vārāṇasī, which is by that time a prosperous city under the reign of king Divodāsa. Śiva instructs a *gaṇeśvara*, named Nikhumba, to trick Divodāsa out of Vārāṇasī.[6]

It is clear from both versions of this story, that Śiva was not originally associated with Kāśī; his occupation of the city seems to have occurred during the creation of the Purāṇas, whose authors may have overlaid the figure of Śiva onto another mythos concerning the city of Kāśī. Diana Eck interprets these passages in a similar manner stating that "When the city was vacant, Shiva arrived and established his residence there ... While Kāśī is the City of Shiva, it clearly does not derive its sanctity from Shiva's presence alone, for in the beginning, it was this place, they say, which attracted Shiva's presence and was chosen by the Lord as his home."[7]

One of the names by which Kāśī is known is that of the title Manikarnika or the Great Burning Ground. This is the name of one of the two great burning *ghats* in Kāśī which is believed to be the permanent abode of Śiva and his consort Pārvatī.[8] The imagery of

[5] ECK, D., *Benares: City of Light*, 95.
[6] BAKKER, H., Construction and Reconstruction of Sacred Space in Vārāṇasī in *Numen* Vol. 43 (Netherlands: Koninklijke Brill NV, 1996), 34.
[7] ECK, D., *Benares: City of Light*, 95.
[8] VIDYARHTI, L. P., *The Sacred Complex of Kashi (A Microcosm of Indian Civilization)*

the burning ghat is not only associated with death, but also with liberation. Kāśī, as a city that grants liberation to its inhabitants, and through its symbolism as Manikarnika, is a Tīrtha that removes sins. This is one of its reasons for being associated with Śiva and, in his form as Bhairava, he is the 'Devourer of Sin'. This is seen in the following extract from the *Skanda Purāṇa.*

> 45. Since you will be eating up the sins of your devotees within a moment, you will have the name of Pāpabhakṣaṇa (Devourer of Sins).[9]

This is taken from the tale in which Śiva decapitates the fifth head of Brahmā and must atone for the sin of Brahmanicide (*brāhmaṇahatyā*). Here, in his fierce manifestation as Bhairava, he is referred to as the Devourer of Sins—this implies that Brahmā himself may have sinned in this episode. It is also noteworthy that the most impure part of the body (the little finger of the left hand) is employed by Bhairava to behead Brahmā, which could also be interpreted as an attempt to demote the status of Brahmā as a deity, whilst promoting that of Śiva. Nonetheless, for the act of Brahmanicide, Śiva must do penance, and it is not until his arrival at Kāśī that he is cleansed of the sin of Brahmanicide. Thus, Kāśī, like Bhairava, is a devourer of sin.

Kāśī not only has the power to remove sin; it also grants liberation from the cycle of life and death. This idea of liberation is also connected with the concept of *amṛtā*, which is sometimes thought of as a type of 'immortality' that can be procured through yogīc practice.

The city's granting of immortality and release can be attributed to its link with the removal of sin. When sin is removed, the cycle of rebirth comes to a halt. The fact that the practice of yoga is linked to Kāśī also connects it with Śiva, who is regarded as the master yogīn. Having transcended death via his practice of yoga and asceticism, Śiva has placed himself beyond the reach of space and time; his

(India: Concept Publishing Company, 1979), 16.

[9] BHATT, G. P., *Ancient Indian Tradition & Mythology, The Skanda-Purāna*, Vol. 58, 327.

transcendence of the mortal state is reflected in the fact that at the time of death, when all beings who die in Kāśī are granted release, it is Śiva who whispers the 'ferry boat' mantra to the deceased in order to transport the soul to liberation, as is written in the *Skanda Purāṇa*.

> 73. There, at the time when the soul comes out, Lord Viśveśvara (Lord of the Universe) himself imparts the Tāraka Brahman (Rāma Mantra of six syllables) Mantra, whereby the individual identifies himself with it (Supreme Being).[10]

Liberation, however, is only one aspect of the bridge between Śiva and Kāśī. The geographic location of the site of Kāśī itself is also of importance for it is found at the confluence of three rivers which possess deep significance.

> 64. The river Sarasvatī is of the nature of rajas; the river Yamunā is of the nature of tamas and the river Ganga here is the nature of sattva. All the three together lead (the devotees) to Brahman (the Absolute) which is free from attributes (rajas etc.).[11]

What this passage is hinting at is that the prominence of the holiness of the site is not because of the physical purifying aspect of water and the rivers—it is because each of the rivers represents one of the three guṇas or strands of cosmic energy that are thought to comprise the totality of existence through a series of complex interactions. Hence, Kāśī is located at the physical confluence of three rivers and, on an esoteric level, it is located at the crossing point of the three guṇas, and therefore a microcosmic model of creation itself. Furthermore, the region in which these three rivers are said to connect is referred to as the trident of Śiva which holds Kāśī aloft.

---

[10] BHATT, G. P., *Ancient Indian Tradition & Mythology, The Skanda-Purāna,* Vol. 58, Part x, 233.

[11] Ibid., 65.

85. O Brāhmaṇa, this holy spot rests on the tip of the trident of Lord Śiva in the intermediate region without touching the ground. Men of deluded intellect do not perceive it.[12]

According to the Kāśī Khanda, where the above quotation is found, the city is not attached to the ground but is suspended in the sky, though this can only be seen by those with the 'divine sight' (*divyadristhi*) of the yogīn.[13] Like the rivers, the trident of Śiva bears the same association and each of the three prongs represents a respective guṇa, thus effectively making Kāśī not just a microcosmic representation of the universe, but also one of Śiva himself. Daniélou also refers to Kāśī as a microcosm, describing its representation as follows:

Kāśī represents the city of knowledge (*jñāna-purī*). In the microcosm "Kāśī" is the name given to the summit of the head, where knowledge is said to dwell. The "lotus of a thousand petals" at the summit of the head is thus *Kāśī-purī* (the resplendent city). This inner "Kāśī" is situated at the point where the three subtle arteries of the body unite. Hence, it is said to stand on the trident of Śiva. Similarly, the earthly Kāśī, the Holy Banaras, is at the point where the Ganges or Milky Way, the earthly river, and the subterranean stream called the "Underworld Ganges" (Pātāla Gaṅgā) meet.[14]

Not only is there evidence of Kāśī being a microcosm of existence, it can also be seen as a microcosm that has transcended existence—like Śiva it has conquered death and time; the city of Kāśī has achieved liberation and is no longer subject to forces of time and space. This is illustrated by a passage from the *Skanda Purāṇā*.

86. There is perpetual Kṛta Yuga here. There is great festivity here forever. There is no defect or adverse condition in the

[12] BHATT, G. P., *Ancient Indian Tradition & Mythology, The Skanda-Purāṇa*, Vol. 58, Part x, 210.
[13] PARRY, J. P., *Death in Banaras* (UK: Cambridge University Press, 1994), 16.
[14] DANIÉLOU, A., *Hindu Polytheism* (UK: Routledge & Kegan Paul Ltd., 1964), pp. 220-221.

> hermitage Viśveśvara, caused by the rise or setting of the Planets.[15]

By the use of the term Viśveśvara it is implied that the Sun, Moon, Mars, Mercury, Jupiter, Venus, and Saturn are all at the initial point of the ecliptic.[16] In order to maintain this state, it is necessary that the planets be no longer moving, which indicates that Kāśī exists outside of the influence of time. The Kṛta Yuga (an alternative name for the Satya Yuga) is the first of the four *kalpas* and when dharma reigned fully. According to Hindu thought, the present age is the Kali age, which is thought to begin at the conclusion of the *Mahābhārata*. By stating that it is a perpetual 'Golden Age' at Kāśī, it implies that Kāśī is outside of the normal constraints of time and space, and hence not subject to the rules of the Kali Yuga. Unaffected by time and space, Kāśī and Śiva operate beyond the power of death, that is why Śiva and Kāśī both possess the ability to grant liberation. Kāśī is also commonly depicted as an embodied being layered in *kośa* or sheaths, and offers a parallel view of layered reality and encompassment.[17] By this depiction, it likens itself to the human body, which is composed of five kośas. Furthermore, if one measures the distance between the kośa of Kāśī the out-most kośa is five *krośas* (a unit of distance equal to about two miles) and is punctuated by one hundred and eight sites, a number sacred in Hindu cosmology as representing the twelve months times the nine *navagraha* (planets), that is, as representing all of time and space.[18] This is illustrated in the subsequent passage:

> 83. This holy spot Avimukta is away from the middle of the Cosmic egg to the extent of five krośas (1 krośa = 3 km), though it is in the center of the Cosmic Egg.[19]

---

15 BHATT, G. P., *Ancient Indian Tradition & Mythology, The Skanda-Purāṇa*, Vol. 58, Part x, 210.
16 UNDERHILL, M. M., *The Hindu Religious Year* (India: Asian Education Services, 1991), 14.
17 HERTEL, B. R., & HUMES, C. A., *Living Banaras* (India: State University of New York Press, 1993), 7.
18 Ibid. 8.
19 BHATT, G. P., *Ancient Indian Tradition & Mythology, The Skanda-Purāṇa*, Vol. 58, Part x, 210.

Not only does the use of the number one hundred and eight have a cosmological significance, the cosmic egg is also representative of the sun. Placing the sun at the center of Kāśī implies that it is the central point of the microcosm itself.

Like a large number of other religious sites, the city of Kāśī also has an association with rivers and water. Of the three rivers around Kāśī, the one most strongly tied to Śiva is the Ganga, which is described in myth as descending to earth through the hair of Śiva himself, and a substantial amount of Kāśī's *mokṣa* granting prowess seems to stem from the city's proximity to the Ganga.

> 24. Whatever holy places are there in the three worlds bestowing cherished desires, they resort to Ganga that flows towards the north at Kāśī.[20]

One Tīrtha site in Kāśī, Omkāra, seems especially linked to both Śiva and the Ganga. Standing on the banks of a large inland lake known as Matsyodarī Tīrtha a thousand years ago, Omkāra was one of the most important Śiva liṅgaṃs in Kāśī.[21] According to Eck, it is possible to pinpoint an extraordinary event that would take place at Kāśī; the river waters would flow backward at certain times. The ramification of this, of course, is that the river waters, which held great status as Tīrthas at regular times, would now acquire an even greater status. Eck describes these events that would take place at Kāśī in the following extract.

> The seasonal Matsyodarī river was a north-flowing tributary of the Varaṇā river. In a rare year of extraordinary rains, however, something extraordinary happened: the river began to flow backward. The Ganges, flooding into the course of the Varaṇā River, would swell the waters of the Varaṇā so that the Varaṇā would begin to back up along the course of the tributary, the Matsyodarī. The strength of the floodwaters pushed back the waters

[20] BHATT, G. P., *Ancient Indian Tradition & Mythology, The Skanda-Purāṇa*, Vol. 58, Part x (India: Motilal Banarsidass, 1996), 263.

[21] ECK, D., *Benares: City of Light* (USA: Princeton University Press, 1982), 112.

> of the Matsyodarī River and reversed its direction. Rather than flowing north into the Varaṇā, the Matsyodarī flowed southward, flooding the Matsyodarī lake, which in turn drained westward into the Mandākinī Lake. From there the waters followed the route of rain drainage through the Beniā Tālāb and into the Godauliā stream, which ran into the Ganges at Dashāshvamedha. In such a year of heavy rain, central Banaras became virtually an island, with the Ganges flowing along its east bank as usual, and the backward flowing floodwaters of the Ganges, the Varaṇā, and the Matsyodarī making another river which circled through the city itself.[22]

The rivers themselves also have a prominent religious significance in their own right in India. The cosmos itself is essentially conceived of as having three layers, the uranic (heavens), the atmosphere, and the earth (chthonic). The atmosphere (*antarikṣa*), reaching as far up as the blue sky extends, is often described as a vast river of space formed as the communication between heaven and earth.[23] Rivers, therefore, are often representative of being a medium between heaven and earth and are conceived of as areas where mortals may communicate with the divine, which serves to explain why a number of holy sites used for pilgrimage are located near rivers or bodies of water. The association of the nāḍīs with rivers can also be seen in other elements, wherein the parts of the geographic landscape are woven into myth and esoteric lore, for Śiva himself has the Ganges (the lunar iḍā) emanating from his head, in the proximity of the crown cakra. As Śiva possesses a strong lunar symbolism (also having the crescent moon in his hair) this association is not coincidental. The myth of how Śiva came to hold the Ganges is also encountered in the tale of King Bhagirath.

> King Bhagirath went to Kailash, there having performed deep ascetic practice, he pleased Śiva. Śiva agreed to stop the flow

[22] ECK, D., *Benares: City of Light* (USA: Princeton University Press, 1982), 117.

[23] ECK, D., *India's Tīrthas: Crossings in Sacred Geography* (USA: The University of Chicago, 1981).

of the Ganges in his locks of hair and afterward she come down gently to the surface of the earth. Śiva was thus valiant and he is praised with the name of "Ganges-Holder."[24]

The rivers of the celestial worlds can also cross down into ours, and India's great rivers are portrayed as originating in the Heavens, flowing down from above. Thus, a river can be a great source of numinous power and a crossing point (Tīrtha) where the boundaries of worlds are at their thinnest and communication with the Gods is the easiest. This is a very old idea in the Hindu Tradition and dates back to the Vedic period. When Indra slays the great serpent Vṛtra, he frees the waters which then proceed to flow to earth. He slew the serpent and sent forth the Seven Rivers opening, as it were, the holes that were blocked.[25]

There are seven sacred confluences, the most important being that of the Ganges and the Yamunā at Prayāga. The site is called Triveṇī, meaning "a confluence of three (rivers), the third being the mythical Sarasvatī river, which is believed to join the two through a subterranean approach."[26] According to White the mystical "hidden nature of the Sarasvatī is brought to the fore in the Purāṇic descriptions of *matsyodarī-yoga*, the "fish-belly conjunction" of Banaras."[27] Moreover, there is also a lake called Matsyodarī, the "Lake of the Fish Belly."[28] This innocuous title possesses a great secret, which portrays both esoteric significance and also geographical symbolism. Abhinavagupta, in his most famous work, the *Tantrāloka*, cryptically mentions Matsyodara in the following passage: "On the level of the highest Kuṇḍalinī is the Emmisional Power which is beautiful because it contains within itself the vibration, there the yogīn should repose devoted to the condition of the belly of the fish."[29]

---

[24] BHARDWAJ, S. M., *Hindu Places of Pilgrimage in India: A Study in Cultural Geography* (USA: University of California Press, 1983), 192.
[25] ECK, D., *India's Tīrthas: Crossings in Sacred Geography.*
[26] BHARATI, A., *The Tantric Tradition* (UK: Rider & Company, 1965), 161.
[27] WHITE, D. G., *The Alchemical Body: Siddha Traditions in Medieval India* (USA: The University of Chicago Press, 1996), 225.
[28] Ibid., 226.
[29] WHITE, D. G., *The Alchemical Body: Siddha Traditions in Medieval India*, pp. 224-225.

This is rendered even clearer by Gorakhnāth who states that: "Holding the breath [when it is] restrained by force (*haṭhāt*) is [called] swallowing into the fish-belly (*mīnodare*)."[30] 'Fish-belly' therefore is a yogīc technique utilized in controlling the breath. The reference to the river Sarasvatī is a reflection of its esoteric symbolism, the confluence of the three great rivers symbolizing the three principal channels of nāḍī and the trident of Śiva.[31]

It is of even greater significance that the site Kapālamochana (the place where the skull of Brahmā is said to have fallen from the hand of Śiva) was precisely at the confluence of the Matsyodarī and the backward-flowing Ganges.[32] This associates the region strongly with Śiva via both the Ganges and the Purāṇic story of Brahmanicide. Rivers also play a significant part in the anthropomorphism of Kāśī for, as can be read in the extract from the *Skanda Purāṇa* below; 'her' arms are named after the rivers Varaṇā and Asi.[33]

> 66. There is a certain noble lady renowned in the worlds as Kāśī. Eager and enthusiastic Arka (Sun-God) and Keśava constitute her tremulous eyes. Varaṇā and Asi are her two arms. This confluence is her *Veṇī* (unornamented single braid of hair). This Kāśī is proclaimed as the source of everlasting bliss.[34]

White elaborates on this further, illustrating the hidden esoteric significance.

> The two vessels are called the iḍā and the piṇgalā are the real *vārāṇ-asī*. The space between them is called Vārāṇasī. There it is said that [Śiva] Viśanāth dwells ... from the right side of the ājñā [cakra] and going to the left nostril flows the iḍā. It is here called Varaṇā, the upward flowing [Ganges] ... Rising

[30] WHITE, D. G., *The Alchemical Body: Siddha Traditions in Medieval India*, 228.
[31] Ibid., 27.
[32] Ibid., 119.
[33] HERTEL, B. R., & HUMES, C. A., *Living Banaras*, 207.
[34] BHATT, G. P., *Ancient Indian Tradition & Mythology, The Skanda-Purāṇa*, Vol. 58, Part x, 65.

> from the left side of the ājñā lotus and going to the right nostril, thisupward-flowing piṇgalā has been called of yore the Asi. [35]

This anthropomorphic form of Kāśī where 'she' is depicted as a noble lady seems to have a strong motif of sun/fire and water, both of which are liminal elements used to 'cross over'. Fire and water also both play a part in the iconography of Śiva.

Another very important manifestation of solar/fire iconography occurs in the tale of the *Jyotirliṅga.* Adi Vishwanath in Kāśī claims to be the original place of Jyotirliṅga.[36] In Kāshī's spiritual tradition, however, it is affirmed that the liṅgaṃ of light did not merely burst forth from the earth in Kāśī, rather it was Kāśī, the "Luminous."[37] This liṅgaṃ, according to the *Śiva Purāṇa,* looked like an endless volume of blazing fire, accompanied by its thousands of flames; it is further said that, if one could have a correct idea of the fierce fire that would destroy the universe at the end of the time of dissolution (pralaya), then, and then only, could one find an equal to this vast column.[38] In the *Śiva Purāṇa,* this Jyotirliṅga is described as *koṭisūryasamaprabha* (lit. emitting effulgence comparable to a crore of suns), which undoubtedly separates it from the sun itself.[39] This statement draws a direct parallel with the sun, with one prominent distinction; the light of Śiva is greater than that of the sun. With regard to solar iconography, it is also important to note the names of the lady Kāśī's eyes, as mentioned in the *Skanda Purāṇa.*

> Kāśī is regarded as a lady with the Sun God Lolārka and Ādikeśava (two famous temples at Kāśī) as her eyes.[40]

There seems to be a certain element of tension at play between Lolārka and Śiva, for Lolārka (from *lola*, "restless, trembling" and

[35] WHITE, D. G., *The Alchemical Body: Siddha Traditions in Medieval India*, 226.

[36] VIDYARHTI, L. P., *The Sacred Complex of Kashi (A Microcosm of Indian Civilization)* (India: Concept Publishing Company, 1979), 15.

[37] ECK, D., *Benares: City of Light*, 109.

[38] SIDDAHANTASHASTREE, R. K., *Śaivism Through the Ages* (India: Munshiram Manoharlal Publishers Pvt. Ltd, 1975), 104.

[39] Ibid., 105.

[40] BHATT, G. P., *Ancient Indian Tradition & Mythology, The Skanda-Purāṇa*, Vol. 58, Part x, 65.

arka, "ray, sun god") is so named because he was made restless from the heat of Śiva's angry eyes.[41] The Tīrtha of the God Lolārka is situated at Lolark Kund in Kāśī—the site of Lolark Kund is the most prominent of the dozen sites in Kāśī that are devoted to the Ādityas, the twelve solar deities born of the Vedic goddess Aditi.[42] Again, the symbolism of light and water is at play in this Tīrtha, for this is a solar god worshiped in the vicinity of a river. The significance of Lolarka is explained by Hertel & Humes in the following passage, which mentions a gradual decline of solar worship occurring in Kāśī that coincided with the God Śiva experiencing a rise in popularity.

> Lolarka is not only the oldest and most famous of Kāśī's Ādityas, but it is perhaps one of the oldest of all sacred sites in Kāśī. Archaeological evidence found at the site includes eighth- and twelfth-century images of Sūrya and an eleventh-century female sun deity, Chakreshvari. But even here at this ancient solar site, devotion to fire on earth and the sun in the sky has been surely and steadily eclipsed by the worship of an even more brilliant source of light in Kāśī: the Purāṇic god Śiva.[43]

To a certain extent, the identity of Śiva and Lolarka seem to have become fused at Lolark Kund; by supplanting Lolarka, Śiva seems to have adopted part of his identity there, and taken on more of a 'solar' demeanor. This solar element, however, is present in Śiva in other stories so it is feasible that this gradual identification of Śiva with older solar deities occurred at locations besides that of Lolark Kund, as is demonstrated in the extract below.

> The melding of Śiva's myths with the fire-solar deities is well known; indeed, some texts identify Śiva-Rudra with Agni directly. In the *Śiva Purāṇa* Śiva's identity is fused with Sūrya even as he is simultaneously declared the sun's lord: At the request of Brahmā, Shiva causes the excess energy wrought

[41] HERTEL, B. R., & HUMES, C. A., *Living Banaras*, 210.
[42] ECK, D., *Benares: City of Light*, 109.
[43] HERTEL, B. R., & HUMES, C. A., *Living Banaras*, 206.

> by his *tapasya* ("heated" self-discipline) to enter the sun since he is "lord of the sun," and he allows Brahmā and all the other immortals to live together in the energy of the sun. At the end of the eon, Śiva agrees to "take the form of the sun and burn this universe."[44]

The connection here is explicit—at the end of time Śiva will take the form of the sun. The *Vāmana Purāṇa* recounts the dispute that took place between Śiva and Sūrya; a dispute that also took place at Kāśī, where Sūrya has to cool himself in the rivers Varaṇā and Asi, for he has been burnt by Śiva's gaze (implying the heat of Śiva is great enough even to burn the sun). The *Vāmana Purāṇa* also speaks of a dispute between Sūrya and Śiva,

> Śiva retaliated with a single stare at Sūrya, proving that his fiery power was more brilliant than that of even the Sun, the "Lord of the Gods." As Sūrya spiraled from the Solar region into the atmosphere, hermits on earth called out, "If you wish to be saved, fall in the land holy to Hari [Vārāṇasī]." The Sun landed between the Varuṇa and Asi rivers. Burning from Śiva's glance, the "Restless sun" or *lulad ravi*, dipped first in the Asi, then in the Varaṇā, and "restless [*lulam*] by the affliction caused by the fire of the eyes of Śiva," he again splashed in the fords of Asi and Varaṇā. The Gods, led by Brahmā, appealed to Śiva on the Sun's behalf.[45]

Here the Sun is subjected to the power of Śiva. It seems intentional that Śiva here dominates the Sun God, and it is quite obvious that Sūrya has been deliberately portrayed as weaker than Śiva. It is likely that, based on the Purāṇic records, the decline of worship for Sūrya began with the rise of Śiva worship, and that the reason Kāśī came to be regarded as the city of Śiva is partially based on the contention that Kāśī was already deemed to be a holy site because of its location at the confluence of three rivers, one of which is the

[44] HERTEL, B. R., & HUMES, C. A., *Living Banaras*, 208.

[45] Ibid., 210.

Ganges. The site of Kāśī appears to have had a colorful history, for it is referred to by Daniélou as the world's oldest city, built by the first king in a forest carpeted with the sacred kāśa grass (*Saccharum Spontaneum*).[46]

As far as the connection between Śiva and Kāśī is concerned, however, it is not before the end of the third century CE that a shift in Hindu religion with respect to Kāśī appears in historical sources.[47] In the oldest edition of the *Skanda Purāṇa* (on Nepalese palm leaf, 810 CE) three chapters are concerned with Kāśī and its mythology of Divodāsa (here called a great yogīn and worshiper of Śiva) in slightly modified form and depict Vārāṇasī as a city of yogīs, especially of the Pāśupata order.[48] This statement is of particular important, for, in a later edition of the *Skanda Purāṇa,* it is King Divodāsa that forbids Śiva to enter the city, and, in order to enter Kāśī, Śiva has to fool Divodāsa. Even though the city is Śiva's, however, Sūrya still remains.

> After many attempts in various guises, the Sun realized it was impossible to tempt the king (Divodāsa). Sūrya abandoned the idea of returning to Śiva's abode for fear of Śiva's anger and instead decided to take the *ashrama* of *kṣetra sannyasa* in Vārāṇasī (to remain forever as a devotee in Kāśī's sacred territory). Sūrya came to be known as "Lolark," for when he saw the beauty of Kāśī, his mind became tremulous of desirous (*loa*). Sūrya-Lolark then dived himself into the twelve Ādityas, the first of which is named Lolark. Lolark constantly looks after the welfare of all Kāśī inhabitants, protecting the purity of the Tīrthas in Kāśī, and the reader is urged to bathe in Lokar Sngam at various times, including the special day of the sixth or seventh of *Margashirsha* when it falls on Sunday.[49]

---

[46] DANIÉLOU, A., *Hindu Polytheism*, 220.

[47] BAKKER, H., Construction and Reconstruction of Sacred Space in Vārāṇasī_in *Numen Vol.* 43 (E.J.Brill, Leiden, 1996), 33.

[48] Ibid., 35.

[49] HERTEL, B. R., & HUMES, C. A., *Living Banaras*, 211.

The history of solar-worship in India is also of note, for it seems to have followed a similar pattern to that found localized at Lolark Kund. This gradual demotion of Sūrya was effected in one of two ways: either by appropriating the mythology of Sūrya (and Agni) or by portraying the Purāṇic deity Śiva, as conqueror and Lord of the Sun.[50]

The sun used to be the center of a flourishing cult in North India and is still venerated by many Hindus. The fourth to the thirteenth centuries was the classical age of solar-worship in India. V. B. Mishra reports that during this time period the Hindu Trinity of Brahmā, Viṣṇu, and Śiva was in some cases "a kind of quadrumvirate," with Sūrya finding a place alongside the three great Gods. Sūrya evidently overshadowed Brahmā and Viṣṇu in some places, as is demonstrated by his replacement of them in some eleventh and twelfth-century sculptures of the Trinity. Finally, some icons of this period combined Sūrya with Śiva as Mārtanda-Bhairava and with Viṣṇu as Sūrya-Nārāyaṇa.[51]

The association of Kāśī with Śiva seems to be a complex one that functions on a number of levels. From the esoteric perspective, he not only resides in Kāśī, he is Kāśī. Śiva's connection with the practice of yoga and liberation from mokṣa also plays a role in the perception of Kāśī as a mokṣa granting city. By virtue of Śiva's status as the master yogīn who has transcended death, Kāśī reflects the abilities of its Lord, who is said to be ever present within the city. Yet, on another metaphysical level, Śiva is the city, for it is a microcosm of himself and the cosmos, which he bears aloft on his trident, the trident being associated with the natural sacred qualities arising from the city's auspicious location at the confluence of the three rivers. The Ganges, which is linked to Śiva, also figures in this, for Kapālamochana (the Place where the Skull fell) is at the confluence of the rivers, one of which is the Ganges, and is thus strongly connected to Śiva. The special relationship between Śiva and the Ganges is important in connection to the Tīrtha at Omkāra,

---

50 HERTEL, B. R., & HUMES, C. A., *Living Banaras*, 208.

51 Ibid., 206.

where at certain times the river water flows backward, surrounding the city with water, an event that was deemed to be extremely auspicious. It seems, though, that the God Śiva actually came to be associated with Kāśī at a later point in history when Kāśī was already a flourishing city. It is important to consider that Śiva chooses Kāśī to be his home but for a time was forbidden entry because of the King Divodāsa. The fact that it was chosen by Śiva himself suggests that Kāśī was already a prominent site. As Śiva gradually grew in popularity due to the distribution of Purāṇic texts which downplayed the role of Sūrya and other solar deities, it appears that Śiva gradually came to supplant Sūrya as a more popular deity. Kāśī, already possessing a strong solar/light motif, permitted the entry of Śiva because he absorbed the qualities of the older solar deities into his own being—thus Śiva came to be the Lord of Kāśī by replacing the older God Sūrya. This also allowed new elements to be added to the iconography of Kāśī, such as its being borne aloft on the trident of Śiva, and its ability to grant liberation. The role of King Divodāsa, however, remains ambiguous for, in the most recent versions of the tale, it is he who forbids Śiva entry to Kāśī, and yet in the *Skanda Purāṇa* found on Nepalese Palm, Divodāsa is referred to as a worshiper of Śiva. Perhaps this seemingly contradictory role occupied by King Divodāsa could best be interpreted as one in which the King at first disapproves of Śiva but at some later point himself converts to the worship of Śiva and, as a consequence of this, allows the God entry into Kāśī. If Sūrya had been the main God of Kāśī prior to the reign of King Divodāsa, then having a royal patron in the city of Kāśī would definitely have helped to boost the ascendancy of Śiva in the city, and provided the God with a very solid connection to the city of Kāśī—one which still holds current to the present day.

In the examples concerning Śiva and the Devī there is a strong connection between them and physical sites. These close links between the divine and the landscape and not just restricted to Śiva and the Devī. In Tamil traditions, Murukan is the "Lord of the Mountains" (Malaikilavōn), more closely identified with the "mountain landscape" than with the son of Śiva in the Saṅgam literature.[52] Notably, many of these sites are in possession of prominent geographical features. It is from the unique quality of the landscape that its sacred essence is derived. In the wider Hindu Tradition, these places, particularly those associated with waters, are often called Tīrthas, and pilgrimage to these Tīrthas is one of the oldest and most prominent features of Indian religious life. A Tīrtha is a "crossing place," a "ford," where one may cross over to the foreshore of a river or to the far shore of the worlds of heaven,[53] as seen in the definition Diana Eck provides.

> Tīrtha—Sanskrit verb *tṛ/tarati*, meaning "to cross over." The noun Tīrtha means a ford, as well as any watering or bathing place. It sometimes means a path or passage generally the root verb *tṛ* includes subsidiary meanings, to master, to surmount, to fulfill, to be saved—as well as its primary meaning, to cross. The noun *tāraka*, also derived from *tṛ*, means a boat or ferry, as well as a pilot or savior. Tīrtha, with its many associations, is a word of passage.[54]

Tīrthas are also a prime example of what Kees Bolle describes as a process of 'topographical religiosity' in which maps of the sacred became entwined with the physical world.

> The liturgical function of the sacred function of sacred places for the "symbolism of being there" is not merely a static imagery. It is alive with what could well be called a "topographical religiosity."[55]

Furthermore, this "symbolism of being there" can be seen as the mainstay of Hinduism in "the vicissitudes of its history."[56] The first major Hindu treatment of tīrtha-yātra is in the Tīrthayātra Parva of

[52] WHITE, D. G., *Kiss of the Yogini: "Tantric Sex" its South Asian Contexts* (USA: The University of Chicago Press, 2006), 176.
[53] ECK, D., *India's Tīrthas: Crossings in Sacred Geography.*
[54] Ibid.
[55] BOLLE, K., W., KITAGAWA, J. M., & LONG, C. H., *Myths and Symbols: Studies in Honor of Mircea Eliade* (USA: University of Chicago Press, 1969), 131.
[56] Ibid., 137.

the *Mahābhārata*, where the Pāṇḍavas, during their forest sojourn, undertake a circuit of the many Tīrthas.[57] The *Mahābhārata* clearly considers going on pilgrimage (tīrtha-yātrā) to be superior to sacrifice: "O thou best of Bharta race, sojourns in Tīrthas which are meritorious and which constitute one of the higher mysteries of the rishis, are even superior to sacrifices."[58] Furthermore, it is clear that tīrtha-yātra is a rite where the place holds the power.[59]

Instead of using the standard terminology of Tīrtha to describe their pilgrimage sites, the Tantrics adopted a different name for these sites in order to preserve their own religious identity and to help distinguish themselves from more orthodox movements. The word the Tantrics chose as a point of reference for their pilgrimage sites is Pīṭha, and the literal translation of the word is *āsana* or seat.[60] The Tantrics refer to their specific shrines, ponds, and other sites as Pīṭhas. The word is loaded for, in the sandhābhāṣā (intentional language) of the Tantras, it connotes the female organ, and the Śiva-linga is always represented as embedded within the Pīṭha, never alone.[61] Śakta Pīṭha is thus translated as a 'Seat of Power'. The different Pīṭhas in India are supposed to be the dwelling places of the Devī (the Mother-Goddess); that is why they are also called Devīsthānas.[62] The Pīṭhas themselves have gained their reputation as pilgrimage sites due to a tale found in the Puraṇās, namely the myth of the death and subsequent dismemberment of Śiva's first wife, Satī, the daughter of Dakṣa. When the corpse of Satī was sliced into pieces by Viṣṇu, the various parts of her body fell to the earth, and the ground on which they fell became Pīṭhas. Therefore, all the Pīṭhas are Devīsthānas, but all the Devīsthānas are not necessarily Pīṭhas.[63] There are also locations that are associated with the Mother-Goddess and yet do not contain any physical part of Satī's body.

[57] ECK, D., *India's Tīrthas: Crossings in Sacred Geography.*

[58] BHARDWELL, S. M., *Hindu Places of Pilgrimage in India: A Study in Cultural Geography* (USA: University of California Press, 1983), 29.

[59] ECK, D., *India's Tīrthas: Crossings in Sacred Geography.*

[60] BAGCHI, S., *Eminent Indian Śakta Centres in Eastern India*, 1.

[61] BHARATI, A., *The Tantric Tradition* (UK: Rider & Company, 1965), 159.

[62] Ibid.

[63] Ibid.

These are known as Upapīṭhas and are distinct from Pīṭhas.[64] The self-sacrifice of the Goddess Satī and the creation of the Śakta Pīṭhas are thus an iconic inversion of a normal sacrifice. Indeed, it is a kind of twisted mirror of the original creative sacrifice described in the Vedas, the sacrifice of the Primordial Person (Puruṣa) recounted in the famous creation myth of the *Rig Veda*.[65] The places where pieces of Satī's dead body fell are said to have become Pīṭhas, i.e., holy seats or resorts of the Mother-Goddess in all of which she is represented as living in some form together with a Bhairava.[66] Some Devīsthānas, on the other hand, are called Siddhapīṭhas, in as much as there lived at least one sādhaka who attained realization or siddhi at the place.[67] Throughout the Tantric tradition, there are many discrepancies regarding the number of Pīṭhas—the number varies widely from text to text, and sometimes within the same text itself different numbers of Pīṭhas are mentioned.

> Śakta Pīṭhas are traditionally associated with the various dismembered parts of the body of Satī—the consort of Śiva … 4 major and 46 minor sacred places are usually recognized. The more venerated shrines are associated with the more magically potent organs of the Goddess. Thus the most important of the Śakta shrines—Kāmākhyā—is associated with the pudenda of the Goddess. Similarly, the skull of the Goddess is venerated at the Temple of Kalighat in Calcutta and the tongue at Jwalamukhi in Himachal Pradesh.[68]

The original number recorded seems to have been four, but with the passage of time, the number gradually increased to seven, eight, nine, ten, fifteen, eighteen, fifty-one and even as high as one hundred and eight.[69]

64 BHARATI, A., *The Tantric Tradition*, 159.

65 URBAN, H., *The Power of Tantra: Religion, Sexuality and the Politics of South Asian Studies*, 35.

66 BHARATI, A., *The Tantric Tradition*, 146.

67 Ibid., 159.

68 BHARDWAJ, S. M., *Hindu Places of Pilgrimage in India: A Study in Cultural Geography* (USA: University of California Press, 1983).

69 BAGCHI, S., *Eminent Indian Śakta Centres in Eastern India*, 3.

The advent of utilization of the number one hundred and eight with regard to the total amount of Pīṭhas was possibly the result of a juxtaposition of traditions, as the number one hundred and eight also plays a significantly prominent role within a number of other Hindu traditions. This is possibly due to its esoteric link with cosmological myth, for the number one hundred and eight is achieved by multiplying the number of the planets (nine) by the portions of the solar calendar (12). Thus, the number can be seen to have widespread importance in India to the sectarian worshipers who often attempted to endow their respective deities with 108 names.[70] Therefore it is reasonable to arrive at the conclusion that the significance of this number is not peculiar to the mythology of the Pīṭhas alone, and was most likely added to the Tantric Tradition at a later point in time. Bharati states that,

> The *Hevajra Tantra*, composed around AD. 690 enumerates the four Pīṭhas, and to my knowledge this is the earliest enumeration: (1) Jālandhara (definitely near the present Jullandur, East Panjab), (2) Oḍḍiyāna (or Uḍḍīyāna, Urgyan in Tib. Misspelled Udyāna, viz., "garden" in the Bengali *Dohakośa* ed. Shahidullah) in the Surat Valley, (3) Pūrṇagiri (the location is doubtful) and (4) Kāmarūpa (Kāmarūpa in Assam) at present the only Pīṭha of the four actually visited by institutionalised Tantrics.[71]

There is also an element of uncertainty in attempting to establish the original locations of the Tantric Pīṭhas, for the locations recorded in the texts also vary. For example, the *Hevajra Tantra* of the Buddhists, composed in the middle of the eighth century CE, enumerates the following Pīṭhas: Jālandhara, Uḍḍīyāna, Pūrṇagiri and Kāmarūpa, while the *Kālikā Purāṇa* mentions several Pīṭhas, including Kāmarūpa, Pūrṇagiri, Jālandhara, and Oḍrā in place of Uḍḍīyāna.[72] The *Kālikā Purāṇa* (chap. LXIV 43-45) calls them (1) Oḍrā, seat at the Goddess Kātyāyanī and the God Jagannātha, (2)

[70] SIRCAR, D. C., *The Śakta Pīṭhas*, 24.
[71] BHARATI, A., *The Tantric Tradition*, 167.
[72] BAGCHI, S., *Eminent Indian Śakta Centres in Eastern India*, 3.

Jalasaila, the seat of the Goddess Caṇḍī and the God Mahānātha, and finally (4) Kāmarūpa, the seat of the deities Kāmeśvari and Kāmeśvara.[73]

According to Hugh Urban, "the region of Kāmarūpa seems to have been identified as an unrivaled center of Tantric culture and the seat of the Goddess' yoni from an early date, mentioned as early as the fourth century in the Allahabad pillar inscription of Samudragupta."[74] Kāmarūpa also has a prominent place in all the lists of four Pīṭhas. This fact may suggest that the Kāmarūpa Pīṭha became unrivaled as a center of Tantric culture by absorbing the popularity of the other Tīrthas of ancient India at a fairly early date.[75] Kāmarūpa is the region of eastern India from where Śaktism is said to have originated and a portion of the body, subtle or concrete, identified with female sexuality.[76] The high importance attributed to the Kāmarūpa Pīṭha site is also clearly denoted by the fact that chapter seventy-nine of the *Kālikā Purāṇa* is entitled 'Places of Pilgrimage in Kāmarūpa'.[77] The *Kālikā Purāṇa* is one of the 18 (Upa) Purāṇas, and it occupies a prominent place in the vast quantity of Purāṇic literature. Though technically an *Upa-Purāṇa*, it is called *Kālikā Purāṇa* or *Kāli-Purāṇa* and was composed to popularize the cult of Śakti, particularly the worship of the Mother Goddess Kāmākhyā.[78] With regard to the worship of the Devī and her sacred sites, the *Kālikā Purāṇa* is a highly important text. By analyzing the accounts of Pīṭhas in the different Tantras it becomes evident that the largest number of Pīṭhas are located in the eastern part of India while the smallest number is to be found within the Madhyadeśa of Manu.[79]

---

[73] BHARATI, A., *The Tantric Tradition*, 167.

[74] URBAN, H., *The Power of Tantra: Religion, Sexuality and the Politics of South Asian Studies*, 38.

[75] SIRCAR, D. C., *The Śakta Pīṭhas*, 15.

[76] WHITE, D. G., *The Alchemical Body: Siddha Traditions in Medieval India*, 235.

[77] SHASTRI, B. N., *The Kālikā Purāṇa*, Part III (Delhi: Nag Publishers, 1992), 1203.

[78] SHASTRI, B. N., *The Kālikā Purāṇa*, Part I (Delhi: Nag Publishers, 1991), 10.

[79] BAGCHI, S., *Eminent Indian Śakta Centres in Eastern India*, 8.

TANTRA, THE KALI YUGA, & THE OCCIDENTAL TRADITIONALIST

Tantrism reached its apex of popularity in medieval India—a time when two very important things occurred which helped to procure its remarkable ascent. One was an interest in esotericism and the other was an increasing belief in the negative effects of the Kali Yuga.

Hinduism adopts a cyclical perspective of time, from the Satya Yuga to the present Kali Yuga. It is a common misconception that the Kali Yuga is named after the Goddess Kālī. Instead, it takes its name from an extremely powerful male demon. This mistake occurs due to errors in English translations of the name Kali—in Sanskrit, the Goddess is named *Kālī* (with long vowels)—the name of the demon is spelled *Kali* (with short vowels). Whilst Tantra does have an intimate relationship with the nature of the Kali Yuga, it is not in the fashion that has been erroneously attributed to it. Rather, Tantrism was devised and constructed specifically to be the main religion in the Kali Yuga.

I. *Explaining the Cycle of Time*

The demonic Kali takes his name from the Sanskrit root *kad* which means to "suffer, grieve, hurt, confound, or confuse." Kali is the arch enemy of Kalki, the 10th avatar of the God Viṣṇu. When

Viṣṇu incarnates as an avatar, so does Kali—in the *Mahābhārata* he is said to be Duryodhana, and in the *Rāmāyaṇa* he is Rāvaṇa. Kali is the great-great-grandson of Lord Brahmā, as well as Adharma who was originally created from Lord Brahmā's back as a *Maleen Pataka* (a sinful object). This is found in the *Śrī Kalki Purāṇa* where it says that "After the annihilation, the secondary creator of the universe, Lord Brahmā, the grandfather of everyone, who was born on the universal lotus flower, created Sin personified, having a black complexion, from his back."[1] An alternate version of Kali's origin states that he was born from the left-over poison that was drunk by Lord Śiva during the churning of the ocean of milk.

Depictions of Kali portray him as both revolting and terrifying. The *Kalki Purāṇa* describes Kali as huge and the color of "soot," with a long tongue and a terrible stench. He carries a bone and has an abdomen that is said to be like that of a crow. Kali is always portrayed as holding his genitals in his left hand and he has a dark complexion, like a black ointment that has been mixed with oil.[2] The *Bhāgavata Purāṇa* also describes him as a Śūdra wearing the garments of a king. Kali's symbol is an owl and he rides a donkey instead of a horse. Kali is very fond of gambling, drinking wine, enjoying the company of prostitutes, and associating with merchants—his whole persona exudes an aura of extreme excess, gluttony, and greed. Kali is also presumed to be responsible for all evil scriptures and badly composed religious texts. The favorite residences of Kali are,

> The playgrounds of ghosts, foxes, and jackals. These places were permeated with the foul odor of decaying beef, and they were infested with crows and owls. Kali's domain can be found wherever there is gambling and intoxication, as well as where women constantly quarrel.[3]

In sum, his domains are those which are deemed impure by Hinduism and are found wherever people lose their rationality,

---

[1] DAS, B., ed. Das, P., *Śrī Kalki Purāṇa* (India: Tai Nitai Press), 5.

[2] Ibid.

[3] Ibid.

generating strife and conflict. It is the influence of Kali that distorts the perception of humanity and lures them from dharma. Kali's association with negative human emotions and antagonism towards dharma is symbolized by the names of his destructive progeny.

> Kali's sister was Durukti, (Harsh Speech). From Durukti's womb, Kali begot a son named Bhaya, (Fear), and a daughter named, Mṛtyu (Death). Bhaya begot a son named Niraya (Hell) from the womb of Mṛtyu and Niraya begot ten thousand sons in the womb of his sister, Yatana (Excessive Pain). Thus, I have described the destructive progeny of Kali, who were all blasphemers of genuine religious principles.[4]

Kali's reign, the Kali Yuga, commences within the *Mahābhārata* and this book is a pivotal text for understanding both the demon and the Yuga. The end of the *Mahābhārata* is traditionally believed to herald the dawn of the Kali Yuga, and it begins when Kṛṣṇa, the avatar of the God Viṣṇu, departs. Based on the astronomical observations of Parāśara, a date of c.1350 BCE can be provided for the *Mahābhārata*.[5]

Kali's presence in the text is subtle, and for the most part, is revealed only through symbolism. Hints of the infernal origin of Duryodhana are hidden within the *Mahābhārata*. Vidura issues warnings of the inauspicious symbols which surround Duryodhana and link him to Kali, saying,

> Listen to me, sire, even if my words are bitter, like medicine to a dying man. When Duryodhana was born he cried like a jackal. He will destroy us all. A jackal stalks our palace. Order Arjuna to kill him. Sacrifice a crow to get peacocks, sire; sell a jackal to buy tigers.[6]

---

[4] DAS, B., ed. Das, P., *Śrī Kalki Purāṇa*, 6.
[5] SIDHARTH, B. G., *The Celestial Key to the Vedas*, (USA: Inner Traditions, 1999), 118.
[6] VYĀSA, trans. Lil, P., *The Mahābhārata of Vyāsa* (India: Vikas Publishing House Pvt Ltd, 1980), 129.

Jackals are one of the animals traditionally associated with both Kali and bad omens. In a different translation of the *Mahābhārata*, Kali's presence is clearly stated.

> Know that Pāṇḍu of unfading glory and distinguished above all others sprung from the Maruts. Kṣattri and Yudhiṣṭhira are both portions of the deity of Righteousness. Know that Duryodhana was Kali, and Śakuni was Dvāpara.[7]

Just as the other main characters within the *Mahābhārata* are avatars of deities, Duryodhana is also the avatar of Kali. The identity of Kali as the villain of the *Mahābhārata* also sheds much light on the actions of Kṛṣṇa, the avatar of Viṣṇu, and the role he plays in teaching Arjuna the Kṣatriya dharma. Kali also appears as Nala in the *Mahābhārata*, who he possesses via a dice game. During the dice game, Nala loses everything and is forced into exile. Kali's possession of Nala ends when the Nāga Karkoṭaka bites him and the venom turns Nala into an ugly dwarf named Bāhuka, who eventually masters the dice game. Learning this enables Nala to exorcise the demon and he vomits Kali from his mouth. The story of Nala is a micro-version of the *Mahābhārata* itself—Duryodhana also lures Yudhiṣṭhira into playing the dice game, unaware that Duryodhana, aided by another demon Dvāpara (who has incarnated as Śakuni) is manipulating the dice so he can take over the kingdom.

> "Challenged, I never retreat," replied Yudhiṣṭhira. "We are pawns in the hand of fate. Let us begin. Who plays against me?" "I will supply the stakes," Duryodhana said. "My uncle Śakuni will play."[8]

Yudhiṣṭhira loses the kingdom, his brothers, himself, and even his wife. The dice game is also of further importance because the Yugas were originally named after the four throws of dice—*Krita*, *Trita*,

---

[7] VYĀSA, trans. Ganguli, K. M., *The Mahābhārata of Kṛṣṇa-Dvaipāyana Vyāsa* (c. 1883–1896), section XXXI.

[8] VYĀSA, trans. Lal, P., *The Mahābhārata of Vyāsa*, 128.

Dvita, and *Kali*—Krita being the best throw and Kali the worst. Therefore, Kali is not only winning the dice game, he is winning the Yuga and declaring it, albeit symbolically, as under his reign and preparing to engage in conflict with his traditional enemy, Viṣṇu who incarnates as Kṛṣṇa in the Bhagavad-Gītā section of the *Mahābhārata.* Despite the defeat of Kali/Duryodhana in the epic, the end of the *Mahābhārata* is the beginning of the Kali Yuga, because it is believed that the very moment Kṛṣṇa left the earth, Kali became active in the world.

Kali will not leave the world again until his nemesis Viṣṇu incarnates as Kalki. The *Kalki Purāṇa* is set at the end of the Kali Yuga and narrates the battle between the final avatar of Viṣṇu and Kali, who is defeated one-third of the way through the text. As Kali's connection to the Kali Yuga is much more explicit in the *Kalki Purāṇa,* the manner in which he influences humanity and dharma is also more obvious. The problems of the Kali Yuga are both moral and ethical, and the central issue of the *Kalki Purāṇa* is that society rejects dharma and Vedic teachings. This is portrayed in Kalki's role vis a vis the *mleccha.* The mlecchas are understood to be,

> Those who do not follow the Vedic principles. In former days, the mlecchas were fewer, and Visvāmitra Muni cursed his sons to become mlecchas. But in the present age, [the] Kali Yuga, there is no need of cursing, for people are automatically mlecchas. This is only the beginning of [the] Kali Yuga but at the end of [the] Kali Yuga the entire population will consist of mlecchas because no one will follow the Vedic principles. At that time, the incarnation Kalki will appear.[9]

It is also stated that,

> The pious Brāhmaṇa have left this country (India), having been chastised by the powerful Kali, who is envious of saintly persons, and who destroys the practice of religious principles.[10]

[9] *Śrīmad Bhāgavatam,* 9:16:33.

[10] DAS, B., ed. Das, P., *Śrī Kalki Purāṇa,* 45.

In addition to the mlecchas multiplying and the Brahmin departing, the caste system also breaks down into a fifth caste that is a result of the other four intermingling, as stated in the *Mahānirvāna Tantra:* "In the Kali Age, however, there are five castes—namely, Brāhmaṇa, Kṣatriya, Vaiśya, Śūdra, and Sāmānya."[11] The effect of the lack of dharma in the Kali Yuga can, therefore, be interpreted as the collapse of traditional law and the negation of all things ethical, moral, or spiritual. The goal of Kalki is not merely to slay Kali, but also to restore dharma and to reinstate Vedic Traditions. Kalki, on the other hand, spreads *adharma* by perverting religious discourse and creating unscrupulous scriptures. This is undoubtedly what Guénon has in mind when he speaks of the "counter-tradition" in the context of the Kali Yuga.

> The reign of the 'counter-tradition' is in fact precisely what is known as the 'reign of the Antichrist', and the Antichrist, independently of all possible preconceptions, is in any case that which will concentrate and synthesize in itself for this task all the powers of the 'counter-initiation', whether it be conceived as an individual or as a collectivity.[12]

The adharmic counter-tradition of the Kali Yuga is also identified with rigid dogma and out of date fundamentalist thinking by Daniélou who writes that, "Visually symbols—that is, the various forms of writing—only begin to be used to fix certain elements of tradition when the evolution of the cycle announces the decline of knowledge."[13] He elaborates further on this stating that,

> Writing is an urban phenomenon, characteristic of the Kali Yuga. To freeze the teachings of "prophets" in books regarded as sacred is to paralyze the spirit of research; it fixes so-called established truths and tends to create blind faith instead of the search for knowledge.[14]

---

[11] AVALON, A., *The Tantra of the Great Liberation* (USA: Dover Publications, 1972).

[12] GUÉNON, R., *The Reign of Quantity & Signs of the Times* (USA: Sophia Perennis, 2004), 270.

[13] DANIÉLOU, A., trans. Hurry, K. F., *Shiva and the Primordial Tradition: From the Tantras to the Science of Dreams*, (USA: Inner Traditions International Ltd., 2003), 103.

[14] DANIÉLOU, A., *While the Gods Play: Shaiva Oracles and Predictions on the Cycles of*

This is very much in line with depictions of Kali (metaphorically) possessing the minds of men to compose scriptures with 'evil intent'. One only needs to read the daily news to see how 'cherry-picked' religious passages can be used to attack ethnic groups, sexes, and sexual orientations. The most obvious modern example would be the deliberate distortion of religious texts to perpetuate political unrest and persecution. But it is only when all spiritual teachings have been eradicated that Kalki will be born, for the *Śrīmad Bhāgavatam* says that "At the end of [the] Kali Yuga, when there exist no topics on the subject of God, even at the residences of so-called saints and respectable gentlemen of the three higher varṇas and when nothing is known of the techniques of sacrifice, even by word, at that time the Lord will appear as the supreme chastiser."[15] It is by restoring dharma, the moral and spiritual essence of society, that Kalki is able to end the Kali Yuga. Kalki says this himself when he announces that "I will then again establish Satya Yuga, and thus reinstate the principles of religion as they were before."[16]

In order to examine the role of Tantrism as a teaching designed specifically for implementation in the Kali Yuga, first of all, a brief explanation of the nature of cyclical time in Hinduism is required, and the respective differences between the ages, especially in relation to their role with regard to dharma, followed by an explanation of the integral role that the Kali Yuga plays within the Western Traditionalist school.

II. *Traditionalism & Tantra*

Ever since mankind discovered the concept of time, predictions of what lies ahead have provided us with a boundless source of fascination—the ability to see into the future. If we could but see forward in time, we could forge our own destinies and compensate for past mistakes. From the beginning of recorded history seers and shamans have crafted techniques to look into the future by means

History and the Destiny of Mankind (USA: Inner Traditions International Ltd., 1987), 87.

15 *Śrīmad Bhāgavatam*, 2.7.

16 DAS, B., ed. Das, P., *Śrī Kalki Purāna*, 16.

of visions and prophecies. A multitude of different predictions have been passed, some originating from dreams, some through prayer and still others have passed from the tongues of the Gods themselves. Each and every prediction tells a story—some tell tales of utopia, others of armageddon. Amongst all of these future events, perhaps none is quite as bleak as that which is drawn from the perspective of cyclical time, which portrays a fixed cycle of events that cannot be changed or prevented by the course of the human intervention. According to this vision of the future, civilization will gradually degenerate until it finally collapses so that the cycle of time may begin again.

The notion of cyclic time is also found outside of the Hindu community, in the idea of a 'Primordial Tradition' which is the core doctrine of the Traditionalist School and Perennial Philosophy. The cycle of Yugas was therefore studied by Traditionalists such as René Guénon, Julius Evola, and Alain Daniélou. Due to their influence, the Kali Yuga was successfully exported into a variety of Western movements and ideologies. According to the Primordial Tradition, the various epochs of human history are reduced to Four Ages, each of which gradually deteriorates. In Hinduism, these are known as the Yugas, respectively titled the Satya Yuga, Tretā Yuga, Dvāpara Yuga, and the Kali Yuga. Each age consists of the main period and two twilight periods. Each twilight period is one-tenth the duration of the main period.[17] An especially interesting point in this system is the inclusion of the two twilight periods, one before and one after, each equal to one-tenth of the main period.[18] These also correspond to the four eras symbolized by the myth of the metals found in Hesiod's *Works and Days*—the Gold, Silver, Bronze, and Iron Ages.[19] Similar versions of this myth are also found in the Persian, Chaldean, Egyptian, Aztec, and Norse Traditions. These Four Ages are part of a greater cycle of existence, known in Hinduism as a *Manvantāra*. Guénon notes that this division of the

[17] SIDHARTH, B. G., *The Celestial Key to the Vedas*, 60.
[18] Ibid., 60.
[19] EVOLA, J., *Revolt Against the Modern World* (USA: Inner Traditions International, 1995), 177.

Manvantāra into four parts is a significant feature of many other cosmic cycles, notably the four seasons of the year, the four weeks of the lunar month, the four ages of human life, and the four points of the compass.[20] It is also common to liken the gradual process of degeneration between the cycles to the image of the Bull of Dharma, which loses its footing as the Ages pass, symbolizing the collapse of dharma or Traditional Law.[21] This example is found in its entirety in the *Laws of Manu*:

> In the Winning Age, religion is entire, standing on all four feet, and so is truth; and men do not acquire any gain through irreligion. But in the other (Ages), through such wrong gained, religion is brought down foot by foot; and because of theft, lying, and deceit, religion goes away foot by foot.[22]

Not only is the Bull of Dharma reduced to standing on one foot alone, this last hoof is also thought to collapse eventually. In the Kali Yuga, only one foot of Dharma remains and it is diminished by the 'feet' of *adharma* (unrighteousness) to such an extent that ultimately it collapses.[23] The Winning Age here is used as another name for the Satya Yuga, for it is also common to compare the Ages to the gambler's dice game, an event which occurs early within the *Mahābhārata*.

According to Hindu Tradition, the commonly accepted lengths of the Yugas are as follows: The Satya Yuga is generally accepted as being 1, 728, 000 human years in duration, the Tretā Yuga is 1, 296,000, the Dvāpara Yuga is 834,000, and the Kali Yuga, being the shortest of the four, is only 432,000 human years in duration.[24] There is, however, some dispute not only as to the length of the Yugas but also the beginning and end points of the cycle. Alain Daniélou derives a different time span for the Yugas than that of the traditional

---

[20] GUÉNON, R., *Traditional Forms & Cosmic Cycles* (USA: Sophia Perennis, 2004), 5.

[21] EVOLA, J., *Revolt Against the Modern World*, 177.

[22] DONIGER, W., & SMITH, B. K., *The Laws of Manu* (UK: Penguin Books, 1991), 12.

[23] TAGORE, G. V., *Ancient Indian Tradition and Mythology, Vol. II, Bhāgavata Purāna* Part v (India: Motilal Banarsidass, 1978), 2139.

[24] DANIÉLOU, A., *Hindu Polytheism* (UK: Routledge & Kegan Paul Ltd, 1964), 249.

Purāṇic model mentioned above. He explains his differences from the Purāṇic model as being based on adjustments made for the earth's gradual orbital shifts:

> The number of days in a year is not constant. The rhythm of the earth's rotation varies over very long periods. A figure of 360 is considered to be average.

Joscelyn Godwin also adopts an astronomical perspective when he states that "one of the recurrent themes of the Golden Age is that during it the earth's axis was perpendicular to the ecliptic … If this were so there would be no seasons, but equal day and night throughout the year."[25] An alteration in time is also noted by René Guénon for the Yugas themselves have "decreasing lengths of the respective durations of the four Yugas that together make up a Manvantāra."[26] The duration of the Yugas decreases proportionally with a ratio of 4:3:2:1.[27] According to Guénon, with regard to the numbers given in different texts for the duration of the Manvantāra and consequently for that of the Yugas, it must be understood that they are not to be regarded as a 'chronology' in the ordinary sense of the word, but rather as expressing a literal number of years; and this is also why certain apparent differences in these numbers do not really imply any contradiction.[28] In Daniélou's version, the lifespan of the Gods is 4,320,000 human years. Eliade also relates the same time span (taken from *Manu I*, 69 *et seq*., *Mahābhārata* III, 12, 826) in which the Satya Yuga lasts for 4,000 years, the Tretā Yuga 3,000 years, the Dvāpara Yuga 2,000 years and the Kali Yuga being only 1,000 'Divine Years' in duration—in human years the figure is the same as that derived by Guénon and Daniélou; the length of the total cycle is 4,320,000.[29] This period is then divided into Manvantāras. Each Manvantāra is divided into four Yugas;

[25] GODWIN, J., Decoding the Cycles of Time: When Does the Kali Yuga End? in *New Dawn Magazine* (Australia: May-June, 2013), 64.

[26] GUÉNON, R., *The Reign of Quantity & Signs of the Times*, 42.

[27] SIDHARTH, B. G., *The Celestial Key to the Vedas*, 60.

[28] GUÉNON, R., *Traditional Forms & Cosmic Cycles*, 6.

[29] ELIADE, M., *Images and Symbols: Studies in Religious Symbolism* (USA: Princeton University Press), 64.

the length of the Yugas then change as follows: The duration of the Satya Yuga becomes 24,195 human years, the Tretā Yuga becomes 18,146 years, the Dvāpara Yuga becomes 12,097 years, and the Kali Yuga is drastically reduced to a mere 6,048 human years, placing in it the modern era. These calculations are extremely similar to those reached by Guénon: Expressed in ordinary years, these same durations of the four Yugas will be respectively 25,920, 19,440, 12,960 and 6,480, forming a total of 64,800 years; and it will be recognized that these numbers are at least within perfectly plausible limits and may very well correspond to the true chronology of present terrestrial humanity.[30] By Daniélou's calculations, the Kali Yuga began in 3012 BCE and will end in 2442 CE.

The first of the four ages is the Satya Yuga, which corresponds to Hesiod's Golden Age. During the Golden Age, presided over by the God Chronos, "mortal men lived as if they were Gods" and no "miserable old age came their way."[31] This was the Age in which the great seers established the basis of their approach to the world's deep reality, which is the foundation of the Primordial Tradition, the expression of universal laws.[32] In other, non-Indian Traditions, this Golden Age is equivalent to the primordial, paradisiacal epoch.[33] The Tretā Yuga or Age of the Three Ritual Fires, saw the constitution of human society, the family, tribe, hierarchy, and royalty—relationships were now formalized in an effort to conform to universal laws.[34] The Dvāpara Yuga saw the birth of various mythologies, philosophical schools, and atheistic doctrines. It was during this period of history that urban civilizations and hierarchies of function developed.[35] The Kali Yuga, or Age of Conflicts, saw the acceleration of the principle of cosmic degeneration. During the Kali Yuga humanity has abandoned its connections with the

[30] GUÉNON, R., *Traditional Forms & Cosmic Cycles*, 8.
[31] EVOLA, J., *Revolt Against the Modern World*, 185.
[32] DANIÉLOU, A., & GABIN, J. L., *Shaivism & The Primordial Tradition* (USA: Inner Traditions International, 2007), 101.
[33] ELIADE, M., *Images and Symbols: Studies in Religious Symbolism*, 63.
[34] DANIÉLOU, A., & GABIN, J. L., *Shaivism & The Primordial Tradition*, 101.
[35] Ibid., 102.

natural world; religion has deteriorated to the mere expression of social codes, the prophets of various sects war with each other.[36] The essential quality of the Kali Yuga is said to be a climate of dissolution, in which all the forces—individual and collective, material, psychic, and spiritual—that were previously held in check by a higher law and by influences of a superior order pass into a state of freedom and chaos.[37] This Age is named Kali after the demon of vice. During this period, the nature of Tradition will be esoteric, and passed between initiates only; it will survive but will remain hidden. The traditional spirit is already beginning to withdraw into itself, and centers where it is preserved in its entirety are becoming isolated and difficult to access; this generalization of confusion corresponds exactly to what must occur in the final phase of the Kali Yuga.[38] During this Age, there will be many conflicts and much strife—there will be conflicts between mysticism and moralism, and also between the religions of nature and of the cities and civic duties.[39] The middle of the Kali Yuga is marked by periods of great upheaval and civil unrest. It was the time of the destruction of Athens, Ur, Babylon, the Persian invasion of Egypt, and also the time during which Rome developed at the expense of the Etruscans.[40] Guénon saw the effects of the Kali Yuga as inevitable, stating that: "we have in fact entered upon the last phase of the Kali Yuga, the darkest period of this 'dark age', the state of dissolution from which it is impossible to emerge otherwise than by a cataclysm, since it is not a mere readjustment that is necessary at such a stage, but a complete renovation."[41] According to Guénon, what characterizes the ultimate phase of a cycle is the realization of all that has been neglected or rejected during the preceding phases. Because of the influence of the Kali Yuga, today's events unfold with a greater speed than in earlier ages, and this speed goes on increasing

[36] DANIÉLOU, A., & GABIN, J. L., *Shaivism & The Primordial Tradition*, 102.
[37] EVOLA, J., *Ride the Tiger: A Survival Manual for the Aristocrats of the Soul* (USA: Inner Traditions International, 2003), 9.
[38] GUÉNON, R., *The Crisis of The Modern World* (USA: Sophia Perennis, 2001), 98.
[39] DANIÉLOU, A., *While the Gods Play: Shaiva Oracles and Predictions on the Cycles of History and the Destiny of Mankind* (USA: Inner Traditions International, 1987), 25.
[40] Ibid., 26.
[41] GUÉNON, R., *The Crisis of The Modern World*, 17.

and will continue to increase up to the end of the cycle, which is something like a progressive 'contraction' of duration.[42] According to the *Bhāgavata Purāṇa,* the Kali Yuga began at the very moment Lord Krishna retired from the earth.[43] The *Bhāgavata Purāṇa* also places this squarely within an astronomical time-frame by stating that the earth entered the Kali Yuga at the moment the Seven Divine Sages (*Ursa Major*) entered the constellation *Magha.*[44]

Many of the predictions held for the Kali Yuga arise from the Hindu scriptures known as the Purāṇas—in particular, the *Linga* and *Bhāgavata Purāṇas* provide lengthy descriptions of the events that will unfold as the Kali Yuga accelerates. An entire section of the *Bhāgavata Purāṇa* is devoted to the evils of the Kali Yuga. Some of the defining points of the Kali Yuga are described as follows:

> In the Kali Yuga, wealth alone will be the deciding factor of [the] nobility of birth, righteous behavior, or merits. And only brute force will be the only standard in the arrangement or decision of what is righteous or just.[45] ... When (in the Kali Age) religion will be predominantly heretical, and kings will be as good as robbers, and men will be earning their livelihood by theft (economic offenses), mendacity, wanton violence to life and such other pursuits.[46] ... Thieves function as kings and kings function as thieves. The chaste ladies cease to exist and wanton sluts increase in number.[47] ... As a result of Kali's influence, mortal beings become dull-witted, unlucky, voracious, destitute of wealth yet voluptuous, and women, wanton, and unchaste.[48] ... In the Kali Age, men will abandon their parents, brothers, friends, and relatives and establish their friendliness on a sexual

[42] GUÉNON, R., *Traditional Forms & Cosmic Cycles*, 42.

[43] TAGORE, G. V., *Ancient Indian Tradition and Mythology, Vol. II, Bhāgavata Purāna,* Part v, 2134.

[44] Ibid.

[45] Ibid., 2130.

[46] Ibid., 2131.

[47] SHASTRI, J. L., *Ancient Indian Tradition and Mythology, Vol. V, Linga Purāna,* Part I (India: Motilal Banarsidass, 1982), 156.

[48] TAGORE, G. V., *Ancient Indian Tradition and Mythology, Vol. II, Bhāgavata Purāna,* Part v, 2140.

> basis. Their affection being centered on their relation with women, they will seek consultations from their wife's relatives (such as sisters and brother-in-laws) and will be miserable.[49] … Killing of fetus and murder of heroes become prevalent.[50] … In Kali Age men excited by *tamoguna* adopt māyā (deception) and jealousy. They do not hesitate to kill ascetics. They are always tormented by jealousy.[51] … In Kali cooked food will be kept for sale in living places. The selling of Vedas and other sacred literature will occur in cross streets; young women will even sell their honor.[52] … Women will be short-statured but voracious, noted for fecundity and shameless. They will be harsh-speakers, given to theft, fraud, and daredevilry.[53]

From these extracts it is clear that a significant amount of the negativity embodied in the Kali Yuga originates from humanity itself under the influence of the tamas guṇa (a materialistic component of existence). In the Kali Yuga, we see an increasing trend towards indulgence on the material plane, such as the abandonment of religion, obsession with sex, and jealousy over the wealth of others. People are respected by their wealth alone, and not for deeper personal qualities such as character or personal achievements. Under the reign of the tamas guṇa, only materialistic pleasures such as sex and money are accorded merit by society in the Kali Yuga. This materialism is also expressed in the passage regarding the abandonment of aged parents and the killing of fetuses—which can be seen in today's increasing trend towards placing one's parents in Retirement Homes, to die amongst strangers rather than accepting responsibility for the elderly. The killing of fetuses can likewise be interpreted as a reference to abortion. Other symptoms include the moral degeneration of the

[49] TAGORE, G. V., *Ancient Indian Tradition and Mythology, Vol. II, Bhāgavata Purāna,* Part V, 2140.

[50] SHASTRI, J. L., *Ancient Indian Tradition and Mythology, Vol. V, Linga Purāna,* Part 1, 156.

[51] Ibid.

[52] Ibid., 157.

[53] TAGORE, G. V., *Ancient Indian Tradition and Mythology, Vol. II, Bhāgavata Purāna,* Part V, 2140.

female to a purely sexual role and a corresponding increase in the growth and social acceptance of prostitution. Perhaps the most unusual prediction here, though, is the one that cooked food will be kept for sale in living spaces—a clear reference to fast food, and the mass consumption of it by the populace at large. A similar picture of civilization slowly decaying from within can be found in the *Viṣṇu Purāṇa. The Viṣṇu Purāṇa* (IV, 24) also tells us that the Kali Yuga is the only age in which property alone confers social rank; wealth becomes the only motive of the virtues, and lust the only bond between the married, falsehood and deception the first condition of success in life, sexuality the sole means of enjoyment, and external ritualistic religion is confused with genuine spirituality.[54] The problems brought by the Kali Yuga are not entirely brought about by moral collapse, however—there are also a set of predictions relating to environmental problems.

> Being oppressed by droughts or famines and heavy taxation and being subjected to excessive cold, biting winds, [blistering] sunshine, [driving] downpour of rain, snowfall, mutual rivalry, the people are going to perish.[55] … As the Yuga draws to a close, men become reduced in number while women increase in proportion.[56] … The earth will be devoid of kings, riches and food grains will not flourish; groups of conspirators will be formed in the cities and countries. The earth will have a short supply of water and will be deficient in fruits.[57] … Suffering from colic they will have their hairs disheveled. Towards the close of the Yuga, people will be born who will be only sixteen years.[58]

The references here to fluctuating extremes of temperature and shortage of water are suggestive of climate change. The mention

54 ELIADE, M., *Images and Symbols: Studies in Religious Symbolism*, 64.

55 TAGORE, G. V., *Ancient Indian Tradition and Mythology, Vol. II, Bhāgavata Purāna*, Part V, 2131.

56 SHASTRI, J. L., *Ancient Indian Tradition and Mythology, Vol. V, Linga Purāna*, Part 1, 156.

57 Ibid., 158.

58 Ibid.

of blistering sunshine likewise suggests the depletion of the ozone layer, making even the sunshine dangerous in the Kali Yuga. It seems likely that the mention of colic and disheveled hair refer to forms of sickness which originate from the effects of the harsh weather and poor diet caused by adverse agricultural conditions. Most disturbing of all is the prediction that at the end of the Yuga, people will die at the tender age of sixteen.

The Kali Yuga also causes moral corrosion, most noticeably in personal behavior and also with bad government. The *Mahānirvāna Tantra* also states that "Those born in the Kali Age are by their nature weak in intellect, and their minds are distracted by lust," implying that the character of people is what causes them to adopt practices which are essentially harmful to both themselves and others.[59] Due to the growing influence of materialism, greed will also become a source of admiration, and only those who are wealthy will be deemed worthy of respect. The *Kalki Purāṇa* states that,

> In [the] Kali Yuga, a person with a lot of money will naturally be respected as a great soul. If a twice-born person earns his livelihood by lending money on interest, he will be considered a pillar of society.[60]

Other human created disasters associated with the Kali Yuga are clearly the result of bad governments. Taxes will increase and political figures will be self-serving rather than protectors of the people. There will also be mass migrations—something that is currently happening as people leave regions for more prosperous and stable countries.

According to the *Bhāgavata Purāṇa,* the Kali Yuga will draw to a close at the occurrence of a specific astronomical event. When the Moon, the Sun, and Jupiter are in conjunction in the same zodiacal house and the star Puṣya is in attendance, the Kṛta (Satya) Yuga dawns.[61] These planets must also enter the zodiacal house

[59] AVALON, A., *The Tantra of the Great Liberation* (USA: Dover Publications, 1972).

[60] DAS, B., ed. Das, P., *Śrī Kalki Purāna*, pp. 8-10.

[61] TAGORE, G. V., *Ancient Indian Tradition and Mythology, Vol. II, Bhāgavata Purāna,* Part V, 2133.

simultaneously, otherwise, this phenomenon would transpire on a twelve year cycle in the sign of Cancer. It is, therefore, the defining point of this prophecy that the three astronomical bodies must enter the zodiacal sign simultaneously to herald the dawn of the new Yuga. Before this occurs, however, the final avatar of Viṣṇu, known as Kalki or Pramiti (Wisdom or Knowledge of Truth) will incarnate at the close of the Kali Yuga, and cleanse the earth to punish those who have fallen prey to the materialistic impulses of the Kali Yuga. Pramiti is the equivalent of Kalki, the last of the ten incarnations of Viṣṇu are mentioned in the *Matsya Purāṇa* (285.67. [277]).[62]

> When the Yuga has come to a close and the period of junction too has arrived, the chastiser of the wicked people will rise up in order to kill all the bad living beings. He will be born in the family of the Moon. He will be called Pramiti by name … He will be surrounded by hundreds and thousands of Brahmins wielding weapons. He will kill the mlecchas (outcast people) in thousands … he will kill those who are not pious and virtuous. He will kill those who are born of different castes and those who depend upon them … He will be killing hundreds and thousands of living beings. By means of this cruel act, he will reduce the entire earth to the seeds ... The subjects who survive the Kali Yuga will be devoid of physical features and mental peace. At that time, the Yuga changes for them overnight, after creating illusion in their minds as in the case of a sleeping or mad man. Thanks to the inevitability and force of future events Kṛta Yuga will set in. When thus the Kṛta Yuga is ushered in, the subjects surviving from the Kali Yuga become those belonging to the Kṛta Yuga.[63]

There is a shred of hope here. Kalki/Pramiti will not slay all beings, just those who have erred from the path. Those who are not judged as sinful by Kalki/Pramiti will survive the onslaught and,

[62] DANIÉLOU, A., *Hindu Polytheism*, 165.
[63] SHASTRI, J. L., *Ancient Indian Tradition and Mythology, Vol. V, Linga Purāna*, Part 1, pp. 160-162.

after an initial period of suffering as the Age draws to a close, they will survive into the dawn of the Satya Yuga. Furthermore, they will be endowed with the mystic powers known as siddhi which are a normal occurrence for all inhabitants of the Age. Their life thereafter shall be long and prosperous. But what of those people who are alive now, who have no prospect of living into the next Satya Yuga? Is there any hope for humanity in the Kali Yuga, given the corruption present in the Yuga? Both Daniélou and Evola saw the path of Tantra as a way to control the currents of the Kali Yuga. Daniélou says that "it is the only method which may bring actual results in the difficult conditions of the age of strife, in which we live."[64]

III. *Julius Evola & the Export of Tantrism to the West*

Daniélou's influence over Traditionalism, however, is dwarfed by that of Julius Evola. Born in Rome during 1898, Giulio Cesare Andrea Evola was the son of an aristocratic Sicilian family, and like many children born in Sicily, he had received a stringent Catholic upbringing. Later in life, he would be a strong opponent of Fascist doctrine. Evola's attempts to curb the destructive elements in Fascism have been wrongly interpreted by some as supporting Fascism when it is clear from his own writing that the opposite was true. Evola was targeted as a 'dissident' and 'subversive' influence. As Evola always said, he was a supporter of traditional aristocracy and one would have to be particularly naive to argue otherwise, given that his theory of culture (which he refers to in the terminology of the era as the "race of the spirit") is designed to *subvert* any form of biological racism and *manipulate* Fascism to conform to his own ideas. The myth that Evola was a 'racist' is only spread by the willfully ignorant, on both the political Left and the Right. As he happened to live in Fascist Italy, his political options were severely limited and he had little choice but to conform with

[64] DANIÉLOU, A., *Hindu Polytheism*, 382.

the government—even advocating traditional aristocracy was enough to put him on the government watch list.

As Evola recalled in his intellectual autobiography, *Il Cammino del Cinabro* (1963, 1972), his favorite pastimes consisted of painting, one of his natural talents, and of visiting libraries as often as he could in order to read works by Oscar Wilde, Friedrich Nietzsche, and Otto Weininger.[65] During his youth, he also studied engineering, and received excellent grades. Evola discontinued his studies prior to the completion of his doctorate, however, because he "did not wish to be bourgeois, like his fellow students." He was also an associate of the Tibetologist Giuseppe Tucci, Tantric scholar Sir John Woodroffe (Arthur Avalon), and an Indian alchemist by the name of C. S. Narayana Swami Aiyar of Chingleput.[66] During this period of history, Indian alchemy was almost completely unknown to the Western world, and it is only in modern times that it has been studied in conjunction with Occidental texts.

Taking issue with René Guénon's (1886-1951) view that spiritual authority ranks higher than royal power, Evola wrote *L'uomo come Potenza* (Man as Power). In the third revised edition (1949), the title was changed to *Lo Yoga Della Potenza* (The Yoga of Power).[67] This was Evola's treatise on Hindu Tantra, for which he consulted primary sources on Kaula Tantra, which at the time were quite obscure. Decio Calvari, president of the Italian Independent Theosophical League, had introduced Evola to the study of Tantrism.[68] Evola was also granted access to authentic Tantric texts from the Kaula school of Tantrism via his association with Sir John Woodroffe, who was not only a respected scholar but was also a Tantric practitioner himself, under the famous pseudonym of Arthur Avalon. Even today Woodroffe is regarded as a leading pioneer in the early research of Tantrism. A substantial proportion of *The Yoga of Power* is derived from Sir John Woodroffe's personal notes on Kaula Tantrism.

---

65 EVOLA, J., *The Yoga of Power: Tantra, Shakti, and the Secret Way* (USA: Inner Traditions, 1992), IX.

66 Ibid., IX.

67 Ibid., XIV.

68 Ibid., XIII.

Evola is of the opinion that the royal or Kṣatriya path in Tantrism outranks that of the Brahmin or priestly path. In this regard, the heroic or solar path of Tantrism represented to Evola a system based not on theory, but on practice—an active path appropriate to the degenerate epoch of the Hindu Kali Yuga, in which purely intellectual or contemplative paths to divinity have suffered a great decrease in their effectiveness. Evola's theories concerning the role of the Kṣatriya varṇa in antiquity are both a 'progression on' and a 'refutation of' René Guénon's work. Despite their sharing the same foundational source in perennial philosophy, there are a number of points on which they differ, the most obvious point of contention being the role of the Kṣatriya in relation to a hierarchical model of civilization. Guénon held that the textual model in Hinduism was correct, with the Brahmin holding all power as the priests/philosophers. Evola, however, declared that this model was theoretical only—in practice the Kṣatriya varṇa held all the power. Normally associated in the West with the military, Evola instead offered a paradigm which depicted the Kṣatriya as the aristocratic caste, composed of the nobility as well as the warriors. Because Evola links the Kṣatriya to the aristocracy, this becomes a central motif in his work. The context of this dispute with Guénon is usually misunderstood, even in Traditionalist circles. The nature of this debate is best explained by Evola himself in *The Path of Cinnabar*,

> Yet, Guénon argued in favor of the legitimate pre-eminence, in the present age, of the priesthood (here associated with 'wisdom' and 'knowledge') over kingship and the warrior caste of the Kṣatriya (associated with action). By contrast, I argued that both poles being the product of recent dissociation, one cannot be regarded as possessing greater dignity than the other: for both poles, I suggested, are equally remote from primordial unity. I also suggested that an orientation towards sovereignty might provide a better foundation for my attempt to reintegrate that condition of centrality (i.e. the condition of the *Absolute Individual*) which Guénon himself had described as the

> primordial condition of humanity. To describe the achievement of this reintegration 'by means of action' (i.e. on the basis of a warrior, vital disposition), I used the term 'heroic' (in the sense in which it was used by Hesiod).[69]

It is clear that Evola is not arguing about the varṇa system simply based on historical evidence, but rather as a medium by which to connect his earlier theory of the *Absolute Individual* with Tradition. Seen in this light, the Evolian model of sovereignty also borrows from European Traditions. The two aspects of his philosophical predisposition Evola is conveying here are, in his words, "an impulse towards transcendence," and the "warrior spirit" (Kṣatriya), which is defined as "a human type tending to action and affirmation."[70] To Evola, this active path to the divine and the model of sovereignty represented the *via umida*, the wet path, which suited the active Western character.[71] It is only in relation to this facet of Evola's philosophy that the emphasis in *Men Among the Ruins* on obedience, loyalty, and the warrior caste can be understood.[72] To a certain extent, these ideas are also supported by the texts themselves, such as the *Laws of Manu* and the *Bṛihādāranyaka Upaniṣad*, which states that: "This is why nothing is greater than the warrior nobility; the priests themselves venerate the warrior when the consecration of the king occurs."[73] This is the concept which Evola grafts onto the Tantric Tradition, which he consequently adapts to his own philosophy. As Evola says,

> During the last years of the 1930s I devoted myself to working on two of my most important books on Eastern wisdom: I completely revised *L'uomo come Potenza* (Man as Power), which was given a new title, *Lo Yoga della Potenza* (The Yoga of Power), and wrote a systematic work concerning primitive

[69] EVOLA, J., *Path of Cinnabar* (UK: Integral Tradition Publishing, 2009), 103.

[70] FURLONG, P., *Social and Political Thought of Julius Evola* (UK: Routledge, 2011), 7.

[71] Ibid., 14.

[72] Ibid., 41.

[73] EVOLA, J., *Revolt Against the Modern World* (USA: Inner Traditions International, 1995), 68.

> Buddhism entitled *La Dottrina del Risveglio* (The Doctrine of Awakening).[74]

Another of Evola's books, *Eros and the Mysteries of Love*, could almost be seen as a continuation of his experimentation with Tantrism. Indeed, the book does not deal with the erotic principle in the normal sense of the word but rather approaches the topic as a highly conceptualized interplay of polarities, adopted from the Traditional use of erotic elements in both Eastern and Western metaphysics. These utilize the erotic principle to transcend the normal limitations of consciousness. Evola describes *Eros and the Mysteries of Love* in the following passage.

> But in this study, metaphysics will also have a second meaning, one that is not unrelated to the world's origin since "metaphysics" literally means the science of that which goes beyond the physical. In our research, this "beyond the physical" will not cover abstract concepts or philosophical ideas, but rather that which may evolve from an experience that is not merely physical, but transpsychological and transphysiological. We shall achieve this through the doctrine of the manifold states of being and through an anthropology that is not restricted to the simple soul-body dichotomy but is aware of "subtle" and even transcendental modalities of human consciousness. Although foreign to contemporary thought, knowledge of this kind formed an integral part of ancient learning and of the traditions of varied peoples.[75]

Following this Evola composed *Ride the Tiger*, which is complementary to this work, even though it was not published until 1961. The title of this book also holds a strong connection with Tantrism and, in many ways, this work is the culmination of Evola's thought on the role of Tradition. The Traditional approach

[74] EVOLA, J., *The Doctrine of Awakening: The Attainment of Self-Mastery According to the Earliest Buddhist Texts* (USA: Inner Traditions, 1996), xi.
[75] EVOLA, J., *Eros and the Mysteries of Love: The Metaphysics of Sex*, (USA: Inner Traditions, 1991), 2.

advocated in the East is to harness the power of the Kali Yuga, by 'Riding the Tiger'—which is also a popular Tantric saying. To this extent, it is not an approach of withdrawal from the modern world Evola advocates, but instead a mastery of the forces of darkness and materialism inherent in the Kali Yuga. *Riding the Tiger,* therefore, deals with the practical existential perspective for the individual who wants to preserve his *hegomonikon* or inner sovereignty.[76] It is the final culmination of Evola's esoteric ideas and the fully evolved theory of his earlier *Absolute Individual.* Underlying the more obvious sources which Evola cites within the text, such as Nietzsche, Sartre, and Heidegger, there are also connections with Hindu thought on the collapse of civilization and the Kali Yuga. Evola is promoting Tantrism to an overtly European audience as a method to deal with the Kali Yuga, which is expressed in the following statement.

> Tantrism may lead the way for a western elite which does not want to become the victim of these experiences whereby an entire civilization is on the verge of being submerged (*What Tantrism means to Modern Western Civilization*, 1950).[77]

Evola expands on this by demonstrating the relation between Tantrism and the Kali Yuga. For Evola, Tantrism offers something which is missing in all other existing Traditions—it is the only genuine esoteric Tradition with a legitimate and unbroken claim to the solar Āryan mythos. It is also known that Evola was not only a Tantric in theory but also practiced certain techniques, some which were appropriated from the Tibetan Buddhist school of Tantra known as *Vajrayāna.* When speaking of Tantra in a Traditionalist context, Evola says that,

> The teachings … that would have been viable in the first age … are no longer fit for people in the following ages, especially in

[76] EVOLA, J., *Men Among the Ruins: Post-War Reflections of a Radical Traditionalist* (Vermont: Inner Traditions, 2003), 89.

[77] URBAN, H. B., *Tantra: Sex, Secrecy, Politics, and Power in the Study of Religion* (USA: University of California Press, 2003), 175.

the last age, the dark age ... mankind in these later ages may find knowledge ... not in the Vedas, but rather in the Tantras.[78]

Furthermore, not only does Evola affirm the role of Tantra in the Kali Yuga, he goes one step further in claiming that Tantrism should be regarded not as Eastern, but as a Western Tradition—more Western than Christianity.

> It is clear with Tantrism the differentiation between liberation and liberty no longer subsists, since, as a general rule Tantrism, in its spirit—leaving out of consideration the framework of local traditions—should be considered distinctly Western. It is more conspicuously Western than Christian soteriology, which proclaims an ideal of salvation from a world that is looked upon as a "vale of tears" and contemplates the destiny of a human nature that has been infected with sin and that stands in need of redemption.[79]

The essence of this is then summarized by a clarification from Evola that he does not intend to proselytize Tantra in the Occident, and he is aware that it is bound up with cultural concerns which are not especially relevant to Europeans, but what he is advocating, however, is that the fundamental concepts employed in Tantrism can be applied to other Traditions in the broader spiritual narrative, all of which are summarized in his major work *Ride the Tiger: A Survival Manual for Aristocrats of the Soul.*

> We may well say that the essence of the way to be followed in the Dark Age is summed up in the saying "riding the tiger." I am not even dreaming of proposing Tantrism to the Western world, or of importing it here in the West so that people may practice it in its original aspects. These aspects, as we have seen, are strictly and inseparably interwoven with local Hindu and Tibetan traditions and with the corresponding spiritual climate. Nonetheless, some of Tantrism's fundamental ideas

[78] URBAN, H. B., *Tantra: Sex, Secrecy, Politics, and Power in the Study of Religion,* 176.
[79] EVOLA, J., *The Yoga of Power*, pp. 187-188.

> may be considered by those who wish to deal with the problems encountered in a new and valid syntheses.[80]

It is perhaps a great irony that Tantrism is today the fastest growing religious movement in the United States, albeit in a non-Traditional fashion. It was, after Evola's death, most definitely imported into the West, but divorced from both the cultural aspects and spiritual aspects (as 'Californian' or 'Pop' Tantrism), thus its import into the Occident remains incomplete. Nevertheless, Tantra is now a rapidly growing Tradition in the West and with correct guidance should be able to evolve beyond the current rudimentary stage of development.

Evola's explanation of the appropriateness of the Tantras as a mode of teaching in the Kali Yuga, is also echoed by Hindu philosophy, whereby the Hindu *Śāstra* (scriptures) are classified into Śrūti, Smṛti, Purāṇa, and Tantra—Śrūti for the Satya Yuga, Smṛti for the Tretā Yuga, Purāṇa for the Dvāpara Yuga, and Tantra for the Kali Yuga.[81] Tantra is the universal scripture (Śāstra) for this Age, and it is therefore considered a *Yuga Śāstra*, for it is only a reinterpretation of the Veda for modern man and therefore is frequently called the *Fifth Veda*.[82] The implication of this statement is that Tantra is the mode of spiritual learning appropriate to the Kali Yuga, due to its emphasis on controlling the forces of materialism. If we are to accept this as true, then our only hope is to '*ride the tiger*'—a popular Tantric saying for controlling the dark forces of the Kali Yuga, rather than avoiding them. The *Mahānirvāna Tantra*, one of the most widely obtainable Tantric texts, repeatedly asserts its dominance in the *Kali Yuga*, declaring its methodology to be more appropriate for practitioners because of the nature of the age.

> In the Kali Yuga, the mantras revealed in the Tantras are efficient, yield immediate fruit, and are recommended for all practices, such as recitation, sacrifice, rituals, and so on. The

[80] EVOLA, J., *The Yoga of Power*, 189.
[81] BERNARD, T., *Hindu Philosophy* (Jaico Books), 27.
[82] Ibid.

> Vedic practices are powerless as a snake lacking poison fangs or like a corpse, though in the beginning, in the Satya Yuga, they were bearing fruit.[83]

The *Mahānirvāna Tantra* says that "when the Kali Age is in full sway for all castes, commencing with the Brāhmaṇas, Tāntrika rites are alone appropriate."[84] Daniélou repeats this sentiment stating that "Only Tantric Yoga methods are efficacious in this age in which values are lost; the rites, asceticism, and virtues of other ages are ineffective."[85] He also believes that the "teachings of Lakuliśa expose the principles of the *Darśana* (the paths of knowledge) in a simple and popular form full of imagery, and suggest patterns of behavior suitable for the final stages of the Kali Yuga."[86] The most simple and effective method of resisting the influence of the Kali Yuga, however, is actually very easy and can be practiced by anyone, for the *Mahānirvāna Tantra* says that,

> In the Kali Age alms are efficacious in the accomplishment of all things. The proper objects of such alms are the poor devoted to meritorious acts.[87]

But what is in Tantra that renders it appropriate for practice in the Kali Yuga where other traditional forms of religion fail to thrive? Firstly, due to events cited earlier resulting from the breakdown of dharma in the Kali Yuga, there are a number of social implications as well as religious one. Dharma plays a part in relation to the laws that govern human society, the nature of the civil duty to society, and even how people interact with one another. Therefore, its effects are both multiple and all encompassing. The Kali Yuga is not merely the end of a cycle it is the end of civilization. Therefore, any weakening of dharma can have a devastating effect. One of

[83] FEURENSTEIN, G., *Tantra: The Path of Ecstasy* (USA: Shambala, 1998), 13.
[84] AVALON, A., *The Tantra of the Great Liberation (Mahānirvāna Tantra)* (USA: Dover Publications, 1972).
[85] DANIÉLOU, A., *Gods of Love and Ecstasy: The Traditions of Shiva and Dionysus* (USA: Inner Traditions International Ltd., 1992), 235.
[86] DANIÉLOU, A., *While the Gods Play*, 120.
[87] AVALON, A., *The Tantra of the Great Liberation (Mahānirvāna Tantra)*.

the first things to collapse is the 'caste' or varṇa system because it represents social order. In the *Mahānirvāna Tantra*, the beginning of the breakdown is predicted via the creation of a fifth varṇa—the *Sāmānya*. The Sāmānya is a hybrid varṇa arising in the Kali Yuga when varṇa rules and regulations are disregarded, and it is formed by the intermingling of the castes. Because of their hybrid classification, they may adopt any profession, except those reserved for the Brahmin, who retains his role as a ritual specialist as is stated here, "O Devī members of the Sāmānya class may for their maintenance follow all occupations except such as especially reserved for the Brāhmaṇa."[88] The Sāmānya therefore, are not a varṇa in their own right, but rather a mixture of individuals who belong to the other four.

> O thou of auspicious vows! In the Satya and other ages there were four castes; in each of these were four stages of life, and the rules of conduct varied according to caste and stages of life. In the Kali Age, however, there are five castes—namely, Brāhmaṇa, Kṣatriya, Vaiśhya, Śūdra, and Sāmānya.[89]

Here Tantric thought goes beyond the religious aspects and into the cultural, defining itself as a Yuga Śāstra because it is written for practice in this era, an epoch of degeneration where civilization begins to break down, and dharma no longer operates as it did in earlier ages. Instead of being counter-traditional, Tantra is therefore *extremely traditional,* and because it retains the Vedic Tradition it also serves to maintain Traditional social roles. What it does do, however, is relocate the impetus of the rituals themselves from orthodox Hinduism to Tantrism by stating that is not a rejection of Vedic thought, but rather a natural progression thereof, designed specifically for the Kali Yuga.

Understanding the role that the Kali Yuga plays in Tantric Traditions is absolutely vital to interpreting the nature of Tantrism itself. Contrary to being opposed to Vedic teachings, Tantra is

88 AVALON, A., *The Tantra of the Great Liberation (Mahānirvāna Tantra)*, 171.
89 Ibid., 158.

merely an extension of them (as is implied by the root *tan* 'to extend') that has been created for the conditions of the Kali Yuga. It is this element that is the defining element of Tantrism, and not any of the 'transgressive' practices which effectively act as a red herring for Occidental scholars, leading to endless over-sensationalism and further misinterpretation by Western audiences. However, certain elements of Tantrism, namely the belief in the Kali Yuga, have penetrated deep into the West via the Traditionalist school—not only through Guénon and Daniélou, but more specifically through the writing of Julius Evola. Whilst his *Yoga of Power* demonstrated a considerable knowledge of Tantra, there are also other factors to consider. For example, there is substantial evidence to suggest that Evola was not merely a scholar, since he practiced a substantial amount of the material that he studied and there is no reason to assume that he did not do the same with Tantra. Belief in the Kali Yuga has also become extremely widespread through a variety of groups connected with Evola and Traditionalism. Other elements have also entered into the Traditionalist school via Hinduism, but by far the most pervasive is the belief that the Kali Yuga is the darkest era of all.

PART II

ORIGINS, RITUALS, & ESOTERIC TEACHINGS

POINT OF ORIGIN

Sacrifice thyself for thine own exaltation.

- *Rig Veda* x.81.5d

Despite Tantrism's tendency to conceal a much more conservative aspect beneath its esoteric trappings of forbidden lore, many of the religious practices found in mainstream Hinduism are also contained in Tantrism. The Vedic Tradition is thought to have its origins in the Golden Age (Satya Yuga) of Hinduism, where every intricate aspect of nature adhered to cosmic design. Tantrism, on the other hand, is believed to belong to a different current; it is thought to be the Śāstra of the Kali Yuga since its ritual actions are transgressive and opt for a view that adopts the world as power to be harnessed, and 'impurity' as a medium by which to gain power. To many it will seem strange to assert that it was precisely the purity and order of the Vedic tradition that gave birth to the rise of Tantrism. It has been claimed in the past that because of its eccentricities and antinomian practices, Tantrism has its origins in the non-Āryan or Dravidian Traditions of India. It is our intention to deliberately oppose this idea and claim the opposite—that the Vedic Tradition itself necessitated the birth of Tantrism. Many of the key ideas inherent in Tantrism are easily found within older Vedic texts. It is often quoted that the Vedas are supposed to contain everything in existence (*yad ihāsti tad anyata, yan nehāsti na tat kva cid,* "that which is found herein exists elsewhere; that which is not, is nowhere").[1] Therefore, it stands to reason that Tantrism too can be found in the Vedas.

Hinduism refers to the origin of the Vedas as *apauruṣeya (*non-human, i.e., its inspiration belongs to the eternal, it is a manifestation of the Word), originating from the numinous through the Devī Vāk.[2] The order within the universe is regulated by *rta*, which is perhaps the most important component of Vedic thought, for it is through rta that all order and structure arises. The best way to describe rta is to adopt Louis Renou's definition which states that "rta, which for convenience sake can be translated by order (cosmic order and moral order) or by law, is, more precisely, the result of correlations, the product of 'adaptation', of the 'fitting together' between the microcosm and the macrocosm."[3] Therefore, rta can be seen as a force of the expression of law in activity which we would call the law of becoming, or transformation, as is contained in the very root of the word itself $\sqrt{ṛ}$ which means to move, to go.[4] Its intimate relationship with the truth (sat) is immediately apparent—there is no difference between the being (sat) of reality and its function (sat and rta). Sat refers to the inner being or truth of reality, and rta to the functioning of that reality.[5] This is the essence of the Golden Age and it is expressed in its name the 'Satya Yuga'. Truth is, in accordance with the functioning of cosmic law, perfectly harmonious and ordered. During the Satya Yuga tapas is the correct mode of religious learning (Yuga Śāstra)—this is expressed in the following statement "Universal order and truth were born of blazing tapas." (*Rig Veda* x.190.1*)*.[6] Tapas is held to be one of the key thoughts of the *ṛṣis*, the great seers who composed the Vedas. Tapas refers to asceticism, or

---

1 RENOU, L. *The Destiny of the Veda in India*, (India: Motilal Banarsidass, 1965), 1.
2 MILLER, J., *The Vision of Cosmic Order in the Vedas* (UK: Routledge & Kegan Paul, 1985), 3.
3 Ibid., 39.
4 Ibid., 38.
5 Ibid., 56.
6 Ibid., 52.

more precisely the inner heat/fire of contemplation that arises during the fervor of extreme asceticism. The heat produced by the body is merely a byproduct of the mental activity, and interpretations of tapas which restrict it to a mere production of heat and flame are a gross oversimplification of the terminology. Through tapas sat becomes visible and rta can be observed. Rta, however, is not just a cosmic function that regulates order in nature, for it also has applications at the social and moral level, and it is through this that the origin of Tantrism can be explained. Rta governs the interplay of human relations, ensuring that moral and ethical codes are kept in order. On this level, rta can be seen to be the expression of the integration of humanity into the cosmic order, of which the social-ethical mode is but a reflection. In its totality, the concept of rta spans over three different spheres of reality (sacrificial, moral, and natural) each of which is a manifestation of the same universal rta.[7] As a principle of cosmic order, rta is similar to the concept of dharma. Though this word did not come into common usage until later, its equivalent terms are readily traceable in the *Rig Veda*.

> Three words in the *Rig Veda* express the establishment, maintenance and working of the law: *dhāman*, *dharman*, *vrata*. The verb 'to establish' (√*dhā*) represents the foundation in full accordance with 'law', it is the laying down of the cosmic law in the space-time world in strict accordance with the rules which stem from, indeed are the expressions of the fundamental order, the inherent harmony at the core of the universe, the blueprint of rta.[8]

This is the main point of difference between rta and dharman. Whilst rta is an undeniable expression of cosmic truth and order, dharman is its expression on the abstract and conceptual plane—it is the social code that reflects the higher truth of the macrocosmic. Through the establishment of laws, this is enacted on the socio-ethical plane, and as an expression of truth, *satya-*

---

[7] MILLER, J., *The Vision of Cosmic Order in the Vedas*, 43.

[8] Ibid., 100.

dharman manifests in human society as social order and right human relationships—which in time becomes dharma.[9] In early Vedic texts, dharman refers to an established or proper mode of conduct that supports or helps maintain the continuing health of the world, with Vedic seers describing dharman as the pillar that props up the universe.[10] Over time, both rta and dharman fell out of popular usage, being replaced by the word dharma, which is still in use today. Miller writes that the notion of *karma* which implies "the setting right of any wrong action, the bringing back into harmony of what has been disharmonized, discordant, out of tune or out of order, is contained in the root idea of rta, inasmuch as rta stands for harmony and orderly process, that right working of all things and the inherent law of the universe which is the basis of manifestation—*anrta*, its opposite, is said to be punished by the Gods who have taken their stand on the side of the cosmic order."[11]

It is only during the Satya Yuga that rta and dharma find their fullest expression; during subsequent Ages, the principle of entropy or chaos causes a gradual degeneration within the cosmic cycle, accelerating until it eventually reaches the point of total collapse. This is expressed in the *Laws of Manu*, where dharma is *explicitly* equated to religion.

> In the Winning Age, religion is entire, standing on all four feet, and so is truth; and men do not acquire any gain through irreligion. But in the other (Ages), through (such wrong) gains, religion is brought down foot by foot; and because of theft, lying, and deceit, religion goes away foot by foot.[12]

The reference to four feet is a reference to the Bull of Dharma, which stands on all four feet only in the Golden Age. The term Golden Age is equivalent to the term employed above—the 'Winning Age'. This is undoubtedly also a reference to the dice game of Yudhiṣṭhira

[9] MILLER, J., *The Vision of Cosmic Order in the Vedas*, 103.
[10] MAHONY, W. K., *The Artful Universe: An Introduction To The Vedic Religious Imagination* (USA: State University of New York Press, 1998), 107.
[11] MILLER, J., *The Vision of Cosmic Order in the Vedas*, 151.
[12] DONIGER, W., & SMITH, B. K., *The Laws of Manu* (UK: Penguin Books, 1991), 12.

in the *Mahābhārata*, as it is within the time-span of this epic in which the Kali Yuga is commonly thought to have dawned. As the son of Dharma, and thus its mortal representative on the earth, it is no coincidence that it is Yudhiṣṭhira who throws the dice for the Pāṇḍavas.

If rta, then, is cosmic order and the inherent truth in universal harmony, and its deterioration is accelerating, with dharma weakening in each subsequent Age, it becomes clear as to what the Kali Yuga actually is: it is not purely the strengthening of the tamas guṇa, as some have stated, but rather an eroding chaos, or creeping entropy. It is a period in which law falters on every level. With rta, it is the breakdown of cosmic laws, which finds expression in the environmental changes that take place in Purāṇic depictions of the Kali Yuga. With the faltering of its socio-ethical counterpart, dharma, it is the breakdown of traditional laws and the established cultural codes of conduct. In both cases, it is the weakening of order and the strengthening of chaos. Though it may not be apparent yet, this belief in a period of unavoidable chaos will be the major contributing factor to the emergence of Tantrism as a rising religion in the Hindu Tradition. By creating a belief in this, the darkest of all ages, Hindu thought needed to create a religion that would provide them with a means to avoid the effects of the Kali Yuga. It is, therefore, our contention that the defining points of Tantrism is not its antinomian elements, but rather its belief in controlling the current of the Kali Yuga, as can be seen in the *Laws of Manu*, where the traditional modes of religion also differ between the ages.

> The religious duties of men are different in the Winning Age and in the Age of Trey and the Age of Deuce; they are different in the Losing Age, in proportion with the decrease of each Age. Inner heat is said to be paramount in the Winning Age, and knowledge in the Age of Trey; they say that sacrifice (is paramount) in the Age of the Deuce, and the one thing in the Losing Age is giving.[13]

[13] DONIGER, W., & SMITH, B. K., *The Laws of Manu* (UK: Penguin Books, 1991), 12.

Therefore, even at the time in which the *Laws of Manu* were composed, it is clearly evident that the traditional modes of communication with the divine were not being expounded or endorsed as practices suitable for the Kali Yuga. It is reasonable to assert that Tantrism did not originate from pre-Āryan or Dravidian elements, for which the historical evidence is extremely scant and dubious at best, but rather out of the scriptural void left by a belief and deep-seated fear in the Hindu mindset of the Kali Yuga. There is very little evidence to suggest that Tantrism existed prior to the 8th century CE. Given the fact that no hard evidence for the existence of Tantrism can be provided before this date, it seems highly unlikely that it arose from a pre-Vedic substratum of India but is instead, a development of existing Vedic thought. More to the point, it is also apparent that the rejection of Tantrism from the more conservative factions stems from their wish to distance themselves from the more controversial practices found in the Left Hand current of Tantrism. However, as we shall see, even some of the acts for which Tantra is usually condemned can be demonstrated within a Vedic context.

One of the grounds on which Tantrism is generally deemed to be on a lower footing than other Hindu Traditions is its association with magic and occultism, for which there is a long and vast history. The Tantras are full of references to magical uses of mantra and yantra to the extent that there are entire texts of spells and magic in circulation. It is because of this connection with magic that some critics refute the authenticity of Tantra as a spiritual tradition. Magic, however, was certainly not unknown in the Vedic religion, and the *Atharva Veda* is full of charms and folklore. Furthermore, in some ways, the *Atharva Veda* may also be a more accurate description of the people's lifestyle than that supplied by other texts from the Vedic period, as is seen here,

> The *Atharva Veda*, the Veda bearing the names of the great worshipers of Agni, Atharvan and Aṅgiras is the Veda of the masses. It can be argued that the AV actually represents the

> life of the ancient Indian agriculturist community, that is the agriculturist himself and his fellowmen in the village together constituting the masses.[14]

The *Atharva Veda* consists of poetry and magic hymns beginning in the later parts, and also with the songs and verses concerning customs of family life.[15] A substantial part of the text is devoted to charms and at this stage of human thought, there is no apparent division between religious and magical practices.

> The sacrificial priests must have promoted and intensified the concept of magic power obtained by sacrifice in order to demonstrate the indispensability of their own art ... Prayer is also part of the sacrifice: if the prayer adopts something from the effects of the magic incantation, then the way in which the sacrifice becomes effective must also be modified accordingly to obtain magic coercive power over Gods, things, and occurrences.[16]

The *Rig Veda* demonstrates that the act of sacrifice is endowed with magic power. This is clearly shown in the hymn of Devāpi for summoning rain which states that "It is seen how the idea slips out of the initial direction: the Gods were supposed to give rain at first in their mercy; now, the priest is pouring it himself by the magic power of his sacrificial act."[17] In another hymn of the *Rig Veda* (10.136.7) the expression *Kunamnamā* (She who is badly bent) is used, which Feuerstein interprets as a reference to *kuṇḍalinī* and is also called *kubjikā* (crooked one) by some early Tantric schools.[18]

On the topic of magical elements within the Vedas, perhaps the best description is that which is provided by Louis Renou,

---

[14] KHARADE, B. S., *Society in the Atharvaveda* (India: D. K. Printworld, 1997), 1.

[15] OLDENBERG, H., *The Religion of the Veda* (India: Motilal Banarsidass, 1988), 8.

[16] Ibid., 186.

[17] Ibid., 187.

[18] FEUERSTEIN, G., *Tantra, The Path of Ecstasy* (USA: Shambala, 1998).

> We should add that the ancient mantras tend to be progressively relegated in personal usage, thus assuming a predominantly magic usage...does not one see the *rgvidhāna* enumerate a mass of formulas or hymns with magical use? The utilization of the *sāmans* in this sense is well known. Thus is accredited the idea of a link between the Vedic mantra and magic, and in popular usage, the *mantra*, whatever may have been its origin, is before all else, an *abracadabra*.[19]

Likewise, it is not hard to imagine how the Nath alchemists of Medieval India would have homologized the material bodies of the microcosm with the Vedic macrocosm when we read phrases such as this found in the *Chāndogya Upaniṣad,*

> What then is that which, dwelling within this little house, this lotus of the heart, is to be sought after, inquired about, and realized? As large as the universe outside, even so large is the universe within the lotus of the heart. Within it are heaven and earth, the sun, the moon, the lightning, and all the stars. What is in this macrocosm is in this microcosm (*Chānd. Up*. 8.12.3).[20]

This concept of replicating the macrocosm within the microcosm will reach its apex in the esoteric teachings of Tantra, and earlier previous echoes are audible in such statements as: "Prajāpati is the sacrifice" and also in the assertion "*puruṣo vai yajñaḥ*" (the sacrifice is the man).[21] These ideas are also perceptible in the Vedic figure of the vrātya, who according to Eliade and Heesterman operated not only as a shaman but also as a proto-Tantric figure.

> An entire book of the *Atharva Veda* (XV) is devoted to them ... it is apparent that the vrātyas practice asceticism (they remain standing for a year, etc.), are familiar with the discipline of breaths (which are assimilated to the various cosmic

[19] RENOU, L., *The Destiny of the Veda in India* (India: Motilal Banarsidass, 1965), 13.
[20] MILLER, J., *The Vision of Cosmic Order in the Vedas*, 31.
[21] MAHONY, W. K., *The Artful Universe: An introduction to the Vedic Religious Imagination* (USA: State University of New York Press, 1998), 144.

> regions), homologize their bodies with the macrocosm... It is permissible to suppose that the vrātyas represented a mysterious brotherhood belonging to the advance guard of the Āryan invaders. But they were not entirely distinct from the Keśins of the *Rig Veda*; in some commentaries, Rudra is called vrātya-pati, and the *Mahābhārata* still uses the term vrātya to designate the Śivaistic bacchantes.[22]

The vrātya date back to the most archaic elements of Vedic society and have been almost completely buried by the past. They constitute part of an older warrior tradition, sharing a number of significant features in common with other Indo-European martial brotherhoods such as the Greeks, Scythians, Persians, Dacians, Celts, and Germans.[23] Until recent times so little has been known about the history of the vrātya that they were assumed to be little more than a collection of outcasts from Vedic culture, dwelling in the forests and on the other fringes of acceptable society and that they were both revered and reviled. It was even once assumed that the vrātya were non-Indo-European in origin. Whilst this statement can now be presumed false, it is certainly true that elements of both Tantrism and yoga can be found in the practices of the vrātya. Evidence of a connection between the practices of the vrātya and those found in Tantrism and Yoga can be seen in Eliade's statement above.

In 1962 new evidence was also brought to light by Jan Heesterman describing the vrātya as an extremely archaic component of a sacrificial society whose role was gradually phased out with the rise of the Brahmin varṇa as sacrificial specialists.[24] In this article, Heesterman submits the hypothesis that the vrātya were then degraded in the later literature and cast in an antinomian, anti-Brahmin mold, with their *sāttra* rites surviving in Vedic initiation rites and in certain periods in the *vrata*, or vow of the *brahmacārin*,

---

[22] ELIADE, M., *Yoga: Immortality and Freedom* (USA: Princeton University Press, 1990), pp. 102-105.

[23] WHITE, D. G., *Myths of the Dog-Man* (USA: University of Chicago Press, 1999), 27.

[24] Ibid., 96.

the Vedic student.[25] Likewise, in the Indra *Śunaḥsakha* tale, there is a reference to the vrātya which claims that their socio-religious status was once as lofty as that of the Brahmin.[26] With the rise of the Brahmin varṇa, the role of the vrātya in ritual was lessened, eventually to such a point that the term itself became degraded and the vrātya were judged to be ritually impure. This decline is attested to by the fact that there is a ritual which is specifically performed to restore the members of the vrātya back to society, removing the impurity from their former actions.

The most striking passage to mention the vrātya is found in the *Chāndogya Upaniṣad* and is named the "[*Samavedic*] *Chant of the Dogs*."[27] The vrātya are not only strongly associated with canine imagery (the texts repeatedly refer to them as 'Dogs') they are also strongly connected with the God Rudra, who acts not only as God of the hunt but is also the deity connected with shamanism and storm. Falk states that the twelve-day sacrifices of the vrātya were the ritual cognate of other Indo-European phenomena, including the Roman *Lupercalia* and the twelve nights of Christmas, in which the wild hunter Wode-Wodin roared through the forests of northern Europe.[28] Furthermore, when the vrātya slay a cow on Rudra's behalf, they are said to be his "dogs" or "wolves", and lupine or canine symbolism is nearly as abundant in Rudra's case as it is in that of Indra.[29] Parallels between the cults of Rudra, the wild hunter of the forest, and those of the Germanic Óðinn/Wodin, as well as the Iranian Aešma and a number of other Indo-European gods associated with the twelve nights of midwinter, are also significant here.[30] The symbolic association with canines also persists in Bhairava (a form of Śiva) who is usually accompanied by a dog. Both Śiva and Bhairava are connected to the God Rudra.

---

[25] WHITE, D. G., *Myths of the Dog-Man*, 96.
[26] Ibid., 100.
[27] Ibid., 96.
[28] Ibid., 98.
[29] Ibid., 101.
[30] Ibid.

The vrātya were simultaneously feared and revered by the community. As strong figures skilled in magic and warfare, the public admired them; but there was also a sentiment of fear aroused by these figures. This attitude of ambiguity towards the vrātya also extended into other areas—it seems that they occupied a boundary line between clearly defined caste roles, as a synthesis of the warrior and priest caste. Given that the vrātya is a particularly archaic figure, this suggests that the original legacy of the vrātya may have its roots in a time prior to the separation of the two primary castes. They seemed to operate under a dual role of being a warrior and a magician or shaman, and it is also suggested by Heesterman that they were an early figure of the Vedic priesthood that came to be replaced by the Brahmin caste. Their social ambiguity can be explained by a simple concept—the symbolism of the vrātya is *liminal*. The word liminal signifies a 'between state' and was coined by Arnold van Gennep to describe states which are 'in-between' or ambiguous. For example, a former member of the vrātya is ceremonially restored and purified before reentering society. It is the liminal nature of their being that makes them dangerous; paradoxically it is also the liminal nature of their being that empowers them. Another illustration of a liminal period can be seen in psychological states—for example, an initiate prior to the performance of an initiation ritual is thought to be a normal person, after the ritual a change of some kind is presumed to have taken place in the psyche of the initiate.

The vrātya, perhaps due to the nature of some of their rituals, probably clashed directly with the rise of the Brahmin caste, for some early textual references afford the vrātya an extremely high social status, however, in subsequent texts from the later Vedic period, the vrātya is regarded to be almost totally impure and not much better regarded than the average outcast from society. Certain other elements of what little we know of the remaining rites of the vrātya appear to contain a decidedly Tantric outlook, such as their connection to the God Rudra/Śiva, the use of the magical arts, and their shamanic or proto-yogīc heritage, coupled with what appears to have been liminal or antinomian ritual practices. The most conclusive evidence that the vrātya were a type of early Tāntrika is provided by the fact that they were accompanied by female practitioners for a sexual rite known as the *vrātya-soma*. During the vrātya-soma, the vrātya were accompanied by a woman going by the title of *puṃścali*, who engaged in ritual intercourse with either the *māgadha* or with a *brahmacārin*.[31] Sexual union is also documented in the *Atharva Veda*, but it does not become a mystical technique prior to the advent of Tantrism. Similar connotations are also expressed in the *Bṛihadāranyaka Upaniṣad*, which makes it quite clear that the religious use of sexual metaphors were present outside of the Tantric Traditions.

> *Bṛihadāranyaka Upaniṣad* (6.4.3): Her genitals are the sacrifice; the altar, her hairs the grass offering, her skin the *soma* press, and her two labia the fire in the center. Verily, as great as the world is for him who sacrifices with the *vājapeya* (strength/liberation) sacrifice, so great is the world for him who, knowing this, practices sexual intercourse. He diverts the good deeds of women to himself. But he who practices sexual intercourse without knowing this—women divert his good deeds to themselves.[32]

In texts from North East India, such as the *Bṛhat Tantrasāra* and the *Prāṇatoṣiṇī Tantra*, sexual union is explicitly described as an analog to the Vedic sacrifice. Here the central act is the ejaculation of semen into the vagina, which is likened to ladling the oblation onto the sacrificial fire. For "sexual union is the libation; the sacred precept is the shedding of semen."[33]

> "I sacrifice [*juhomi*]" into the "fire of the Self, which is radiant with the oblation of *dharma* and *adharma*." Then finally, reciting the *mantra*, "I sacrifice into the fire that is full of the bodily fluids of *dharma* and *adharma*", he should release his semen.[34]

[31] FEUERSTEIN G., *Tantra, The Path of Ecstasy.*
[32] *Brihad-Āranyaka-Upanishad* (6.4.3).
[33] URBAN, H., *The Power of Tantra: Religion, Sexuality and the Politics of South Asian Studies* (USA: I. B. Tauris & CO Ltd, 2010), 109.
[34] Ibid.

The strongest evidence for a Vedic origin of Tantrism, however, lies in the *Atharva Veda* where it says that,

> The lotus bloom with nine doorways, encircled by three strands;
> What a wondrous marvel—the Self—
> Lies within it![35]

The symbolism here is strikingly similar to the Tantric cakra system. Tantra utilizes nine entry/exit points by which the winds or breaths may enter or exit the body. The body itself also contains three nāḍī in Tantrism, the iḍā, piṅgalā, and the suṣumṇā which symbolise the lunar, solar, and royal currents used to arouse kuṇḍalinī. In David Gordon White's opinion, however, the earliest Hindu reference to the cakra system is found in the *Bhāgavata Purāṇa* where six sites (*sthāna*) are listed at the naval (*nābhi*), heart (*hṛt*), breast (*uras*), root of the palate (*svatālumūla*), the place between the eyebrows (*bhruvorantara*), and the cranium (*mūrdha*).[36] The earliest reference to an eight-part cakra system, according to White, is the *Kaulajñāna-nirṇaya*.[37] Gavin Flood, however, maintains that a five part cakra predates both of these references cited by White.

> Five cakras used in early Tantra, attribute to five elements ... In fact, it [the system of six cakras] is found in none of the early traditions mentioned. Instead, we find there a great variety in the division of the vertical line of the central power (*suṣumṇā*). There are six 'seasons', five 'knots' (*granthayaḥ*), five voids (*vyomāni*), nine wheels (*cakrāni*), eleven wheels, twelve knots, at least three sets of sixteen loci (*ādhārāḥ*), sixteen knots, twenty-eight vital points (*marmāni*), etc.[38]

In this regard, it seems quite likely that the cakra system simply differs in esoteric symbolism between texts and schools within the

[35] MAHONY, W. K., *The Artful Universe: An Introduction to the Vedic Religious Imagination*, 174.
[36] FLOOD, G., *The Tantric Body: The Secret Tradition of Hindu Religion* (USA: I. B. Tauris & Co. Ltd, 2006), 158.
[37] Ibid.
[38] Ibid.

broader framework of Tantrism, and that the number was probably increased as the theoretical teachings of Tantrism expanded. For example, the earliest definitive references to cakras are not found within Hindu Tantra, but in Tibetan Buddhist Tantra, and there they begin with four centers only. Furthermore, in the Tibetan Tradition, it is clearly emphasized that the four cakra are created within the body of the initiate and they do not exist in the same manner as the organs of the body. This serves to explain the differing number of cakras found in Tantric texts. There is, therefore, no reason to assume that references in the *Atharva Veda* are not indicative of a type of proto-tantric practice in the early Vedic period, despite the fact that the cakras are not directly referenced. Rather it appears probable that the original premise which the cakra system was later developed upon was essentially an internalized mapping of the cosmos onto the human form allowing the Tantric adept to homologize the microcosm of their physical body with the universal macrocosm and thus 'yoke' themselves to the nature of the divine in the same fashion as other yogīc practitioners.

It is generally accepted that Tantrism began to emerge much later than this, at the time of the composition of the Purāṇas. The Purāṇas are often considered as the successors of the Vedas, but occasionally they are also placed at the same rank and even on a higher rank. They are sometimes said to form part of the Vedas, probably due to an ambiguous phrase in an Upanisaḍic text. It is also stated that these texts are a means of access to the Veda, therefore, they are intermediaries, if not intercessors.[39] One of the interesting points of the Purāṇas is that they repeat many myths from the Vedas, but retell them in a new context. One example of this, which is of significance, is that of Dakṣa/Prajāpati,

> According to a legend found in the AB (3.33-34), in order to punish Prajāpati for establishing an illicit sexual relationship with his own daughter, the Gods out of their most fearful forms fashioned a divine being called Bhūtavat who he pierced with

[39] RENOU, L., *The Destiny of the Veda in India*, 8.

> his shaft. This Bhūtavat is none other than Rudra, for in the ŚB (1, 7.4.1-8) version of the same legend the task of piercing Prajāpati was assigned by the Gods to Rudra. The legend later developed into the well-known story of the destruction of the sacrifice of Dakṣa-Prajāpati by Śiva, also called Rudra.[40]

In the Purāṇic version of this myth, the sacrifice of Dakṣa is disrupted by Śiva following the 'death' of Satī, Dakṣa's daughter. In connection with the four ages of the world, it is stated that, while asceticism (tapas) and knowledge (*jñāna*) are appropriate to the first and second ages respectively (the Satya and Tretā Yugas), sacrifice (*yajña*) is appropriate to the third (Dvāpara).[41] As a deity, Dakṣa is the God of sacrifice par excellence; it is he who performs the cosmogonic yajña that ensures the continuation of the cosmos. Thus, when Śiva transgresses this particular ritual, it is not only the disruption of a ceremony but the disruption of the entire rta or cosmic order which is perpetuated by the yajña. This myth is highly symbolic, in that the Tantric God Śiva has disrupted the very act that perpetuates existence in the Dvāpara Yuga. It is entirely possible that this also bears significance to the transition of the Yugas, as the death/rebirth of Satī also signifies the loss of a lunar month from the calendar. In this regard, it may also be a myth that depicts the end of the Dvāpara Yuga and the beginning of the Kali Yuga, though this is not stated explicitly within the passage.

The Purāṇas, however, did not mark the beginning of the end of the Vedic period, that is done by the Upaniṣads themselves, which begin a new orientation with their Kṣatriya tendencies, and their teachings carried beyond ritual.[42] It is with these ideas that we really begin to see the first real evidence of Tantra emerge, and lay witness to its meteoric rise to power in medieval India.

---

[40] BHATTACHARYYA, N. N., *Indian Demonology: The Inverted Pantheon* (India: Manohar, 2000), 38.

[41] HEESTERMAN, J., *The Broken World of Sacrifice: An Essay in Ancient Indian Ritual* (USA: University of Chicago Press, 1993), 13.

[42] RENOU, L., *The Destiny of the Veda in India*, 5.

SACRED TRANSGRESSION

The best way to describe the public perception of Tantra is as an 'over-sensationalized' one. Wherever it goes, and whatever it does, the commonly perceived image of Tantra is one that creates a stir. Some writers overplay the sexual element, some overplay violence, whilst others use shock tactics such as the occult or transgression—but because they write from an etic perspective (outside of the Tradition) they write about what they see rather than what they know and in the process damage the real essence of the Tantric Traditions. Tantra is not a movement for promoting sexual promiscuity, degenerate social behavior, or anti-social elements. It is first and foremost a spiritual Tradition and it is this primary characteristic which must be studied and understood. The sexual elements are present simply because Tantra does not renounce the physical form and integrates the body into ritual use, rather than attempting to stifle natural functions. The body itself becomes a ritual tool and, instead of attempting to repress human sexual elements, Tantra seeks to control and subvert the animal urges to a higher purpose. Such an act is only perverted in the minds of the perverted. When sexual elements do occur in Tantric rituals, they are so controlled by rituals and procedures that they are a controlled performance instead of an erotic act. The sexual drive is therefore sublimated by the will towards the sacred rather than the mundane act. Tantra is not a teaching of sexual excess, but rather one of extreme control of the sexual impulse—it redirects this energy towards a divine purpose rather than a worldly one. This is the reason why it must be kept secret to prevent misuse by unqualified individuals.

All this is complicated even further by the fact that Tantrism has, within its broader perspective, a number of different schools all with different teachings. Perhaps the most important basic distinction to recognize is that Tantrism operates primarily in two forms, a 'Right-Hand' mode and a 'Left-Hand' mode, one of which will utilize symbolic methods in ritual whilst the other sometimes will not. In theory and practice, the difference between the two modes is not as vast as one would expect, and if anything, the shared common ground is greater than the differences. The only difference between the two is in terms of ritual practice; in terms of ethics or theory, there is none. At the theoretical level both the Right Hand and the Left-Hand schools of Tantra are the same, and within its set ritual framework, one will find a very precise set of what can only be termed as antinomian standards. Antinomian comes from the Latin *anti*—the accepted norm and *nomos—law*. The Tantric texts themselves reflect this use in words like *pratiloman* (against the grain) and *parāvritti* (inversion).[1] This, of course, leads us to the topic Tantrism is most famed for in the West: sex.

To begin with, Tantric sex is both more extreme and less extreme than occidental audiences have imagined it to be. It is, for example, much more intense than the current 'sacred sex' genre of books which inundate lackluster Western bedrooms, and, on the other hand, is much less 'sexy' when actually practiced because it involves ritual observations. Tantra is not just a means to induce or postpone orgasms for inept sexual partners.

The *Yoni Tantra* and *Kāmākhyā Tantra* describe at least three different contexts in which sexual rites might occur: the *abhiṣeka* or initiation of a new member into the Tantric lineage (*kula*); the ritual of *yoni puja* or worship of the female sexual organ; and the *cakra puja* or "circle worship," involving multiple male and female

[1] FEUERSTEIN, G., *Tantra, The Path of Ecstasy* (USA: Shambala, 1998), 8.

participants who collectively engage in the Five M's.[2] Yoni puja is obviously very far removed from the concept of sacred sex, for, though it incorporates sexual elements, it involves no act of coitus. Interestingly enough the texts also describe the nine types of women (*Navakanya*) who are suitable for this—both Brahmin and Śūdra women are included, but Kṣatriya and Vaiśya women are conspicuously absent from the list.

What actually makes the sex powerful in Tantric ritual is, first and foremost, not the sex itself, but the forbidden nature of the ritual. The notorious rite of the Five M's is a deliberate and powerful psychologically destructive ritual that is intended to be profoundly shocking in its use of forbidden substances. Thus, the approach to the sex is entirely different; the European looks upon the Rite of the Five M's (*pañcamakāra*) as pleasurable whilst the Hindu views it as dangerous. The notorious 'Rite of the Five M's' began as the smaller 'Three M's' (*makāratraya*), namely the consumption of wine (*madya*), meat (*māṃsa*), and sexual fluids resulting from their union (*maithuna*), which is performed as a kula rite by a sādhaka and his *dūtī*. According to Jayaratha, sexual substances are actually passed from mouth to mouth in the rite (a practice which is based upon a Kaśmiri marriage custom of passing food from mouth to mouth).[3] These initial three were later expanded into the famous 'Five M's' or substances (*pañcatattva*) of later Śākta Tantrism, with the addition of fish (*matsya*) and parched grain (*mudra*), which, in the Śrī Vidyā Brāhmanical response to the earlier tradition, were substituted with 'pure' substances (*pratinidhi*).[4]

The reason the rite of the Five M's is viewed as dangerous and not pleasurable is because it utilizes substances and techniques that are considered to be harmful and polluting such as the consumption of meat, alcohol, and sex. Moreover, the sex is not always performed with an attractive or desirable woman, but sometimes with a low

[2] URBAN, H., *The Power of Tantra: Religion, Sexuality, and the Politics of South Asian Studies* (USA: I. B. Tauris & CO Ltd, 2010), 105.
[3] FLOOD, G., *The Tantric Body: The Secret Tradition of Hindu Religion* (USA: I. B. Tauris & Co. Ltd, 2006), pp. 168-169.
[4] Ibid.

caste prostitute—in short, someone who is normally classified as repulsive. According to the *Yoginī Tantra*, the traditional rule for sexual relations is to remain within one's social class: "Brāhmaṇa women for Brāhmaṇs, Kṣatriya women for Kṣatriyas, Vaiśya women for Vaiśyas, O Deveṣī—that is the traditional rule for sexual union."[5] It is therefore considered polluting because the males are violating caste restrictions and taking partners well beneath their own status in most circumstances. Furthermore, the sexual position (*viparīta-rata)* is inverted implying that the female has dominance over the male. The position was therefore not viewed as socially 'acceptable' by the culture of this era. Thus, the position itself is also 'forbidden.' Add to this the religious practices involving mantra and one has a situation not involving ritual sex but instead *sexualized ritual*. The key aspect of the ritual is not sex itself, but the transgressive nature of sex and this is the element that Western emulations of Left-Hand Tantra lack. In the West, where nothing sexual is forbidden and every excess is encouraged, any forbidden and transgressive element is disempowered to the very point that the Right-Hand mode of worship starts to take on an antinomian precedent.

Just as there are obvious differences in biology between males and females, there are also differences in terms of practice when the sexual rituals do occur. Regarding the nature of sexual practices within Tantrism, for males, it is an exceedingly difficult observance (*asidhārāvrata*), and it is mainly the preserve of the non-Saiddhāntika traditions, although it is not wholly unknown within the Siddhānta.[6] The sexual forces which are desirable in a male are the exact opposite in a female because Tantrism advocates a balancing of polarities and harmonized opposites—therefore, it is much easier for a female to practice Tantra. It is extremely different to another type of sexual rite, the *kula prakriyā*, which requires that the couple have a requisite qualification (*ahikāra*), which means having undergone an initiation into the practice but also having

[5] URBAN, H., *The Power of Tantra: Religion, Sexuality, and the Politics of South Asian Studies*, 117.

[6] FLOOD, G., *The Tantric Body: The Secret Tradition of Hindu Religion*, 164.

certain personal levels of receptivity, such as displaying signs of possession (trembling or loss of consciousness) during initiation.[7] The practice was thus clearly restricted to those who had the required disposition and had a certain level of training beforehand. It was not merely a means of instant sexual gratification, but rather a complex methodology which transformed the body into a ritual tool for the sacred. According to Sanderson, this mode of worship could also be enacted in an external manner:

> On a red cloth upon the ground, in a circle filled with vermilion powder and enclosed with a black border, on a coconut substituted for a human skull, a vessel filled with wine or other alcohol, or on a *maṇḍala*. It may also be offered on the exposed genitals of the dūtī [female practitioner], on one's own body, or in the act of sexual intercourse with the dūtī. Later tradition emphasizes the possibility of worshiping the deities in the vital energy (*prāṇa*)—one visualizes their gratification by the 'nectar' of one's ingoing breath. We are told that the seeker of liberation may carry out this worship in thought alone (*sāṃvidī puja*). However, even one who does this must offer erotic worship with his dūtī on certain special days of the year (*parvas*).[8]

As mentioned earlier, however, Tantric practices differ drastically from school to school, and the various schools do not adopt the same methodology. For example, a late Hindu text, the *Kālīvilāsa Tantra*, condemns the ritualistic use of women, wine, etc., stating that the Tantras mentioning Left-Handed ritual are "prohibited in our era" (*kalau varjitāni*).[9] Paramahamsa Ramakrishna, the famous Bengali saint of the late nineteenth century, used to warn his disciples to stay away from the two great evils, *kāminī kāñcana* (woman and gold), in spite of the fact that he himself had been initiated into Tantric sādhanā by Bhairavī Brāhmaṇī. Also, some

---

7 FLOOD, G., *The Tantric Body: The Secret Tradition of Hindu Religion*, 168.

8 Ibid., 165.

9 BHARATI, A., *The Tantric Tradition* (UK: Rider & Company, 1965), 71.

fierce deities such as Ugratārā, Caṇḍī, Ucchiṣṭa, Bhairavī, and Bhairava can only be worshiped in the Left-Hand mode.[10]

Hugh Urban maintains that, if understood from their correct context, Tantric sexual rites are really not primarily about "sex" at all—at least not in the contemporary understanding of it as pure sensory gratification. Rather Urban believes that "the Tantric offering of sexual fluids in secret ritual, the *kulayāga* or esoteric sacrifice,"[11] is the esoteric counterpart to the public offering of blood sacrifice. Here Urban is drawing on an older correlation between blood and social impurity which is inherited from Vedic Tradition. Blood is something which is not normally seen; its presence belongs within the body, and when it is visible blood represents the breaking of a taboo or a deviation from the normal biological condition. The visible esoteric significance is blood that of violence, transgression, and of danger. The only circumstance under which blood is normal and harmless during the cycle of human existence is during menstruation, where it is linked to female fertility and to sexuality. Blood, therefore, has a link not only to transgression but also to sexuality, for it is the ovum, the fertile part of the female that is lost during menstruation—precisely the thing that is praised in Tantrism. It is not just the transgressive aspect of blood which is of importance, it is also important because menstrual blood is the physical counterpart to semen. Just as semen represents the male creative power, menstrual blood in Tantra is the female creative power. The following passage from the *Kāmākhyā Tantra* makes it clear that this is why semen and blood are praised.

> Listen, O Goddess, I am telling you the great secret knowledge. I am semen, and you are indeed blood. The whole world consists of these two. But just as the whole pure world is born of semen and blood, even so, that essence goes forth in the body of the child.[12]

---

[10] URBAN, H., *Power of Tantra: Religion, Sexuality, and the Politics of South Asian Studies*, 103.

[11] Ibid., 100.

[12] Ibid., 135.

However, despite Tantrism's worship of this obvious biological truth, menstrual blood is still viewed as a highly impure substance. Classical Indian law books such as the *Gautama Dharma Sūtra* and *Vasiṣtha Dharma Sūtra* are quite clear that sexual intercourse with a menstruating woman is a highly polluting act that requires arduous penance to be purified. Sexual union with a menstruating woman is associated with all manner of negative outcomes, including the birth of the cursed demon king, Naraka who was conceived during the Earth's menstrual flow. The *Brahmavaivarta Purāṇa* likewise contains several cautionary tales about children born of women during the menstrual period, who are therefore inherently unclean (*aśauca*), degraded, and tainted by the sin of menstruation (*ṛtu-doṣata*).[13] Therefore, it is not only an exhalation of natural creative power, it is also, in Hindu society, a powerfully transgressive act which appears to have been utilized in certain rites, and even the term *caṇḍālī* (which is widely used in Tantra) can also be used to designate "a woman on the first day of her menses."[14]

The controversial part of Tantra where it will differ dramatically from what drifts around in 'sacred sex' circles is the ritual consumption of the sexual fluids following the act. In some texts, this is more important and emphasized more strongly than the sexual act itself. Sex alone is not transgressive nor is it a spiritual act. The combined sexual fluids become an immensely powerful substance because they represent the combined energy of the God and the Devī. They are at once possessed of the numinous power of the sacred and the forbidden. The texts themselves reaffirm the importance of the substance itself:

> *Kāmākhyā Tantra* states that the "The remnants of the śakti [*śakty-ucchiṣṭa*] should be consumed; otherwise, one goes to hell. What one offers to the śakti, O Goddess, is offered to the Gods." Likewise, the *Bṛhat Tantrasāra* declares that the combined sexual fluids or *kula dravya* is the most awesome and

[13] URBAN, H., *Power of Tantra: Religion, Sexuality, and the Politics of South Asian Studies*, 116.

[14] Ibid.

> dangerous of substances. As the ucchiṣṭa or sacrificial left-over, it is the very essence of this secret offering and ritual meal: With the sacrificial elements, the semen, unbroken grains of rice, perfume, flowers, O Deveśī, he should worship the Goddess in the vagina ... With incense, lamps and various food offerings, the kula adept should honor her in veracious ways, and then he should [consume] the remnants [ucchiṣṭa] himself.[15]

The sexual rites are, however, a minor aspect of Tantrism and are only present in a very small number of Tantric schools. The vast majority of Tantrics do not engage in any sexual form of practice and, even amongst the schools who do, rituals involving sex are rare and performed infrequently. The *Kālikā Purāṇa* acknowledges (but only briefly mentions) sexual rites and even the *Kaulajñāna Nirṇaya* does not describe the details of sexual intercourse, not even when it mentions the consumption of sexual fluids, but in the *Yoni Tantra* and *Kāmākhyā Tantra*, the sexual union becomes central.[16]

Sexual transgression is also very minor compared to other aspects however, which have not yet permeated Western culture. In India, Tantrism is associated with much more sinister and extreme modes of behavior, such as black magic, necrophagy, and human sacrifice. These unfortunate associations are due to the esoteric nature of Tantrism which prevents its true nature from being disclosed to those outside of the Tradition. Some of these are liable to be shocking to Western audiences, as is the fact that Tantra, far from being a Tradition based on 'sacred sex', has a much more sinister side. Early in the formative period of Tantra, for example, human sacrifices are known to have been offered. This was not a matter however of capturing victims and using them as ritual instruments—rather it seems to have been linked to political power, and only someone with royal sanction could order a human sacrifice. Therefore, although the victim is ritually slain, the process

[15] URBAN, H., *Power of Tantra: Religion, Sexuality, and the Politics of South Asian Studies*, 112.

[16] Ibid., 101.

itself is more akin to a 'state execution' and it was usually reserved for opponents and prisoners of war as stated here,

> The prince, the minister, the counselor, and the *sauptika*, etc., may offer human sacrifice [in order to attain] kingship, prosperity, and wealth. If one offers a human being without the permission of the king, he will find a great misfortune. During an invasion or war, one may offer a human being at will, but only a royal person [may do so], and no one else.[17]

The fact that the majority of the victims were largely members of invading armies is supported by the above statement. The preferred human victims, moreover, are said to be neither a priest nor an untouchable, but ideally "the mercenaries of enemy lands, who are captured in battle."[18] Ritual sacrifice in Tantrism, therefore, was the sacralization of military executions. Given the fact that India went through periods of enormous political unrest and aggressive foreign incursions, and that there was no economic system around to support the prisoners of war, it seems human sacrifice was brought in as a way of reducing the number of captured prisoners. In the notorious act of *Thugee* (ritual sacrifice to the Goddess Kālī), the victims were not random either—they were exclusively non-Indian and male. Again, they were foreigners in India, which means that there was an undying political motivation behind the cult of Thugee too. The problem with interpreting actual accounts of Thugee is that it is difficult to discern fact from fiction. On the one hand, they certainly were professional assassins. On the other hand, the historical records contain heavily biased British colonialist accounts. Thugee differs substantially from other forms of Tantric sacrifice because it does not spill the blood, instead it maintains the blood is be sacred, which is why strangulation was advocated instead of decapitation (the more commonly used form of sacrifice). For sacrifice to Kālī, this is radically different, and the

[17] URBAN, H., *Power of Tantra: Religion, Sexuality, and the Politics of South Asian Studies*, pp. 92-93.
[18] Ibid., 93.

'Thugs' are not the norm in this regard, nor are they the norm for any form of worship of Kālī.

The head is the most important part of the human body, and it is for this reason that decapitation was the preferred form of sacrifice. On occasion, it was also viewed as a form of augury, and omens were read into the distance and direction in which the severed head fell. The *Kālikā Purāṇa* provides a long list of various good and bad omens associated with its direction, the sound it emits and how the blood flows out, along with their portents for the future of the kingdom.[19] The following passage describes how one can gain victory by offering a severed head to the Goddess. By standing in an all-night vigil holding the severed head as the supreme gift to the Goddess, the king achieves the highest fruit of sacrifice,

> If the adept stays awake all night holding the head of a human being in his right hand and the vessel of blood in his left, he becomes a king in this life, and in after death, he reaches my [Śiva's] realm and becomes lord of hosts.[20]

Similarly, during the ritual decapitation of a buffalo, at the moment of decapitation the buffalo is explicitly identified with a human enemy, and via sympathetic magic (to use Fraser's terminology) it is hoped that the death of the buffalo correlates to the defeat or death of an opponent.

However, the notoriety of the dark side of Tantra transgresses even the boundaries of death, for many Tāntrikas are also believed to be powerful magicians who are particularly adept at necromancy. Even today Kāmākhyā has a sinister reputation for the practice of *śava sādhanā* which requires a fresh human corpse. As Dehejia writes, "in the town of Kāmākhyā people rarely leave a corpse uncremated overnight for fear of losing it to Tantric practitioners."[21] Such rites not only use the forbidden to harness the power of impurity in ritual, they

19 URBAN, H., *Power of Tantra: Religion, Sexuality, and the Politics of South Asian Studies*, 94.
20 Ibid.
21 Ibid., 173.

also utilize elements found in 'black' magic and 'necromancy proper'. The association with necromantic practices probably developed as an extension of existing mortuary practices in Tantra, such as the association with cremation grounds as sites of contemplation. It is well known that the Aghori sect has a ritual involving necrophagy (eating the flesh of a corpse—not an act of murder) and live in cremation grounds. Historical evidence also suggests that human skulls were a ritual instrument in early Tantrism—just as they were in Buddhism—not because they symbolized death, but because they symbolized detachment and renunciation from the normal mode of human existence. It is especially important to note that in these instances of necromancy and necrophagy, no individuals were actually harmed or killed—the corpses were those of people who had died from other means. However repulsive some people may find these acts, they are transgressive only in an aesthetic sense as no violent crimes were committed. This also separates the occult side of Tantra from the political organizations which could authorize human sacrifices or assassinations. In time, the transgressive elements in Tantra were toned down and sexual practices were brought in as a 'lesser' transgression to replace mortuary practices. The ritual sacrifice of prisoners of war also decreased as society became increasingly urbanized and drifted more towards large scale civilizations rather than numerous small kingdoms and villages.

Understanding the role of transgression in ritual is a complex one, which is not easily understood by observation from those outside of the Tantric Traditions. From an outside perspective, such behavior could easily be dismissed as simply abnormal or perverse acts with an ultimately hedonistic objective. Normally, the majority of orthodox spiritual traditions (including those outside of India) advocate abstinence from objects and acts which are believed to be 'impure'. By handling material that is normally forbidden or impure, the Tāntrika gains power because these acts are no longer psychologically disempowering. Instead of avoiding them, the Tāntrika heroically conquers them. Therefore, it is difficult to disagree when Brooks says that,

> The Tāntrika conceives of the world as power. The world is nothing but power to be harnessed.[22]

The way 'power' is utilized here is not the way in which it is sometimes interpreted, as a type of malign narcissism cultivating worldly power. Rather, it is an acknowledgment that all objects contain an equal quantity of 'power'. That which is impure is in truth no different to that which is not, and this is the form of gnosis which the 'transgressive' acts are intended to imbue in the adept. In the case of three modes of practice (*pashu*, *vīra*, and *divya*), this can be realized in three different modes—symbolic repetition, ritual practice, or purely through wisdom itself. As Sanderson writes, even the high-class Brahmin Tantrics like Abhinavagupta and Bhāskararāya engaged in the "occult manipulation of impurity" in order to release the dangerous, wild, and chaotic power of what is forbidden and unclean.[23] One reference, however, states that;

> Impure substances like wine and meat can only be consumed by non-twice born castes; above all, a Brahmin must never compromise his purity by consuming meat or wine. "The offering of [wine] is only for Śūdras: a Brahmin should never offer wine to the Great Goddess. No Brahmin should ever consume wine or meat."[24]

This statement implies very much that varṇa was not denounced by all Tantric sects. To quote Hugh Urban again, "The Tantric does not simply abolish the duality of purity and impurity, but on the contrary exploits this duality by first intensifying and then transgressing it."[25] More simply put: to gain 'power' from the

---

[22] URBAN, H. B., The Power of the Impure: Transgression, Violence and Secrecy in Bengali Śakta Tantra and Modern Western Magic in *Numen*, Vol. 50 (Netherlands: Koninklijke Brill NV, 2003), 275.

[23] URBAN, H. B., Elitism and Esotericism: Strategies of Secrecy and Power in South Indian Tantra and French Freemasonry in *Numen*, Vol. 44, Issue 1 (Netherlands: Koninklijke Brill NV, 1997), 18.

[24] URBAN, H. B., The Power of the Impure: Transgression, Violence and Secrecy in Bengali Śakta Tantra and Modern Western Magic in *Numen*, Vol. 50, 279.

[25] URBAN, H. B., Elitism and Esotericism: Strategies of Secrecy and Power in South Indian

handling of forbidden substances, the substance must be forbidden. This is one of the reasons why Tantra in the 'Western Transmission' remains an anemic interpretation of the original—the 'forbidden elements' either do not exist at all or have no cultural restrictions in the West, leading to a dull interpretation of 'sacred sex' which does not serve the same purpose nor use the same techniques as the original form. Culturally speaking, the use of the 'forbidden' in India does not correlate with that of the West, where very little is 'forbidden'—in most European countries one would be more 'transgressive' if they did not consume alcohol, practiced celibacy, and denounced football.

Although the use of sacred transgression tends to overshadow the rest of Tantra, this reputation does not always cross over into the world of the mundane. There is no reason to assume that transgressive ritual practice is analogous to transgressive social behavior. Whilst the two attributes may manifest together, neither is logically a precondition for the creation of the other. Despite some of the instances cited above, much of the inner core of Tantrism itself remains rooted in Vedic Tradition, and despite Tantrism's denial of varṇa, much of its power structure remains inherently Brāhmanic and is therefore not 'transgressive' at all. As Hugh Urban also notes, some of the most prominent Tantric figures are Brahmin, which could be interpreted as a continuation of their spiritual authority rather than as an overt denunciation of it. Notable examples of this are Raghunandana, Kṛṣṇānanda, Abhinavagupta, and Bhāskararāya. Despite Tantra's reputation for violating social norms, all four instead depict a conservative approach to Tantra. Douglas Brooks also suggested in his study of the Śrīvidyā Tradition that South Indian Brahmins became especially interested in the rituals of Tantra precisely at a time when Brāhmanical power was being threatened by the rise of *bhakti* and Śaṅkara's Vedānta.[26] If Brooks is correct, then it simply means that Brahmins simply revised existing material to perpetuate their own role. As André Padoux says,

Tantra and French Freemasonry in *Numen*, Vol. 44, Issue 1, 19.

[26] Ibid., 5.

"Even though Tantrism is ... notable for transgressive practices in violation of caste ... it does not appear at all socially egalitarian, and still less revolutionary."[27] Moreover, in some cases whilst varṇa may be denied externally, a new hierarchical power structure is created with the Tantric group itself and "When the adept is initiated into this system, and when he passes through this hierarchy in ritual or meditation, he is simultaneously inscribing the hierarchy of the Tantric lineage upon his own body and consciousness."[28] The adept, therefore, becomes not only part of the social structure but has the hierarchy remapped onto the physical medium of the body. Thus via Tantra, the Brahmin varṇa were able to retain their role as religious experts in time when traditional authority was on the wane. The *Mahānirvāna Tantra* also reinforces its role as a *Yuga Śāstra* by stating that Tāntrika rites alone are appropriate for practice in the Kali Yuga. It also mentions the Brahmin directly.

> Shrī Devī said: Thou hast Thyself said, O Lord, that when the Kali Age is in full sway for all castes, commencing with the Brāhmaṇas, Tāntrika rites are alone appropriate.[29]

This statement performs two very important functions: it preserves the traditional role of the Brahmin and affirms Tantra's legitimacy as part of the Hindu Tradition and the spiritual descendant of the Vedas. Vedic elements are not denounced by Tantrism instead, they are absorbed and restructured into a new model of religious thought to conform with the Hindu model of cyclical time as we see in the extract below where the *Brahma-Sāvitrī* mantra is referenced,

> In the Kali Age, all observations bear the fruit of enjoyment and liberation when done according to the rites of the Tantras. The *Brahma-Sāvitrī*, though known as *Vaidika*, should be called

[27] URBAN, H. B., Elitism and Esotericism: Strategies of Secrecy and Power in South Indian Tantra and French Freemasonry in *Numen*, Vol. 44, Issue 1, 6.

[28] Ibid., 20.

[29] AVALON, A., *The Tantra of the Great Liberation (Mahānirvāna Tantra)* (USA: Dover Publications, 1972), 167.

> *Tāntrika* also, and is appropriate in both observances. It is, therefore, O Devi, that I have said that when the Kali Age is in full sway, the twice-born shall be entitled to the *Gāyatrī*, but not the other mantras. In the Kali Age, the *Sāvitrī* should be said by the Brāhmaṇas, preceded by the *Tāra*, and by the *Kamalā* and *Vāsbhava Bījas* respectively.[30]

Tantra, therefore, came to power not by denouncing its Vedic heritage or setting itself up as a rival to Vedic Tradition; rather its strategy was to take existing Vedic teachings and incorporate them into a new religious model which was suitable for dealing with the dangerous forces of the Kali Yuga, and to allow adepts to control these forces rather than vainly struggling to oppose them. This is especially clear in the case of Bhāskararāya who,

> Also defended certain Tantric texts [and] above all, an esoteric work known as the *Tripurā Upaniṣad* as being revealed scripture (śrūti), having the same origin and the same inherent authority as the Veda itself. The *Tripurā Upaniṣad* was claimed to be part of both the *Rg Veda* and the *Atharva Veda* while at the same time having the sacred efficacy of both a Tantric and Vedic text.[31]

The central premise is that previously the Tantric teachings had been hidden implicitly within the Vedas, but now because human beings have sunken to such a bestial level, it is necessary to proclaim them explicitly due to the effects of the Kali Yuga.[32] It is made quite clear that the Tantric Tradition is thought to be the mode of practice for the Kali Yuga, where Traditional Law (Rta and dhāman/dharma) is degraded to the point of non-existence and that, under these conditions, Traditional Law can only be held and maintained by a Tradition which can control the dark forces of the Kali Yuga, rather than shy away from confronting them because,

---

[30] AVALON, A., *The Tantra of the Great Liberation (Mahānirvāna Tantra),* 168.
[31] URBAN, H. B., Elitism and Esotericism: Strategies of Secrecy and Power in South Indian Tantra and French Freemasonry in *Numen*, Vol. 44, Issue 1, 12.
[32] Ibid.

> Non-Tantric Hindu interpretations of the Veda … fail to meet the needs of the degenerate Kali Age … As a remedy, Tantrics teach the necessity of … esoteric (*rahasya*) forms of knowledge.[33]

Tantra, on the contrary to being antagonistic to the Vedas, is instead a continuation of the same ideas, rewritten for a 'modern audience' burdened by the effects of the Kali Yuga, and it is in this context alone that the most unorthodox practices of Tantra can be understood. Rta, the principle of the cosmic law/order remains eternal, but in the Kali Yuga, its mortal counterpart, dhāman/dharma erodes and the original meanings of the Vedas become obscured and, finally, all is forgotten. Because this Yuga is tied to the tamas guṇa (which represents the aspects of materialism) Tantra aspires to conquer the materialism of the age by 'riding the tiger' rather than attempting to oppose a force that is believed to be unstoppable. Because the Kali Yuga is part of a cyclic theory of time, Tantra is deemed to be the efficacious method in the Kali Yuga, because it uses the energy of the Kali Yuga against itself by controlling the impurity of the age to conquer it. The role that transgression plays in such a context is to permit one to channel the impurity of the age within the controlled environment of the ritual space. That is not to say that this is the primary purpose of the rituals themselves, however, as other aspects are also utilized. Any sort of transgressive ritual act is not the primary purpose of the ritual but merely an action that expedites the understanding of the ritual itself, by taking the meaning beyond the symbolic and into the physical world.

[33] URBAN, H. B., Elitism and Esotericism: Strategies of Secrecy and Power in South Indian Tantra and French Freemasonry in *Numen*, Vol. 44, Issue 1, 13.

LEXICOGRAPHICAL GNOSEOLOGY

India contains a rich heritage of texts concerning aesthetic theory, mantra, and the religious use of sound. These ideas occasionally overlap, as can be seen in the writing of the Kaśmir Śaivite Abhinavagupta, who drew inspiration from the earlier rasa theories of Bharata Muni. Abhinavagupta is one of the most highly regarded philosophers to emerge from the Tantric Tradition, and a descendant of Atrigupta, whom King Latitaditya invited to live in Kaśmir in the eighth century.[1] Abhinavagupta, being a natural polymath, wrote on a broad range of subjects including philosophy, religion, dramaturgy, aesthetics, and literary criticism. The *Tantrāloka* is regarded as his most important work and is believed to embody the essence of Śaivism. Abhinavagupta's contribution to Śaivism is one of immense significance, and his use of mantric formulas is deemed to be complex, combining many of his previous ideas into a single form. In this regard, the influence of Bharata Muni on Abhinavagupta's thought is important, as Abhinavagupta's ideas on dramaturgy link it to the Śaivite Tradition:

> The actions of the actor have been devised in order that the spectator might obtain an aesthetic experience that is appropriate to direct perception (as in drama). This is why Bharata has sanctioned the use of music, etc., in order to

[1] PANDIT, B. N., *History of Kashmir Saivism* (India: Utpal Publications, 1990), 47.

> break the knots of the heart that is filled with the anger and sorrow indigenous to it. For the text (the Natyasastra?) includes everything (or: is meant for all people).[2]

Abhinavagupta expands on these ideas in his religious writings by incorporating *rasa* theories into Kaśmir Śaivism. The original meaning of rasa was 'sap' or 'taste', but its meaning is best understood if the word rasa is interpreted as 'dramatic sentiment' or 'aesthetic enjoyment'.[3]

Abhinavagupta, however, understands Bharata's rasa-sūtra as meaning that rasa is produced from the combination of *vibhava, anubhava,* and *vyabhichari-bhava*, which means that rasa comes from the force of one's response to something that is already existing, not something that is produced.[4] Just as an object can be obscured, so too can the rasa of a performance. To fully experience a performance, Abhinavagupta lists certain obstacles (*vighnas*), which must be removed. The obstacles he cites are the same as those which serve to maintain the image of the 'I' or the ego, illustrating how his rasa theory is connected to Kaśmir Śaivism. This spiritual dimension arises from the connection with the Śaivite tradition, in which Śiva and Śakti are conceptualized as cosmic playwrights, the creators, and observers of the unfolding drama of existence. This is particularly apparent in the Sahaja Vidyodaya of the *Spanda Kārikās*, in which Śiva's dynamic aspect is revealed and found to be identical with the essential self of all individuals. In the fifth verse of the Sahaja Vidyodaya it is written that one who possesses such knowledge of the self sees the whole world as the play of Śiva, which is the same as that of the individual self, as is explained by Singh.

> He, who has this retaliation (viz. identity of his Self with the whole universe), being constantly united with the Divine, views

[2] MASSON, J. L., & PATWARDEN, M. V., *Śāntarasa and Abhinavagupta's Philosophy of Aesthetics* (India: Bhandarkar Oriental Research Institute, 1969), 16. Comments by translator.
[3] HABERMAN, D., *Acting as a Way of Salvation* (UK: Oxford University Press, 1988), 13.
[4] Ibid., 20.

> the entire world as a play (of the Self identical with Śiva), and is liberated while alive. There is no doubt about this.[5]

This idea is closely entwined with the concept of the *Heart of Śiva*. The Heart embodies the paradoxical nature of Śiva[6] and, according to Muller-Ortega, in order to understand the heart of Śiva there must be a replication of tantric sādhanā.[7] With regard to this Wulff notes the connection between Abhinavagupta's aesthetic theory and his practice of Kaśmir Śaivism,

> In aesthetic experience, as in yogīc trance and in final release, subject and object disappear, and one transcends all desires and limited, ego-bound perceptions. Abhinavagupta terms the highest state of *vigalitavedyantara*, "one in which the object of knowledge has dissolved."[8]

Of all the rasas described by Abhinavagupta, it is the ninth rasa, *śāntarasa*, which Abhinavagupta praises as the highest rasa, identifying it with Śiva. Śāntarasa, the tranquil sentiment, conveys a sense of world-weariness and a desire to transcend the cycle of existence. Abhinavagupta refers to śāntarasa as being the natural state of one's mind, when it is freed from outside interferences and able to discover its true self as identical with the self of Śiva. Described in such a manner, śāntarasa bears some similarity to the concept of the 'Clear Light' in Vajrayāna Buddhism. Śāntarasa is a blissful state of neutrality, where one has the same attitude towards all living creatures, and there are no emotional states. Śāntarasa is untainted by external experiences, regardless of whether the emotions experienced are positive or negative, as they all, to a certain extent, originate from the ego. Experiencing these emotions

[5] SINGH, J., *The Yoga of Vibration and Divine Pulsation* (India: Motilal Banarsidass, 1992), 119. Comments by translator.

[6] MULLER-ORTEGA, P. E., *The Triadic Heart of Siva* (USA: State University of New York Press, 1989), 82.

[7] Ibid., 3.

[8] WULFF, D. M., Religion in a New Mode: The Convergence of the Aesthetic and the Religious in Medieval India in *The Journal of The American Academy of Religion* 54 (UK: Oxford University Press, 1986), 677.

reveals the persistence of the ego, something which an adept of the Śaivite tradition should be beyond. The importance of śāntarasa in this process is clearly demonstrated by Abhinavagupta in the following quotation,

> He should display the eight rasas in the places allotted to the eight gods. And in the centre he should display śāntarasa in the place of the supreme God (Śiva).[9]

Abhinavagupta's descriptions of states of consciousness and ideas on śāntarasa relate to the Heart of Śiva, and it is for this reason that it occupies the position allocated to Śiva.

The Heart of Śiva not only contains a revelation of mystic experience, it also provides a highly developed philosophy of sound which is interwoven with an elaborate system concerning the construction and encoding of mantras.

The importance of sound, and consequently of the verbalization of language, is often neglected in comparison to that of sight. Humans usually have a strong preference for visual stimuli, but our reliance on the visual sense is also a limitation—it shackles us to the world of physical form, to the detriment of other sensory stimuli such as sound. Within Tantra, the visual and audiological senses become the Path of Sound and the Path of Objects.[10] The Path of Sound deals with the concept of *parāvāk*, for as Abhinavagupta states, the universe consists not only of visible phenomenon, but also of parāvāk, the verbal power of the Divine. In this theory, there is no distinction between the word and the symbol, instead

> The word is the symbol. The four stages of *vāc*[11] as *parā*, *paśyantī*, *madhyamā* and *vaikhari* represent a gradual descent

[9] MASSON, J. L., & PATWARDHAN, M. V., *Śāntarasa and Abhinavagupta's Philosophy of Aesthetics*, 139.

[10] FLOOD, G., *The Tantric Body: The Secret Tradition of Hindu Religion* (USA: I. B. Tauris & Co. Ltd, 2006), 129.

[11] Speech.

> (or ascent) from the undifferentiated, transcendental level to the differentiated, gross level.[12]

This is further divided into principles of expansion and contraction, which are also homologized into the corporeal microcosm via the rising and falling of breath during meditative states. Furthermore,

> Śiva's Supreme Speech (parāvāk) emanates into all the phonetic components of mantras and corresponding cosmic principles (tattvas). At the Para, "Supreme," level of Abhinava's Trika rubric, Śiva subsists in unity with the Goddess Para Śakti who is the same as Supreme Speech. As such, Śiva is also called "Bhairava, the collectively of sound (*sabdarasibhairava*)," for he contains within his unity all the undifferentiated phonemes as well as the archetypal bimbas of all the tattvas.[13]

Though it reaches its apex of complexity in Abhinavagupta, the importance of language and speech remains constant in all forms of Tantrism, due to the prominence of mantras in Tantrism. These combinations of letters into encrypted mantras can be best understood as elaborate esoteric formulas. In addition to this, the texts are also sometimes overlaid with *sandhābhāṣā* or "twilight language" which is deployed to obfuscate the structure of rituals for the uninitiated. Agehananda Bharati provides some examples of the terminology used to encrypt mantras below:

> Oṃ is called *praṇava, tāra, setu*, bridge, etc.
> Hrīm is called '*māyā-bīja*'.
> Raṃ is called '*vahnī*' (fire, syn. Of Agni), '*rakta*' ('red')
> Hūṃ is called '*kūrca*' ('bundles', 'heap')
> Aiṃ is called '*vahnijāyā*' (i.e. wife of Agni—the Vedic termination mantra '*svāhā*' is said to be the exoteric name of Agni's consort); '*vāgbhāva*' ('she of speech-existence'), '*vahni-*

[12] ABHINAVAGUPTA, trans. Singh, J., *Parā-Trīśikā-Vivaraṇa: The Secret of Tantric Mysticism* (India: Motilal Banarsidass, 2005), xv.
[13] LAWRENCE, D. P., Remarks on Abhinavagupta's Use of the Analogy of Reflection in *Journal of Indian Philosophy* (Netherlands: Springer, 2005), 595.

kāntā' ('beloved of Agni').
Klīṃ is called '*kāmabīja*' (i.e. bīja of Cupid), but more often simply '*kāma*' or any of its synonyms (*madana, manmatha, ratipati*)
Krīṃ is called 'ādya' (incipient) and also '*Kālī-bīja*'
Śrīṃ is also called '*Laksmī-bīja*' or simply 'Lakṣmī'
Huṃ is called '*varma*' ('warrior')
Phaṭ is called '*astra*' ('weapon, already discussed')
Em is called '*yonī-bīja*' ('womb-bīja').[14]

Without knowledge of meaning of the mantra, they are well-nigh useless to the uninitiated. Meditation and repetition are barren of rewards, for as the *Kulārṇava Tantra* states,

> Mantras without consciousness are said to be mere letters. They yield no result even after a trillion recitations.[15]

This sentiment is also echoed by the *Śrī Kanthīya Samhitā*, which suggests that the practitioner must be fully immersed in the mantra to succeed.

> So long as the mantrin is distinct from the mantra, he cannot be successful. Wisdom alone must be the root of all of this; otherwise he is not successful. [16]

However, in some instances it is sufficient for a practitioner to possess a general understanding of meaning of the mantra without knowledge of its specific formal nuances, for the desired result to be achieved.

> What if the verbatim meanings are not known? Enough if the sense as a whole of the whole sentence is understood. The accepted theory in this matter is that the spirit is quite different from the letter.[17]

---

[14] BHARATI, A., *The Tantric Tradition* (UK: Rider & Company, 1965), 119.
[15] FEURENSTEIN, G., *Tantra: The Path of Ecstasy* (USA: Shambala, 1998), 192.
[16] Ibid., 192.
[17] MAHKIN, B., (trans.) Sastri, P. S., *Varivasyā-Rahasya and its Commentary* (India: The

In general, however, knowledge is a prerequisite for wisdom, and this cannot be attained without understanding the mantra. This has two implications. Firstly, the control of knowledge functions as a restriction of power and ensures that this knowledge remains under the control of the Tantric tradition, and impervious to the ruminations of external observers. Secondly, the restriction of knowledge also produces a negative effect because it renders the tradition vulnerable to misinterpretation by outsiders. Given Tantra's association with the occult and antinomian practices, this secrecy which obscures Tantra from outsiders has rendered it particularly susceptible to misinterpretation, even by so-called 'religious experts' who usually research material through the lens of their own culture, and not that of Hinduism. Despite the secrecy surrounding Tantrism, the regulations used for safeguarding the mantras were not always complex, and sometimes it merely involved reversing the order of the text or,

> Interchanging the syllables of a line (*vyākulitākṣara*), or paraphrasing it. ... The most extreme involved various forms of encoding that required possession of a key, and knowledge of a procedure, before decoding would be possible. The best examples of this about which I am aware are the devices known as *prastāra* and *gahvara*, which are specific to the tradition of the Kulālikā or Paścimāmnāya ... This involves secreting the mantra through something like a "substitution cipher."[18]

Furthermore, recitation of the mantra itself is not deemed to be sufficient for it to be efficacious. The mantra must also be awakened (*prabuddha*) in a process known as "mantric consciousness" (*mantra-caitanya*).[19] This operates at a metaphysical level similar to that of neuro-linguistic programming, in order to render the cognitive disparity between the subject and the object obsolete.

Adyar Library and Research Centre, 1934), 119.

[18] MULLER-ORTEGA, P. E., Ciphering the Supreme: Mantric Encoding in Abhinavagupta's *Tantrāloka* in *International Journal of Hindu Studies,* Vol. 7 (Netherlands: Kluwer Academic Publishers, 2003), 7.

[19] FEURENSTEIN, G., *Tantra: The Path of Ecstasy*, 192.

Identification with the mantra has to be sufficiently intense to cause a change at a subliminal level, evoking the desired response in a butterfly effect—a minor alteration in consciousness becomes a catalyst that elicits a massive effect on the psyche.

The process of studying mantras is further complicated by their method of construction, which utilizes a framework revolving around the concept of a seed (bīja) mantra. Mantras contain seed sounds in meta-Sanskrit that transcends ordinary speech and, as their name suggests, they are the "seeds" of all sounds.[20] According to the *Mantra-Yoga-Samhitā,* there are eight primary seed mantras: *Aim, Hrīm, Klīm, Krīm, Shrīm, Trīm, Strīm, Hlīm,* although there are also seed syllables such as *lam, vam, ram, yam, ham, hum, hūm* and *phat.*[21] Not only do these all possess inherent encrypted meanings, their use is also tied to specific correspondences. The *Mantra-Yoga-Samhitā,* for example, cites the following *kula-akula-cakra associations*:

Wind	*Fire*	*Earth*	*Water*	*Ether*
a, ā	i, ī	u,ū	ṛ, ṝ	ḷ, ḹ
e	ai	o	au	aṃ
ka	kha	ga	gha	ṅa
ca	cha	ja	jha	na
ṭa	ṭha	ḍa	ḍha	ṇa
ta	tha	da	dha	na
pa	pha	ba	bha	ma
ya	ra	la	va	śa
ṣa	kṣa	la	sa	ha[22]

[20] BROOKS, D. R., *The Secret of the Three Cities: An Introduction to Hindu Śakta Tantrism* (USA: University of Chicago Press, 1990), 61.
[21] FEURENSTEIN, G., *Tantra: The Path of Ecstasy*, pp. 196-7.
[22] Ibid., 104.

Abhinavagupta also provides a lexicographical representation of cosmology based on groupings of the Sanskrit alphabet—this system consists of a classification of letters. Jaideva Singh explains this by describing the associations of letters with their respective esoteric meaning,

> Trika philosophy maintains that the entire manifestation is an expression of parā śakti or parāvāk or transcendental logos. This parāvāk is creative energy. Every letter of the alphabet represents energy in the same form. The letters of the alphabet are arranged in two schemes in *Trika*, viz., *Mātṛkā* and *Mālinī* ... The main difference between the two consists of the arrangement of letters. In Mātṛkā, they are arranged in a regular order, i.e., the vowels come first and the consonants come next in a serial order. In Mālinī, they are arranged in an irregular way, i.e., the vowels and consonants are mixed and no serial order is observed.[23]

It is obvious that there are two different techniques used for encrypting the mantras. The first method, Mātṛkā means the little mother[24] or phonematic creative energy. The second technique is named after the Goddess and Mālinī literally means the Devī who wears a *mālā* or garland consisting of the letters of the Sanskrit alphabet.[25]

The arcane lore of mantra encryption is full of complex cosmological correspondences in the philosophy of language. The phonemes that compose the mantras are expressions of the most fundamental cosmogonic forces of reality. According to Muller-Ortega,

---

[23] ABHINAVAGUPTA, trans. Singh, J., *Parā-Trīśikā-Vivaraṇa: The Secret of Tantric Mysticism*, XVI.

[24] The symbolism of the Mātṛkā relates to form of proto-Tantric worship involving localized groupings of female deities referred to as 'Mātṛkās'. The iconography of the Mātṛkā is strongly linked to fertility hence it's the innate creative power of this method of verbalization.

[25] ABHINAVAGUPTA, trans. Singh, J., *Parā-Trīśikā-Vivaraṇa: The Secret of Tantric Mysticism, Parā-Trīsika-Vivarana*, 137.

> It is no accident that chapter 30 of Abhinavagupta's *Tantrāloka* (as well as major portions of his *Parātriṃśikāvivaraṇa* and *Parātrīśikālaghuvṛtti*) are given over to explanation of these fundamental linguistic, conceptual, and world-building correspondences. The complex linkages between tattvas (fundamental principles) and varṇas (phonemic linguistic elements) are central to an understanding of what Abhinavagupta entails in the process of encoding.[26]

In other texts Abhinavagupta also establishes a set of correspondences between the thirty-six tattvas and the fifty phonemes which he achieves by setting the sixteen vowels as equal to Śiva.[27] This is then coupled with a scheme for gender division which separates the vowels and consonants into male and female aspects, as stated here,

> In this realm of letter, Śiva i.e. the group of vowels, is said to be bīja, i.e., germ or semen, and Śakti, or the group of consonants is said to be the womb or receptacle (M.V. III, 12). The realm of letters has two aspects (1) bīja and (2) yoni. Of these, the vowels are considered to be bīja and the consonants beginning with 'k' are considered to be yoni (M.V. III, 10).[28]

Śri Vidyā is another branch of Tantrism which utilizes a detailed system of mantric formulas involving intricate linguistic theories. Śri Vidyā differs from Kaśmir Śaivism by attempting to legitimate its spiritual authority by reinforcing Vedic elements in order to present the tradition as a Yuga Śāstra, and as the teaching that is appropriate for obtaining enlightenment in the Kali Yuga. One of the ways in which Śrī Vidyā attempts to illustrate its spiritual lineage is by incorporating into its practice the *Gāyatrī* mantra,

[26] MULLER-ORTEGA, P. E., Ciphering the Supreme: Mantric Encoding in Abhinavagupta's Tantrāloka in *International Journal of Hindu Studies*, 24.

[27] MULLER-ORTEGA, P. E., *The Triadic Heart of Siva* (USA: State University of New York Press, 1989), 132.

[28] ABHINAVAGUPTA, trans. Singh, J., *Parā-Trīśikā-Vivaraṇa: The Secret of Tantric Mysticism*, 122.

which is one of the holiest mantras in Hinduism. It is the mantra which "causes the sun to rise" and is dedicated to one of the oldest Vedic gods, the solar deity Savitṛ.[29] In this branch of Tantra, the *Gāyatrī* mantra has been transformed into a new 'revised' mantra—the *Śrī Vidyā*.

> The fourteen Vidyā's have been declared to be the expedients in this world to understand Her. Even among them the most essential are the Veda's and therein indeed *Gāyatrī*.[30]

Drawing its name from this, Śrī Vidyā Tantrism considers the *Śrī Vidyā* mantra to be superior in essence to the older *Gāyatrī* mantra because it consists of "indestructible seed" syllables rather than words, and transcends such "mundane" considerations as a semantic meaning.[31] This viewpoint is not unusual in Tantrism, and it is common for a purely bīja[32] mantra to be regarded as both esoteric and inherently superior. The *Gāyatrī* therefore retains its Vedic heritage and innate power, but is refined and adapted to a form suitable for Tantric practice. To quote a Śrī Vidyā adept:

> Because it is purely seed syllables (*bījākṣaras*), *Śrī Vidyā* is the purest form of mantra. It does not make a request or praise the God; it is God's purest expression. *Gāyatrī* is great but it cannot match *Śrī Vidyā* because it is still in language; it is Veda and mantra but when transformed into the *Śrī Vidyā* its greatness increases.[33]

The esoteric explanation of the syllables also links cosmological patterns of creation to yogīc concepts and practices. For each sound

[29] Savitṛ represents the anthropomorphized power of the sun and thus the highest incarnation of human consciousness and creativity. He is the father of Mitra, whom would later become Mithras.

[30] MAHKIN, B., trans. Sastri, P. S., *Varivasyā-Rahasya and its Commentary*, 7.

[31] BROOKS, D. R., *Auspicious Wisdom: The Texts of Traditions of Śrī Vidyā Śakta Tantrism in South India* (USA: State University of New York Press, 1992), 5.

[32] Seed mantra, composed of syllables.

[33] BROOKS, D. R., *Auspicious Wisdom: The Texts of Traditions of Śrī Vidyā Śakta Tantrism in South India*, 95.

within the mantra there is a series of identifications with different parts of the universe's subtle and physical forms. Each of these corresponds to aspects of human consciousness and parts of the body. The mantra's syllables are then identified with the emergence of the universe in the form of Śrī Cakra.[34]

The implementation of mantras is directly linked to the concept of primordial sound and closely tied to the emanation of Godhead in both Śrī Vidyā and Kaśmir Śaivism. The construction of mantras entails a detailed process of cosmological correspondences in which letters and syllables are identified with different facets of the universe and its creative processes in an intricate meta-narrative. A mantra permits Tantric adepts to possess a direct connection to the primordial resonance of creation itself. Vāk becomes Brahman-as-sound (śabdabrahman), which, according to Tantric theory, has gradually devolved from a state of transcendent unity into subtle and increasingly more mundane forms of sound and language.[35] The *Śrī Vidyā* mantra is in this regard, a perfect expression of the 'primordial sound' (vāk or śabda), just as it is linked to the Vedic *Gāyatrī*.[36] The 'Primordial Sound' can also be traced back to a Vedic origin embodied by Vāk the Goddess of Speech, to whom some also attribute the entire narrative of the *Rig Veda*.[37] There is a hymn within the *Rig Veda* dedicated to Vāk which is reproduced below.

> I move with the Rudras, with the Vasus, with the Ādityas and all the Gods. I carry both Mitra and Varuṇa, both Indra and Agni, and both of the Asvins.
>
> I carry the swelling soma, the Tvastr, and Pūṣan and Bhaga. I bestow wealth on the pious sacrificer who presses the soma and

[34] BROOKS, D. R., *Auspicious Wisdom: The Texts of Traditions of Śrī Vidyā Śakta Tantrism in South India* (USA: State University of New York Press, 1992), 98.

[35] Ibid., 60.

[36] BROOKS, D. R., *The Secret of the Three Cities: An Introduction to Hindu Śakta Tantrism Secret of the Three Cities*, 92.

[37] Some authors use the absence of female figures in the *Rg Veda* to claim the inferiority of women in India—this idea is erroneous, as is shown by the presence of Vāk who is clearly not a minor Goddess.

> offers oblation. I am the queen, the confluence of riches, the skillful one who is first among those worthy of sacrifice. The Gods divided me up into many parts, for I dwell in many places and enter into many forms.
>
> The one who eats food, who truly sees, who breathes, who hears what is said, does so through me. Listen, you whom they have heard: what I tell you should be heeded.
>
> I am the one who says, by myself, what give joy to Gods and men. Whom I love I make awesome; I make him a sage, a wise man, a Brahmin.
>
> I stretch the bow for Rudra so that his arrow will strike down the hater of prayer. I incite the contest among the people. I have pervaded sky and earth.
>
> I gave birth to the father on the head of this world. My womb is in the waters, within the ocean. From there I spread out over all creatures and touch the very sky with the crown of my head.
>
> I am the one who blows like the wind, embracing all creatures. Beyond the sky, beyond this earth, so much have I become in my greatness.[38]

From this hymn it is obvious that Vāk is the embodiment of the creative power inherent in words and language, which is why the 'authorship' of the *Rig Veda* is sometimes attributed to her. Vāk represents the primordial power of sound and words—and their ability to create and influence the course of history. As L. L. Patton says, "To put it in the terms of poetry, the study of imitation in mantric usage can contribute to an understanding of Vedic poetry as not only metaphoric but also metonymic or associative in nature."[39] Metonymy is defined here as,

---

[38] DONIGER, W., (trans), *The Rig Veda* (UK: Penguin Classics, 1981), 63.

[39] PATTON, L. L., Viniyogavijñāna: The Uses of Poetry in Vedic ritual in *International Journal of Hindu Studies*, Vol. 4 (Netherlands: Kluwer Academic Publishers, 2000), 242.

> a relationship of concomitance or continuity, between two categories, that formerly or usually named by the word and that to which the word is transferred. This is to be distinguished from metaphor, which is the transfer of a name that belongs to something else, either from the genus to the species, or from the species to the genus, or from one species to another (Jakobsen and Halle 1971: 243).[40]

Another example of this can be seen in the mystical mantra stanza by the Tamil Siddha Civavākkiyar:

> Like so many forms he stands, by reason of the sound *a*,
> Having dressed himself in shapes, by reason of the sound *u*,
> The illusory world, by reason of the sound *ma*;
> The *civāyam* became realized, by reason of the sound *ci*.[41]

It is from this idea of the transcendent principle present in language that the Tantric schools create their increasingly complex philosophies of sound and wordplay. The philosophical importance and the practical value of the mantras rests on two facts. Firstly, the yogīc function of sounds were used as 'supports' for concentration (*dhāraṇā*) and secondly, in the internalized Tantric liturgy, the 'mystical sound' itself has a specific function, yielding its meaning only to the initiated during mediation.[42] This implies that the mere repetition of the mantra is not always guaranteed to produce favorable results, for, as Bhāskararāya says,

> The utterance of sound without a knowledge of the [true] import bears no fruit, [even as] the offering thrown over ashes in the absence of fire does not burst into flame. Those who are merely reciting the different sounds without knowledge of their meaning are like asses carrying loads of sandalwood.[43]

[40] PATTON, L. L., Viniyogavijñāna: The Uses of Poetry in Vedic ritual in *International Journal of Hindu Studies*, 242.
[41] ZVELEBIL, K. V., *The Poets of the Powers* (UK: Rider & Company, 1973) 23.
[42] Ibid., 52.
[43] BROOKS, D. R., *Auspicious Wisdom: The Texts of Traditions of Śrī Vidyā Śakta Tantrism in South India*, 98.

Bhāskararāya is a primary figure within Śrī Vidyā Tantrism. Out of the six esoteric meanings (*artha*) of Śrī Vidyā in the *Yogīnīhṛdaya,* it is Bhāskararāya's explanation which is the most widely known:

> The *bhavārtha* or "existential meaning" refers to the ontological identity of the mantra's sounds with ultimate reality. The *sampradāyārtha* or "traditional meaning" identifies the syllables with the five physical elements and the thirty-six tattvas or categories that make up reality. *Nirgarbhārtha* is the "hidden meaning" is explained as the identity of the Self, the guru and Śiva while the *kaulikārtha* or "meaning according to the Kula") sets forth the identity of Self, Guru, and Goddess, in addition to establishing a relationship between the mantra's components and the microcosm/macrocosm. In *rahasyārtha* the "secret meaning" the mantra is identified with the body's yogic centers, thus completing the macrocosm/microcosm analogy of the previous meaning. *Mahātattvārtha* is the final level of meaning, the "meaning of ultimate reality." At this stage, all duality is to be transcended.[44]

In Bhāskararāya's analogy, the microcosmic and macrocosmic elements of the mantra are clearly juxtaposed, with the mantra also serving as the medium to bridge the ontological rift betwixt form and formlessness with the ultimate aim of transcending existential duality. This is achieved by ascribing esoteric formulas to the Sanskrit alphabet such as the forty-eight (or fifty-one) phonemes of the Sanskrit language, the mātṛkās or "little mothers." Furthermore, when discussing the relationship between Śrī Vidyā and the primordial sound, Bhāskararāya states, "That [initial] modification [of the One into many] is [technically] called śānta [literally, "peaceful"] because it is the aggregate form of [the four emanations of evolving primordial sound (śabda) technically called *paśyantī, madhyamā* and *vaikhari*]."[45]

---

[44] BROOKS, D. R., *Auspicious Wisdom: The Texts of Traditions of Śrī Vidyā Śakta Tantrism in South India*, 99.

[45] BROOKS, D. R., *The Secret of the Three Cities: An Introduction to Hindu Śakta Tantrism*, 61.

It is especially pertinent that Bhāskararāya links śāntarasa to the primordial sound, in a similar fashion to Abhinavagupta. The experience of śānta as an emotive sensation is related to the *Heart of Śiva*, and the idea of *spanda* or vibration is central to Abhinavagupta's thinking. This begins with a spontaneous sound (*dhvani*) which as the great Heart that produces the universal vibration (*sāmānya-spanda*), it is the emanation of consciousness present in perception. The term dhvani is rendered here as "sound" because it conveys the eternal resonance, the primordial sound that is set up by this movement within the ultimate reality.[46] As Abhinavagupta says,

> The pure and spontaneous cognition of the mantra is the "I" itself. Thus say the ancient masters. This is the very capacity for illumination of light. This, in fact, is the very force of all the mantras, whose nature is the Heart. Without this [potency of the mantras] they [the mantras] would be inert, like living beings without a heart (*Tantrāloka* 4.192-93).[47]

The *Heart Mantra* is therefore one of the most potent mantras in Kaśmir Śaivism—and also the one most closely linked to the *Heart of Śiva* and the Primordial Sound.

Abhinavagupta states the following on the Heart Mantra,

> He who is not born of the yoginī, who is not Rudra, does not clearly obtain this Heart of the God of Gods, which immediately grants both liberation and union … He who obtains this seed mantra, in the very moment he obtains it, is no longer a bound creature. Because, when this seed-mantra is obtained, for him this Heart is produced. This Heart is the very condition of Bhairava.[48]

---

[46] MULLER-ORTEGA, P. E., *The Triadic Heart of Siva* (USA: State University of New York Press, 1989), 120.

[47] MULLER-ORTEGA, P. E., Ciphering the Supreme: Mantric Encoding in Abhinavagupta's *Tantrāloka* in *International Journal of Hindu Studies*, Vol. 7, 25.

[48] MULLER-ORTEGA, P. E., *The Triadic Heart of Siva*, 163.

The primordial essence of totality is reflected back via the Heart, as Abhinavagutpa informs us here:

> Thus this whole world-egg shines [in the heart] like a face in a mirror. Though appearing as separate, this [world-egg, actually] is not separate and consists of self-recognitive apprehension [*svavimarsamaya*].[49]

The structure of the *Heart Mantra*, however, is tripartite:

> This is the great Heart, the triangle, the Ultimate, filled by its three parts each of which is higher than the last, that is the phonemes S, AU, and Ḥ. The great Heart has at its basis the never obstructed capacity for carrying out hundreds of openings and closings of the All, as shown by the power of contraction and expansion whose essence are the functions of appearing, that is blazing forth, and disappearing, that is dissolving down. This Heart thus has three parts or portions.[50]

Of these three phonemes, it is Ḥ (*visarga*) which appears to have been allocated the greatest importance by Abhinavagupta. Translated as *Emissional Power*, visarga is an essential component of the meaning of the Heart—which Abhinavagupta calls the Rudra-dyad. It is a phoneme, the last of the vowels, which is believed to be present in all the other fifteen vowels. As such, it forms the immortal aspect of the sixteen parts of the moon, the lunar stations with which the vowels are equated. The location of visagra in the Heart represents the power of consciousness itself, and according to Kaśmir Śaivism, the highest power of consciousness is its freedom. Visarga, therefore, expresses the freedom of the highest reality in rhythmical expansion and contraction, which functions on all layers of reality. The structure of the Heart Mantra is hinted at by Kṣemarāja in the *Parā-prāveśikā*,

---

49 LAWRENCE, D. P., Remarks on Abhinavagupta's Use of the Analogy of Reflection in *Journal of Indian Philosophy*, 598.

50 MULLER-ORTEGA, P. E., *The Triadic Heart of Siva*, 121.

> Thus says the eternal tradition which holds that this world is within the seed of the Heart formed of the supreme noble lady. How?
>
> Just as the nature of pots and vessels and so on made of clay is nothing but clay, and just as the nature which is in the various kinds of fluids such as water is the same liquid element, so when the true nature of all principles, beginning with earth and ending with māyā, is being considered, we find they are nothing but Being (sat).
>
> With respect to that word sat which is formed merely of the uninflected word, if we eliminate the portion of the suffix which makes clear the meaning of the stem word under consideration, what remains is only the phoneme S. This is the essential reality of the thirty-one principles and is hidden within them. Then come the principles (tattva) of Śuddhavidyā, Īśvara, and Sadāśiva, whose essence are the energies of knowledge and action. Because of the predominance of energy, these principles are contained in that which is composed of the energy of the Supreme, and we thus arrive at the phoneme AU. The phoneme Ḥ, the *visarjanīya*, then occurs in the form of the manifestation which is both above and below. The essential nature of this Heart-seed thus constituted is the Supreme Śiva, who is both transcendent of all and yet immanent within the universe. This is because it is the place of repose of all and that from which all arises, and its nature is the supreme mantra (AHAM). He who truly knows such a seed-mantra and is absorbed in it, he is initiated into the highest reality and, without abandoning his life, continues to exist like the ordinary man.[51]

This is further complicated by the fact that there are in fact two heart mantras—the *Heart of Emission* and the *Heart of Reabsorption*. Abhinavagupta describes the processes involved in the *Heart of Reabsorption*.

[51] MULLER-ORTEGA, P. E., *The Triadic Heart of Siva*, pp. 178-9.

> The seed of reabsorption is as follows; the ether (KH) stands in the heart, the flowery (Ph) is a labial, the fire (R) is a cerebral, the triangular (E) is palatoguttural, and the bindu (ṃ) resides in the higher sphere. The awakened one who employs this method and is wholly devoted to the recitation of the phonemes without long delay penetrates into the abode of the Supreme, he is the wise one. According to certain texts, for example, the *Dīkṣottara-tantra*, the word varṇa refers to colors, blue and so on. He who remembers in his own Heart the reabsorption (Kṣ), the man (M), the fire (R), and the wind (Y), is united with practice. This is a fire which, awakened by this seed, flames violently in the lotus of his Heart, like a flame made variegated by sparks of different colours—blue, yellow, red—which surround it. The bindu shines flaming like a flame, just like the sun without clouds.[52]

From this passage it should be clear that the heart mantra also has a secret esoteric technique which accompanies it. Jayaratha also provides some clues for understanding the secrets of mantra encryption, citing the following equivalences:

> *Bodhāgnīnd: agnibījsya*: the fire of awakening, the fire seed, the phoneme RA.
>
> *Khātmantvam: vyomātmanaḥ khavarṇasya:* the ethereal state, the void state, the phoneme KHA.
>
> *Nāda: kuṭavarṇasya*: the crooked consonant. This is the least explicit and most ambigious (if not controversial) clue. From evidence elsewhere, it is reconstructed as the phoneme PHA, which is covertly given in the commentary several times in the word "*prasphurita*."
>
> *Śaktitritaya: yonibījasya*: the triad of powers, the womb-vowel, that is, the vowel E. Here a different vowel is intended by the same encoding expression—śaktitritaya—that is used to decode the vowel in the first mantra.

[52] MULLER-ORTEGA, P. E., *The Triadic Heart of Siva*, 181.

> *Vedanātmakatām: bindvantavarṇa*: the pure knower, having the phoneme bindu or ṃ at its end.[53]

By understanding the esoteric meaning of the phonemes, knowledge of a mantra can be ascertained, and without knowledge of the encryption process the mantra is almost completely useless. The role of language and sound in Tantric ritual is a primary one, around which practice is constructed. It also serves to bind the objective principle to the subjective, which is the basis for the cognitive division from which the illusion of duality arises. The Heart Mantra, which contains the ultimate truth for the school of Kaśmir Śaivism, provides us with the required ingredients for gnosis in a single mantra. The same method of overlaying cosmological truths onto a narrative of phonemes is found in Śrī Vidyā Tantrism, which reinforces its ritual strength by claiming Vedic ancestry from the *Gāyatrī* mantra.

> This is because it is the place of repose of all and that from which all arises, and its nature is the supreme mantra (AHAM). He who truly knows such a seed-mantra and is absorbed in it, he is initiated into the highest reality and, without abandoning his life, continues to exist like the ordinary man.[54]

In this regard, Tantrism can be seen as a spiritual tradition which developed out of a Vedic background, and not a tradition which runs contrary to it. By reinforcing the *Gāyatrī* within the Tantric framework, and modifying it, Śrī Vidyā is not rejecting the Vedas, but simply modifying earlier techniques which are no longer deemed to be efficacious in the Kali Yuga.

The sheer complexity of Tantric mantra formulas makes the subject difficult to approach theoretically, as there are a number of different techniques for assessing the suitability of a mantra for individual practitioners, as well as more versatile mantras suitable for use by more than one person. The mantras for individuals

[53] MULLER-ORTEGA, P. E., Ciphering the Supreme: Mantric Encoding in Abhinavagupta's Tantrāloka in *International Journal of Hindu Studies*, 16.

[54] MULLER ORTEGA, P. E., *The Triadic Heart of Śiva*, pp. 178-9.

are often drawn diagrammatically, with a specific order that will occasionally utilize other factors, such as the practitioner's natal astrological chart, which then requires additional knowledge of astrology (*Jyotiṣa*).

This chapter is only a very brief introduction to the implementation of mantras within the Tantric Traditions. The theories behind both Śrī Vidyā and Kaśmir Śaivism regarding the teachings of primordial sound, mantric formulas, and encryption processes in general, is one which cannot be explained at length in a single chapter. However, it is a mandatory requirement for readers to have a basic understanding of how mantra and sound is utilized before proceeding to the next chapter, which deals with the siddha traditions and magical formulas, and requires extensive knowledge in regard to the use of mantras.

MAGICO-RELIGIOUS PRACTICES

> The sin born of the black magic deed perishes at the utterance (of blessings) of the Brahmins.[1]

Ever since the occident first discovered the ancient wisdom of India, our fascination with the country's occult mysteries has been both deep and flawed. Currently, the Western world has an extremely low comprehension of genuine Tantric practices, preferring to concentrate on illusionary 'sacred sex' aspects of Tantrism which have been constructed out of Freudian repression rather than any actual Tantric occult rituals—which are usually very far from the popular perception of 'sexy'. Most of the current obsession with sex in Western occultism was evoked directly from the prudish Victorian era of magicians such as Aleister Crowley, Paschal Beverly Randolph, and the "Omnipotent Oom."[2] All of these versions of Neo-Tantra are based on a profound misunderstanding of Tantrism, and completely ignorant in regards to Tantra's occult techniques.

What actually occupies the dominant role in Tantrism is its focus on the 'attainment of worldly power' which is to be made manifest in this lifetime via preternatural occult power. Even the word śakti literally translates as power. More often than not, this

---

[1] MAHIDHARA, trans. A Board of Scholars, *The Mantramahodadhi of Mahidhara* (India: Sri Satguru Publications, 2014), 576.

[2] "The Omnipotent Oom" was one of the names used by Pierre Arnold Bernard.

power manifests through abilities referred to as siddhi (attainments or perfections). The siddhi correspond exactly to the phenomena referred to as 'psychic powers' in the current era. In contrast to most Western belief systems, these are considered to be a normal by-product of yoga in Hinduism and are not strictly 'supernatural'. This association between siddhi and yoga is even found in the *Yogatattva Upaniṣad.* Moreover, the nature of the Kali Yuga is thought to actually make the attainment of siddhi easier, and thus it is more common than in prior ages.

However, the importance placed on siddhi over the benefits of enlightenment and spiritual progress can also be a terrible hazard, for the siddhi themselves can become an impediment to further spiritual progress, and bind the practitioner to the wheel of saṃsāra. Even Patañjali warns the reader that the possession of siddhi is ultimately an obstacle to the attainment of true samādhi since all possession implies bondage to the thing possessed.[3] This is the reason why one who 'rides the tiger can never dismount', for, like the Kali Yuga, the forces the Tantric is channeling are extremely dangerous if control is relinquished. The Tantras themselves state that one who performs Tantra for the sake of gaining siddhi will never attain enlightenment, and this is why Tantra is linked so strongly to the sphere of the occult in India: there are countless 'fallen' practitioners who have turned to the occult instead of embracing the spiritual side of Tantrism, and they have become highly skilled black magicians as well as 'sinister yogīs'. The extraordinary occult abilities of the Tantrics are discussed in the 49th Chapter of the Śaṅkaravijaya of Ānandagiri:

> Through our special knowledge of [various powers of our sorcery], and our special expertise in gaining mastery over [each of the five elements], and by virtue of drinking poisons, drinking mercury, and drinking [specially prepared] oils … [and] by means of special forms of yogīc practice, [we effect] the removal of accidental or untimely death. By means of special [acts of] sorcery (*kriyā*) … through special Śaktis …

[3] ZVELEBIL, K. V., *The Poets of the Powers* (UK: Rider & Company, 1973), 62.

> Yakṣiṇīs … [and] Mohinīs, by means of the various divisions of Kakṣ[y]apuṭa knowledge, iron-making, copper-making, silver-making, gold-making, etc., by various means of various types of metallurgical expertise… [and] through the special use of black mercuric oxide, roots, and mantras, magic, and great magic, we can strike people blind and blind lions, śarabhas, and tigers. By means of this panoply of specialized practices, we are, in fact, omniscient.[4]

Furthermore, during the Middle Ages, which were the apex of power for the Tantric Tradition, many of these magicians enjoyed court privileges and were employed by kings for the purposes of divination, astrology, and even the magical murder of political opponents, as can be seen in this example:

> A king may offer sacrifice for his enemies. He should first consecrate the sword with mantra, and then consecrate the buffalo or goat with the name of the enemy. He should bind the animal with a cord around his mouth, reciting the mantra three times. He should sever the head and offer it with great effort to the Goddess. Whenever enemies become strong, more sacrifices should be offered. At such times he should sever the head and offer it for the destruction of his enemies. He should infuse the soul of the enemy into the animal. With the slaughter of this [animal], the lives of his unfortunate enemies are also slain. "O Caṇḍikā, of terrible form, devour my enemy, so and so" this mantra should be repeated … This hateful enemy of mine is himself in the form of the animal. Destroy him, Māhāmārī, devour him, devour him, *spheṇg spheṇg*!" With this mantra, a flower should be placed on his head. He should then offer the blood, with the two-syllable [mantra].[5]

---

[4] WHITE, D. G., *Kiss of the Yoginī: "Tantric Sex" its South Asian Context* (USA: The University of Chicago Press, 2006), 162.

[5] URBAN, H. B., *The Power of Tantra: Religion, Sexuality and the Politics of South Asian Studies* (USA: I. B. Tauris & CO Ltd, 2010), 90.

In addition to this example, there are also Tantric texts which are almost exclusively devoted to the occult, some of which resemble the European grimoires. However, the nature of the rituals involved are much darker and make the grimoires appear quite harmless by comparison. The most notorious Tantric text which deals exclusively with the occult is the *Mantramahodadhi of Mahidhara* (c.1588 CE). The *Mantramahodadhi* is regarded as an especially potent text, and even modern editions of this work come with a warning that the translators accept no responsibility for any damage incurred as a result of using its content. It is also worth remembering at this point, that an "Aspirant should not even open and read the scriptures containing these practices (*prayoga śastra*) without the guidance of a master."[6] Other well-known texts that deal with the occult and siddhi include the *Dattatreya Tantra* and the *Vīṇāśikhatantra*. There are many other texts which also approach the occult in a more indirect fashion such as the *Kāmarūpī Tantrasāra*, *Kāmākhyā Tantrasāra*, *Ādio Āsal Kāmākhyā Tantrasāra* (The Original and True Essence of Kāmākhyā Tantra), and *Kāmarūpīyā Tantramantra Āru Ouṣadh* (The Tantra, Mantra, and Medicine of Kāmarūpa).[7] These texts serve a purpose similar to a liturgical vessel just as the Western grimoires do; when a formula is read from them, the power of the text is enhanced by the sacrality of the book from which it is read.[8] In light of this, however, the books cannot be separated from the cultural conditions which gave them birth. This means that not only do the texts themselves require study, they are also related to other forms of Hindu esotericism and operate within this framework, just as the grimoires are only appropriate for use within the Judeo-Christian Tradition.

The occult aspects of Tantrism did not emerge from a vacuum. Their spiritual ancestry can be traced to the Vedas themselves. Magic

---

[6] TIGUNAIT, P. R., *Tantra Unveiled: Seducing the Forces of Matter & Spirit* (USA: Himalayan Institute Press, 1999), 14.

[7] URBAN, H., *The Power of Tantra: Religion, Sexuality and the Politics of South Asian Studies*, 173.

[8] KIECKHEFFER, R., *Forbidden Rites: A Necromancer's Manual of the Fifteenth Century* (UK: Sutton Publishing, 1997), 5.

was certainly not unknown in the Vedic era, and the *Atharva Veda* is stocked with a plethora of charms which testify this. Instances of magical acts in the Vedas are often employed in such a manner that there is, at this stage of religious development, no apparent division between religious and magical practices. The *Rig Veda* also demonstrates the inchoate magic power embedded in the ritual sacrifice of gifts or homage. One of the many examples of this can be seen in the hymn to Parjanya for obtaining rain:

> Give us rain from heaven, O Maruts. Make the streams of the seed-bearing stallion overflow as they swell. Come here with your thunder, pouring down waters, for you are our father, the bright sky-god.[9]

Though it is phrased in religious terminology, the act itself still verges on occultism because it requests a physical manifestation as the result of the ritual, as opposed to a purely spiritual effect. This is the defining principle of demarcation which separates magic from religion—magic seeks to attain a worldly effect (telluric), and religion a spiritual one (uranic). In regard to this presence of magical elements Louis Renou writes that "the mantra, whatever may have been its origin, is before all else, an *abracadabra*." He does not imply this in a derogatory fashion, rather it is a concession to the fact that the word 'abracadabra' was originally a magical term constructed in the same way the mantra is, prior to being imported into popular culture. Moreover, the implementation of alphabetical constructs to create a sacred language for magico-religious purposes is a common practice found in many different cultures, and even the 'barbarous names'[10] which appear in magical texts are similar encryptions.

In some ways, however, the *Atharva Veda* provides a more accurate description of people's lifestyle than other texts from the

[9] DONIGER O'FLAHERTY, W., trans. *The Rig Veda: An Anthology* (UK: Penguin Books Ltd., 1981), 173.

[10] 'Barbarous' from the Greek *barbaroi* implying from foreign sources, usually Egyptian, Hebrew, or Persian magical sources that did not translate easily into Greek.

Vedic period. The *Atharva Veda* mentions many charms from herbs (*apā mārga, rohiṇī, dūrva, auduṁbara, palāsa,* etc.) and animal products (antelope's horn, tiger's paw, wild boar's tooth) and metals (copper, iron, gold, etc.)[11] An example of a charm from the *Atharva Veda* is provided by Shah,

> Considered one of the most potent of all charms is that made from the wood of the Sraktya tree (*Clerodendrum Phlomoides*). A piece of wood is cut, then shaped into something representing the object of one's desire. For victory in battle the supplicant fashions a sword or spear from the wood. In many cases, however, a simple disc is made, bearing radiating lines to indicate the cakra—an ancient Indian sun-sign.[12]

And in another example,

> A charm is first made, from the Gangida tree, and over it this spell is intoned:
>
> "The seers, while speaking the name of Indra, gave to man the Gangida. It had been made a remedy by the Gods from the beginning, and a destroyer of the Vishkandha. Protect us, Gangida, for we look after his treasures, verily the Gods and the Brāhmaṇas made him a protection that nullifies evil forces!
>
> I have approached the evil eye of the inimical; O thousand-eyed one, destroy all these! Gangida, thou art our refuge.
>
> The Gangida will protect me from the heavens, from the earth, from plants, from the air; and now from the past, and from the future. I am to be protected in every direction!
>
> May the all-powerful, protective Gangida render all the magic of Gods and men weak and powerless!"[13]

---

[11] TIGUNAIT, P. R., *Tantra Unveiled: Seducing the Forces of Matter & Spirit*, 8.

[12] SHAH, S. I., *Oriental Magic* (UK: The Octagon Press, 1992), 113.

[13] Ibid., 117.

It is clear that this charm possessed an animist component, as is seen in the reference to the tree 'spirit' Gangida. In general, such spirits were deemed to be responsible for all the issues which afflicted the human race. Other prominent animist entities include Chaṇḍā, Arāi, Koka, Durnāma, Arjuṇī, Grāhi, Niṛṛtu, Sadāhva, Ugajihvā, Malimlucha, Pramāli, and Kakūrabha.[14]

The *Atharva Veda* also recognizes two forms of magic, *śānta* which is associated with holy magic and *ghora* which is 'black magic'. It is owing to this twofold magic that verses in the *Atharva Veda* verses are believed to possess the power 'to bless, to appease, and to curse.' In this regard,

> The Vedic sacrifices with the chanting of Rig Veda mantras might have developed into the later Tāntrik mystical rituals. They are efficacious in the attainment of worldly prosperity, removal of hurdles and ailments and other practical benefits.[15]

The benevolent (śānta) category includes śāntī (pacification of evil spirits), *paushṭika* (nourishment of the individual) and *bheshaja* (cure of disease and restoration of health).[16] The malefic (ghora) category includes *vaśīkaraṇa* (attracting the affection of people by coercion), *staṃbhana* (arresting the movement or speech of opponents), *vidreshaṇa* (causing enmity and ill-will among friends), *uccāṭana* (dispersing enemies by occult means) and *māraṇa* (death).[17] Collectively, śāntī, vaśīkaraṇa, staṃbhana, vidreshaṇa, uccāṭana, and māraṇa are also referred to as the Six Acts (*ṣaṭkarman*) of Tantrism, with five of the six being classified as ghora or 'black magic' because they impair the will or activity of another human being.

Within the Tantras, magic is also deployed to recreate cosmological events on the microcosmic level of the individual through the use of symbolic representation in mantra and yantra.

[14] TIGUNAIT, P. R., *Tantra Unveiled: Seducing the Forces of Matter & Spirit*, 7.

[15] MAHIDHARA, trans. A Board of Scholars, *The Mantramahodadhi of Mahidhara* (India: Sri Satguru Publications 2014), IX.

[16] TIGUNAIT, P. R., *Tantra Unveiled: Seducing the Forces of Matter & Spirit*, 8.

[17] Ibid., 11.

For example, there are nine minerals, nine gems, and nine groups of herbs that correspond to the nine planets, and these groups of nine correspond to the nine constituents of the human body: chyme, blood, flesh, bone, marrow, seminal fluid, *ojas* (vitality), and *jiva* (soul).[18] The yantra acts as the visual representation of the ritual and mantra is the aural representation. The composition of both are highly formulated, and rules for symbolism are stringently applied to these ritual components.

Although the topic of mantra was discussed in the previous chapter, it is necessary to revisit the subject in relation to the occult, because the way it is utilized is different, even though the linguistic formula remains as an essential aspect. Any word, spoken or written, can possess powers which operate at a sacred level as well as at a mundane one. When dealing with the oral component in magical rites, and in particular mantras, language is used as the bridge between the subject and the object, the real and the ideal, in order to draw the immaterial into the realm of the manifest. The implementation of standardized sets of ritual formulas serve to enhance this ability, and ideas such as this are by no means restricted to the Tantric Tradition. For example, the *Corpus Hermeticum* also explains the interactions betwixt speech, ritual, and the numinous.

> God has endowed man beyond all mortal creatures with these two gifts: *Nous* and Speech, both as much valued as immortality. If he uses these gifts rightly, he will be no different from the immortals, and on departing from the body he will be guided by both to the realm of the gods and the blessed ones … For *Agathos Daimon*, the blessed God, has said that the soul is in the body, Nous in Soul, and the Word in Nous, and that God is the father of these … The Word is an image of Nous, and Nous is an image of God; just as the body is an image of an idea, and the idea is an image of the soul.[19]

[18] TIGUNAIT, P. R., *Tantra Unveiled: Seducing the Forces of Matter & Spirit*, 55.

[19] SALAMAN, S., VAN OYEN, D., & WHARTON, W. D., trans. *The Way of Hermes: The Corpus Hermeticum & The Definitions of Hermes Trismegistus to Asclepius* (UK: Duckbacks, 2001), 77.

In certain European ceremonial magic texts, ritual aspects are also encoded in a similar manner to mantras, for example, the names for God derived from Hebrew or Greek liturgical formulas, such as AGLA, which is the common magical acronym for the Hebrew "*Ata gibor leolam Adonai.*"[20] The effect of oration in such rituals operates in an analogous fashion to mantra with the word becoming the transitional point between subject and object and conjuring the desired goal of ritual into manifestation.[21] The oral ritual formula acts as an operative mechanism by which ritual specialists can transcribe their will, serving as a catalyst to conjure the symbolized event into existence in the physical world. It is the transitory point between the existent and that which has not yet existed—the power of the word or speech evokes the desired goal of ritual into the realm of physical manifestation.

In the Tantric Tradition, each mantra carries its own specific and unique meaning. The Tantras view the Sanskrit alphabet as the network of abstract and primordial sound-units (*bīja-aksharas*) with each sound unit (or letter) representing a specific form of energy[22] and which can be combined together in a cosmogonic sequence to act as a magical operative betwixt the sacred and the mundane, in an almost Mercurial fashion. This is illustrated by the *Parā-Trīśikā-Vivaraṇa* which states that "The difference between the word and its referent is, in the stage of *madhyamā*, only in a subtle mental state, it has not yet been externalized."[23] The bīja contains the essence of the mantra and the main mantra represents the form of the deity divided into six main limbs (*aṅga*).[24] These mantric components are then structured in such way that they construct a codified formula known only to those inside the Tradition. By the process of repetition, the mantra then acts in a similar way to neurolinguistic

[20] KIECKHEFFER, R., *Forbidden Rites: A Necromancer's Manual of the Fifteenth Century*, 139.

[21] LADRIERE, J., trans. Barden, G., *Language & Belief* (UK: Macmillan, 1972), 177.

[22] TIGUNAIT, P. R., *Tantra Unveiled: Seducing the Forces of Matter & Spirit*, 6.

[23] ABHINAVAGUPTA, trans. Singh, J., *Parā-Trīśikā-Vivaraṇa: The Secret of Tantric Mysticism* (India: Motilal Banarsidass, 2005), 10.

[24] GUPTA, S., Worship of Kali According to the Toḍala Tantra in ed. White, D. G., *Tantra in Practice* (USA: Princeton University Press, 2000), 472.

programming and the power of the words becomes an instrument of the practitioner's will, removing the arbitrary distinction between the subject and object.

***

The majority of Tantric occult formulas begin with a procedure called *nyāsa* (keeping or placing), which involves a mapping of the divine or sacred onto the human body. There are various forms of nyāsa, all of which have a specific purpose. These forms include (but are not limited to) *mātrika-nyāsa* (placement of the alphabet) *jīva-nyāsa* (placement of life), *ṛṣi-nyāsa* (placement of the seer), *kara-nyāsa* (placement of the hand), *aṅga-nyāsa* (placement of the ancillary), and *pīṭha-nyāsa* (placement of the sacred sites). The *Parā-Trīśikā-Vivaraṇa*, by way of example, mentions another form, stating that;

> The knowers of mantra, in order to achieve the desired object of the followers of mantra and Tantra should practice in matters of nyāsa, the nyāsa of Mālinī which is free of particular prescription (of rites) and has a mixed arrangement of vowels and consonants, for the sake of the Śakta body.[25]

Nyāsa is not restricted to occult use, and it is a widely used procedure as a preliminary stage for many different practices. Nyāsa is best thought of as an ancillary procedure, and not part of the main ritual itself, even though it is often required within a magical framework as well as within more general modes of practice.

The yantra is equally as important as the aural and linguistic elements found in mantras. In terms of construction and implementation, the yantra follows a similar method and each element found in a yantra possesses an innate meaning, just as phonemes within mantras do. By itself, the yantra is not an exclusively occult practice, since it is a visual element which can be

[25] ABHINAVAGUPTA, trans. Singh, J., *Parā-Trīśikā-Vivaraṇa: The Secret of Tantric Mysticism*, 123.

used for worship, meditation, magic, or tailored to awaken siddhi. The mantra and the yantra should be considered as complimentary ritual constructs, with yantra functioning as the visual causative principle and mantra as the aural. The unifying energy between the aural and visual components is the deity they are connected to, for, as Kaulāvalli says, "The yantra has a mantra as its soul and the deity is the soul of the mantra."[26] The yantra also establishes a connection between the numinous and its creator, and if any harm befalls the yantra, misfortune is relayed to the one who created it, for it remains linked to them through spiritual energy. As such, the yantra is a potent ritual tool, which, in etymological terms, is related to the word instrument and is derived from the root *yam* (*Uṇādi* 4, 133) or alternatively from the form '*yantrati*' (or '*yantrayati*') (*Dhātu-pātha*, 32, 3), the meaning in both cases being "to restrain," "to compel," "to bend."[27] Early instances of the word yantra were used in relation to mechanical appliances and blunt surgical instruments, such as '*yantra-gṛha*' (oil mill), '*yantra-putrikā*' (puppet or doll which is moved by strings),[28] '*tata-yantra*' (discs with handle), '*nādī-yantra*' (tubular appliances), and '*śālākya-yantra*' (thin probes).[29] Given these associations, the yantra should be considered as a ritual instrument or tool.

As with other forms of magic in India, occult yantras also fall into the categories of the beneficial (*saumya* or *aghora*), and the malevolent (*krūra* or *ghora*).[30] Yantras for peace and prosperity are also known as *śantika-paushtika*[31] whereas "vengeful missiles" are called *abhicāra* and are used for "violent acts" (*kṛtyā*).[32] It is worth noting that the 'love/lust' spells to procure the affection of a woman or a man also fall into the category of malevolent magic because they compromise the will of a sentient being. There are also yantras

[26] RAO, R. S. K., *The Yantra: Text with 32 Plates* (India: Sri Satguru Publications, 1988), 24.
[27] TIGUNAIT, P. R., *Tantra Unveiled: Seducing the Forces of Matter & Spirit*, 10.
[28] RAO, R. S. K., *The Yantra: Text with 32 Plates* (Delhi: Sri Satguru Publications), 10.
[29] Ibid., 11.
[30] Ibid., 20.
[31] Ibid.
[32] Ibid.

which combine both malefic and benevolent aspects such as *bhūta-ucchāṭana* or *bhūta-āveśa-nigraha* (exorcism).[33] The deities which are frequently depicted in occult yantras include Hanumān, Chaṇḍī, Durgā, Sastā, Kālī, Bhairava, and Gaṇeśa.

There are also preliminary steps to be followed prior to constructing the yantra, such as immersing the material on which the yantra is to be constructed in fluids such as milk, curds, ghee, honey/sugar, and water. Once this has been done, there are two methods of construction. One method of drawing the yantra is commenced from the center (expansion), and the other method begins with the outer points of the yantra (contraction). These two methods also represent creation (*sṛshṭi*) and destruction (*saṁhāra*).[34] If the yantra is to be used for benevolent purposes, the lines in the yantra are to be drawn from East to West and this is reversed for malefic magic. In a similar fashion, a progressive yantra is crafted with an upward ascent, and a non-progressive yantra is written in a descending manner.

The focal point of the yantra is the bindu located near a seed-syllable (*bīja-akshara*), and if the yantra is also associated with an individual, its name or initial is placed in close proximity to this. Once the yantra has been fully created, it is usually covered with a cloth until the time of consecration. However, if the yantra is to be worn on the body, consecration is not always required. After its creation, the way the yantra is used is determined by its elemental type, for instance, "Fire yantra [are] burned or buried near the hearth, air suspended from a height, Water thrown into [the] water, [and for] Earth mountains, crossroads, [and] cremation grounds."[35]

The yantra is also required to be created at the correct time of day and astrological time, in correspondence with the deities and planetary bodies who govern the hours (*horā*) of the day. This excludes the outer planets of the solar system, for as Chawdhri informs the reader,

---

[33] RAO, S. K., *The Yantra: Text with 32 Plates*, 22.

[34] Ibid., 31.

[35] CHAWDHRI, L. R., *Practicals of Yantras* (India: Sagar Publications, 1998), 4.

> Astronomical bodies past Saturn are not included in traditional horā divisions because in the past they could not be observed as the pertinent technology to discern their existence had not been discovered. Thus the planets which are allocated to the horā are the Sun, Moon, Mercury, Venus, Mars, Jupiter, Saturn—which also correlates with the days of the week.[36]

This is mirrored precisely in the European calendar and also in Western ceremonial magic, which also uses a system of planetary hours for occult purposes. There are, however, differences between Western and Eastern astrology which manifest in the construction method. The Western system follows only a solar calendar and Hinduism also has a lunar calendar incorporated into its schema of cosmic cycles in which lunar periods are referred to as *nakṣatra*. Not only does the creation of the yantra require the use of these astrological calculations, certain magical procedures also utilize the phases of the moon (for which either the *amānta* or *pūnimāṇta* system is used). This revolves around the division of the lunar phases into light and dark halves of the moon, depending on whether the moon is waxing or waning.

***

The emphasis on the siddhi, is unsurprisingly, particularly prevalent within the Siddha teachings, and as Zvelebil relates, "The doctrines of the Siddha, in their blend of yoga and magic Tantrism, represent a very archaic modality of spirituality which has survived nowhere else, and which has remained in existence down to our day, as a kind of 'living fossils,' strangely modern."[37] Tirumūlar defines the Siddhas as those "who have experienced divine light (*oli*) and divine power (*catti*, Sanskrit śakti) from within and through samādhi."[38] David Gordon White also asserts that the Siddha were more prevalent in Śrīśailam (Kurnool District, Andhra Pradesh),

[36] CHAWDHRI, L. R., *Practicals of Yantras*, 49.
[37] ZVELEBIL, K. V., *The Poets of the Powers* (UK: Rider & Company, 1973), 120.
[38] Ibid., 27.

Kedārnāth (Chamoli District, Uttar Pradesh), Mount Abu (Sirohi District, Rajasthan), and Girnār (Junagadh District, Gujarat).[39] Furthermore, the *Haṭhayogapradīpikā* also contains a list of Siddhas, including Matsyendranāth, Gorakhnāth, and Nāgārjuna, all of whom were prominent figures associated with Tantrism. Kaula Tantrism even claims that its spiritual ancestry arises directly the Siddha doctrines, as is stated in Bhairava's text, the *Bringing Forth of the Kaula Gnosis.*

> From the *Mahākaula* [arose] the *Siddha Kaula*; from the Siddha Kaula the Fish-Belly. It was uttered by me upon each of the divisions of the four ages (yugas). In the first [age] the bringing forth (*nirṇiti*) [was made] to the Kaula; in the second to the [Kaula] known as Mahat; in the third, to the [Kaula] named Siddhāmṛta [and] in the Kali [age] to the Fish-Belly.[40]

The name 'Fish Belly', aside from being decidedly unglamorous, refers not only to a sacred confluence of waters, but also to the yogīc technique of breathing and control over the nāḍī, and is associated with Matsyendranāth, whose other name Matsyendra translates as 'Lord of the Fishes'. His major work was the *Kaulajñānanirnāya (*Discussion of the Knowledge Pertaining to the Kaula Tradition) and Gorakhnāth was one of his disciples.

The use of siddhi, however, is not restricted to the Siddha doctrines. As they are considered to be a normal by-product of yogīc practice, any and all advanced practitioners of authentic yoga[41] should be automatically assumed to possess siddhi to a certain degree. Even the *Mahābhārata* speaks of the power of accomplished yogīs to perceive the life force of the recently deceased person

---

[39] WHITE, D. G., Mountains of Wisdom: On the Interface Between Siddha and Vidyādhara Cults and the Siddha Orders in Medieval India in *International Journal of Hindu Studies,* Vol. 1, (Netherlands: Kluwer Academic Publishers, 1997), 88.

[40] WHITE, D. G., *Kiss of the Yoginī: "Tantric Sex" its South Asian Context* (USA: The University of Chicago Press, 2006), 25.

[41] 'Authentic yoga' does not include the current use of it in an American context, where it has become a form of exercise.

departing from the physical body.[42] Whilst many of the siddhi correspond directly to what are currently referred to as clairvoyance, telepathy, and astral projection, etc., there are a few references to far more sinister practices, which are clearly a perversion of normal yogīc teachings, such as performing subjugation (one of the Six Acts which falls under the rubric of black magic) by entering another's body through the yogīc arteries.[43] This process is described in the *Netra Tantra*, which details how to perform a psychic assault on the victim.

> Having mounted an assault (ākramya), out through the upper or lower entrance [of his subtle body], into that other body's living self (*jīvam*), which is situated in that person's heart, and having attacked its integrity, [the yogī] should go to work on [that self's] equanimity [and then], attaching [himself] to its prime mover (śakti), he should smash … encapsulate … and annihilate that self's energy. Thereupon … the connoisseur of yoga … should heat up [the other body's self] with … the solar nature of his mind-stuff (*citsūryatvena*). Situated in the other [body's heart], it will melt away [the other self's] rays in the same way as the sun, with its rays [melts away the rays of the moon]. He should then yoke, in the [other body's heart], all of the action organs, beginning with the organ of speech … [and he should yoke] from every side those [organ's associated] elements, [which have become] liquefied … [And then], having laid hold of the accumulated debris of [the other body's] inner organ (*antaḥkaraṇa*) with his own consciousness, the yogīn should then enter [that body with his own self], assaulting (ākramya) that body-capital from every side. He should quickly bring all that has been melted down and captured into his own self's place [i.e., his own body heart]. At that very moment, he [also] brings the [other body's] living self [into his own heart], through the yokings of seal and spells.[44]

[42] WHITE, D. G., *Sinister Yogīs* (USA: The University of Chicago Press, 2009), 161.

[43] GOUDRIAAN, T., *The Vīṇāśikhatantra* (India: Motilal Banarsidass, 1985), 39.

[44] WHITE, D. G., *Sinister Yogīs*, 163.

On a similar note, Kṣemarāja also summarizes a lost work entitled the *Tattvārthacintāmaṇi* (a text attributed to Kallaṭabhaṭṭa) saying that,

> The yogīn can reduce himself to the size of a globule[45] and through breath control enter into the body of another person. After remaining there for a period of one hundred *morae*, he then mounts an assault on the "city of eight" (*puryaṣṭakam*) with his own city of eight, by means of his breath, whose energy-based power has been protectively augmented.[46]

This practice also appears in the *Vīṇāśikhatantra*.

> The clever man, having meditated on his own [name's] bīja and that of the victim as well as on those of the four or five deities (?), as being present within the yogīc duct (iḍā?) in a state of intermingling, and having caused them to enter by the way of the yogīc duct into the victim's body, will by means of this practice bring the threefold world under his power.[47]

Given that three different sources describe this technique of performing subjugation via yoga, one can only assume that it was a reasonably widespread practice. To make it all the more sinister, a particularly powerful yogīn was also believed to be able to perform this on more than one individual at a time, and that by doing so he could burn off any negative karma accumulated from the practice of black magic at an expedited rate:

> According to Vyomaśiva, a yogīn could, by virtue of his power to take over multiple bodies simultaneously, use his fire of knowledge to burn off his accumulated karma at an accelerated pace. In another context, Vyomaśiva argued that the all-pervasive character of each individual self is the necessary precondition for a yogī's ability to inhabit multiple bodies simultaneously.[48]

45 *Gulika*.
46 WHITE, D. G., *Sinister Yogīs*, 163.
47 GOUDRIAAN, T., *The Vīṇāśikhatantra*, 115.
48 WHITE, D. G., *Sinister Yogīs*, 161.

Furthermore, White also suggests that the gnosis arising from the use of siddhi also accumulates rapidly because the use of siddhi allows direct perception of what is distant or hidden to humans normally.[49] This also implies that there is a distinction between magic, which does not offer direct perception—only knowledge of the result—and the use of siddhi where the perception of the event is direct.

The technique of psychically projecting oneself into the body of another (*parakāyāveśa*), is also linked to necromancy, and a similar technique can be implemented to 'reanimate' a corpse for occult purposes. As with different forms of necromancy in other cultures, this does not entail the physical resurrection of a corpse, but rather the use of spirits as intermediaries between the natural and supernatural realms. For example, siddhi was also believed to be obtainable with the help of a ghost (*preta*) evoked by a ritual involving a corpse.[50] Again, this form of practice falls exclusively into the realm of 'black magic' and the ritual use of impurity/transgression. The *Vīṇāśikhatantra* describes a necromantic rite thus:

> Human flesh with unhusked grains added to it, together with the milk of a black cow, this mixture he should sacrifice into the mouth of a corpse without delay until the ghost of the decreased rises and says to him: "What can I do?"
>
> One may then beg of him the possessions one desires, O Illustrious One, a magic pill, gold and a buried [treasure] or even a kingdom (if he happens to be an exiled prince);
>
> And methods to conquer even Indra; magic ointment for the feet (which enables one to fly through the air) or the elixir of life; [the ghost] presents him with only one of the mentioned goods before he leaves; not by another method.[51]

---

49 WHITE, D. G., *Sinister Yogīs*, 157.

50 GOUDRIAAN, T., *The Vīṇāśikhatantra*, 40.

51 Ibid., 117.

The *Mantramahodadhi of Mahidhara* also cites another rite which, despite not involving necromancy, still involves mortuary practices.

> 38-39. Now other Kālī Mantras are being mentioned. They are all bestowers of supernatural powers. Twice Māya-Twice Kūrca etc. are being explained in the commentary. The mantra thus arrived at is as follows:
>
> It has twenty-one syllables. The initiatory rites are as before "Om Hrīm Hrim Hūm Hūm Krīm Krīm Krim Dakṣiṇe Kālike Krīm Krīm Krīm Hūm Hūm Hrīm Hrīm."
>
> 40. The devotee shall seat himself on a corpse at the root of a Bilva tree or Vaṭa tree (Banyan) and repeat this mantra one *lakh* (1,00,000) times. He shall become the master of all supernatural powers.[52]

Necromantic or mortuary practices such as this also occur in other forms, and, according to Hugh Urban, Kāmākhyā persists in having a sinister reputation for its continued practice of the Tantric rite of śava sādhanā.[53] Fortunately, there is another procedure to acquire siddhi in the *Mantramahodadhi* which does not involve corpses, and, like the previous one, this is also associated with the Goddess Kālī:

> Now I shall mention the Mantras of Kālī that accord the supernatural powers of speech immediately. If they are properly propitiated, men obtain all their desired things in this world.
>
> (As explained in the commentary) the Mantra becomes a Twenty-two syllabled One as follows:
>
> "Krīm Krīm Krīm Hūm Hūm Hrīm Hrīm Dakṣiṇe Kālikā.
>
> Krim Krim Krim Hūm Hūm Hrim Hrim Svāhā."

[52] MAHIDHARA, trans. A Board of Scholars, *The Mantramahodadhi of Mahidhara*, 58.
[53] URBAN, H. B, *The Power of Tantra: Religion, Sexuality and the Politics of South Asian Studies*, 173.

> There is no necessity for the purification by means of Siddha and Sadhya procedures. Nor is there the necessity of taxing the mind too much or performing the *Purascaraṇa* (Initiatory Rites). This is the Queen of Mantras. By merely remembering this One gets the Eight Supernatural powers.
>
> The Sage of this Mantra is Bhairava, the meter is Uśṇik, the deity is Kālī, the Bijā is Māyā (i.e. Hrim) and śakti is *Dīrgha Varm* (i.e. Hūm). Intelligent men have said so.
>
> The *Aṅga Nyāsa* is to be performed with the initial Bīja along with the Six Long Vowels.[54]

****

Another occult practice which is linked to the Siddha doctrines is that of alchemy, which flourished in India from 900 CE to 1600 CE,[55] along with early scientific experiments with chemistry and sought to synchronize new discoveries in the natural world with spiritual beliefs. The most famous alchemical text in India is the eleventh-century *Rasārṇava,* which explicitly describes the acquisition of supernatural powers from the consumption of chemical products. Alchemy, via ingested chemical substances, aims at bodily transmutation, as is stated in the *Rasārṇava*:

> As in metal, so in the body. Mercury ought always to be employed in this way. When it penetrates a metal and the body, [mercury] behaves in the same fashion: first test [mercury] on a metal, then use it in the body.[56]

---

[54] MAHIDHARA, trans. A Board of Scholars, *The Mantramahodadhi of Mahidhara*, 54.

[55] HELLWIG, O., A Chronometric Approach to Indian Alchemical Literature in *Literary and Linguistic Computing*, Vol. 24, No. 4, (Germany: Freie Universitat, 2009), 374.

[56] WHITE, D. G., Mercury & Immortality: The Hindu Alchemical Tradition in ed. Cheak, A., *Alchemical Traditions* (Australia: Numen Books, 2013), pp. 218-219.

The consumption of mercury by an alchemist is known as *khecarī jāraṇa* (flight calcination) and is presumed to produce the ability of magical flight, just as the yogīs could via siddhi (*Rasārṇava* 11.104b-6, 12.337).[57] Moreover, the two different forms of esoteric practice appear to be linked, as the two supreme deities of the *Rasārṇava* (Rasabhairava and Rasāṅkuśī) are iconographically identical to the Tantric deities Svacchanda Bhairava and Bālā Tripurasundarī according to David Gordon White.[58] Śiva is also connected with the alchemical substance mercury which is described as *rudra-virya* the "semen of Rudra."[59] This association between alchemy and bodily secretions continues in *haṭha yogīc* teachings:

> The seminal fluid (mineral or human), transformed by a heat source located above, drips down to remain (held there by gravity) in the reversed upper chamber of the apparatus or, in the yogīc case, the cranial vault. This posture also evokes the *viparītakaraṇī* or 'reverse' practice of yoga, which Gorakhnāth praises in his *Gorakṣa Śataka* as a fool-proof method for retaining in one's head the precious nectar one has so carefully distilled from 'raw' semen.[60]

Furthermore, in another method,

> A classic haṭhayogīc technique, called the *jālamdhara bandha*, the 'lock of the net-bearer,' uses this network of channels to seal off the head as the bearer or recipient (*dhara*) of the nectar that is held up in the cranial vault. The haṭhayogīc 'Hermetic seal of Śambhu' (*śāmbhavī mudrā*) or 'Wizard apparatus' ([*vidyā*]

[57] WHITE, D. G., Mountains of Wisdom: On the Interface Between Siddha and Vidyādhara Cults and the Siddha Orders in Medieval India in *International Journal of Hindu Studies*, Vol. 1, 83.

[58] WHITE, D. G., Mercury & Immortality: The Hindu Alchemical Tradition in ed. Cheak, A., *Alchemical Traditions*, 227.

[59] TRELOAR, F. E., Ritual Objects Illustrating Indian Alchemy and Tantric Religious Practice in *Isis*, Vol. 58, No. 3 (USA: University of Chicago Press, 1967), 396.

[60] WHITE, D. G., Mountains of Wisdom: On the Interface Between Siddha and Vidyādhara Cults and the Siddha Orders in Medieval India in *International Journal of Hindu Studies, Vol.* 1, 80.

> *dh[a]ra* yantra) described in this verse is an upside-down version of the 'lock of the net-bearer': the two chambers of the alchemical apparatus are the head and torso of the yogīn; the mud-smeared layers of cloth stretched across their mouths the network of channels in the throat, and the nectar that is held in the head is the mercury that condenses on the incurred inner surface of the down turned upper chamber.[61]

Examples such as these demonstrate that there was a significant amount of overlap between scientific method and esoteric practice, which formed what is referred to as alchemy today. Moreover, the names of India's most famous alchemists include Nāgārjuna, Nandin, Carpaṭi, Manthāna Bhairava, and Svacchanda Bhairava, which correspond to the legendary founders of the Tantric traditions.[62] According to White the Kapalika school of Tantra were also considered to be experts in alchemy (*dhātuvāda*) and practiced the transmutation of metals.[63]

The alchemical operations found in Tantrism are marked by a predominant use of mica and sulphur which are related to the Devī, and mercury which originates from Śiva. The minerals, particularly mica, were used for transubstantiations of the body and the transmutation of the metals (*dehalohakara*).[64] Though we are in effect dealing with the same substances found within other branches of the alchemical tradition, one of the main differences that will be encountered is the obvious use of sexual imagery employed here. Mercury is equated with semen, and the following correlations are found to be related to the fluids of the Devī: sulphur (*gandhaka*/uterine blood), mica (*abhraka*/sexual emission), and red arsenic (*manaḥśilā*/uterine blood).

---

[61] WHITE, D. G., Mountains of Wisdom: On the Interface Between Siddha and Vidyādhara Cults and the Siddha Orders in Medieval India in *International Journal of Hindu Studies, Vol. 1*, 79.

[62] WHITE, D. G., Mercury & Immortality: The Hindu Alchemical Tradition in ed. Cheak, A., *Alchemical Traditions*, 228.

[63] DANIÉLOU, A., *While the Gods Play: Shaiva Oracles and Predictions on the Cycles of History and the Destiny of Mankind,* (USA: Inner Traditions International, 1987).

[64] RAY, M., Gems in Indian Alchemy in *Indian Journal of the History of Science* (India: Indian National Science Academy, 1991), 145.

However, although there are correspondences between alchemy and Tantra, they should not be perceived as identical, for it would be a grievous case of 'cultural appropriation' to refer to Tantra as an Indian form of alchemy, which would serve to objectify Tantrism as a mere extension of the Western esoteric corpus. Whilst Tantrism undoubtedly borrowed the terminology from early chemistry this is by no means a primary feature of Tantra, nor is alchemy an over-arching esoteric Tradition or an element of perennial philosophy. The presence of alchemical symbolism in esoteric traditions occurs because the elements in the periodic table are empirically observable via the natural laws of chemistry, which are the unifying principles at work. The fact that alchemy reached its peak simultaneously in different cultures suggests that it did so because of emerging scientific discoveries in the field of chemistry. These newly discovered chemical reactions appeared similar to magic, and therefore were of value to those with an interest in esoterica as well as science. This is particularly evident in the fact that the majority of alchemical lore found in Tantrism is deliberately presented as an alternative method for the acquisition of siddhi. As such, it is likely that alchemy developed as an alternative to older methods as part of a deliberate effort to incorporate the newly emergent study of chemistry into pre-existent spiritual traditions. Therefore, whilst alchemy is certainly an aspect which was overlaid onto the Tantric Tradition, it is by no means one of the most important, and simply overlays new terminology onto pre-existing practices.

***

At the beginning of this chapter we mentioned the basic distinction between benevolent and malevolent magic in India, along with references to the Six Acts, which, rather than being a set of specific prescribed rituals, are instead a standardized set of formula for the creation of magical rituals. The Six Acts, as the name implies, are composed of six different types of magic as is indicated by Mahidhara,

> 1-3. I shall now mention the Six types of (Rites) activities (Pursued by Devotees for Achieving Desired results). By proper application, they all bestow great powers and fulfillment of desires. They are (a) Śāntī, (b) Vaśyam, (c) Staṃbhanam, (d) Dveśam, (e) Uccāṭanam and (f) Māraṇam.[65]

The Six Acts are not only one of the most erudite ritual formulas ever designed, they can also be seen as extremely devastating in terms of application. Even if these rites were not always effective, one has to take into accord the psychological effect that would be produced from their performance. Despite this, even Tantrics such as Krishnananda devoted a good deal of attention to the Six Acts,[66] and a substantial amount of rituals in Tantric occult texts deal with either subjugation or the outright murder of enemies.

As unpleasant as these acts are, they still involve precise ritual guidelines and involve highly disciplined procedures which are not always cited within the text. It certainly would not be a stretch of the imagination to suggest that these techniques were performed by advanced practitioners within the Tantric Tradition. Not only do the Six Acts of magic all have specific correspondences concerning elements, days, yogīc postures, mantras, mudras, and breathing, they are also clearly constructed for people who understand these correspondences or, in other words, advanced magicians operating in the Tantric framework.

In regard to the Six Acts, it is necessary to revisit the topic of mantras yet again, this time with particular emphasis placed on their use in an exclusively magical environment. The structure of each mantra not only follows the rules which were established

---

65 MAHIDHARA, trans. A Board of Scholars, *The Mantramahodadhi of Mahidhara,* 570.

66 URBAN, H. B., The Power of the Impure: Transgression, Violence and Secrecy in Bengali Śakta Tantra and Modern Western Magic in *Numen*, Vol. 50 (Netherlands: Koninklijke Brill NV, 2003), 282.

previously, each type of magic follows a particular formula. Mantras are composed according to the following guidelines:

> Appeasement – The method is *granthana* (one letter of the mantra alternates with one letter of the spell's recipient's name).
>
> Subjugation – The method is *vidarbha* (two letters of the mantra alternate with one letter of the victim's name).
>
> Immobilization – The method is *samputa* (the mantra is repeated before and after the victim's name).
>
> Enmity – The method is *rodhanna* (the mantra is inserted at the beginning, middle, and end of the victim's name).
>
> Eradication – The method is *yoga* (the mantra appears at the end of the victim's name).
>
> Liquidation – The method is *pallava* (the mantra is followed by the victim's name).

Furthermore, the *Vīṇāśikhatantra* states that,

> During liquidation the syllables [are] in reverse order, ending and beginning (?) with hūṁ phaṭ. During the rituals of subjugation and of attraction, one should pronounce oṃ [before] and svāhā, respectively namas [after] the bījas.
>
> One should always sacrifice in this way, and the wise man should not omit any aspect of the ritual. The pronunciation of *namas* is taught for the end of the recitation, that of *svāhā* for the sacrifice.[67]

There are further derivatives of the formulas in the *Vīṇāśikhatantra* which customize the mantras even further, based on the desired end result. By way of example, for lesser acts of black magic which are merely vexatious but not particularly harmful, the structure is different from those whose purpose is purely destructive.

[67] GOUDRIAAN, T., *The Vīṇāśikhatantra*, 121. Comments by the translator.

a) For liquidation: within a *ma*. (The name and syllable are) written with yellow orpiment.

b) For silencing opponents: within a *sa* (293).

c) For attraction: within an *ā* (294f.)

d) For wealth: within an *e* (296ab).

e) For subjugation: within a *va* (296cd).

f) For various respectable objectives including final release: within the haṃsa (297).

g) For destruction of enemies: within a *bha* (298)

h) For liquidation: within (text: "at the end of") the word *phat*.

i) For dissension: within the *ja*.

j) For eradication of the enemy's family: at the end of *hūṃ phat*.

k) For "small" objectives (teasing or harming the enemy): within a *ya*.[68]

Another text provides a variation on the mantric formulas for the Six Acts in the following list, which possesses some similarity but not the same depth of complexity as the descriptions found in the *Vīṇāśikhatantra*.

Appeasement – *namaḥ*
Subjugation – *svāhā*
Immobilization – *vaṣaṭ*
Enmity – *vausat*
Eradication – *hum*
Liquidation – *phat*[69]

68 GOUDRIAAN, T., *The Vīṇāśikhatantra*, pp.42-43.

69 BÜHNEMANN, G., The Six Rites of Magic in ed. White, D. G, in *Tantra in Practice* (USA: Princeton University Press, 2000), 45.

The similarity between the formulas, such as the standard ending for liquidation and eradication suggests that the Six Acts did not develop in isolation and that different schools of Tantrism were in communication with each other. More importantly, it suggests that there was an original version of the Six Acts which was disseminated through the different branches, which would make it a very archaic technique indeed.

Not only do the endings themselves hold an innate purpose for magical operations, the mantras also have three genders: masculine, feminine, and neuter. This is cited in the *Mantramahodadhi*.

> 93-97. Mantras ending with Vaṣaṭ or Phaṭ come under the male category. Those that end with Vausat or Svāhā come under the female category. Mantras ending with Hum or Namaḥ come under the neuter category.
>
> In the rites of Vaśya, Uccāṭana, and Rodha (i.e. Staṃbhana) the mantras of the male category are the bestowers of benefits. In minor rites as well as those of dispelling sickness the mantras of the female category yield benefits quicker. In Abhicāra (black magic) the mantras of the neuter category are recommended.[70]

The reasoning for this distinction is explained by Bühnemann,

> Some authorities distinguish three sexes of mantra used in desire-orientated rites based upon the final syllable(s). Mantras ending in huṃ and/or phaṭ, the sound of breaking, are considered masculine; those ending in svāhā, the exclamation used for making an offering into the fire, are feminine; and those ending in namaḥ ('obeisance') are neuter. The ritual application for these mantras accords with the flow of breath (svara) in the three most important nāḍīs, piṇgalā, iḍā, and suṣumṇā. Masculine mantras are successfully employed in "cruel rites," like liquidation.[71]

[70] MAHIDHARA, trans. A Board of Scholars, *The Mantramahodadhi of Mahidhara*, 559.

[71] BÜHNEMANN, G., Selecting and Perfecting Mantras in Hindu Tantrism in *Bulletin of the School of Oriental and African Studies*, Vol. 54, No. 2 (UK: Cambridge University Press, 1991), pp. 304-305.

In addition to requirements for mantras, the *Mantramahodadhi* mentions nineteen items which are required to be prepared prior to commencing any practice of the Six Acts. This consists of:

(1) Deity

(2) The color of the deity

(3) Season

(4) The quarter of direction

(5) The day

(6) The Seat, Posture

(7) The Vinyāsas or special setting

(8) Maṇḍala (Zero)

(9) Mudrā (Gesture)

(10) Akṣara (Letter)

(11) Bhūtodaya (Rising of the Element)

(12) Samidhā (Sacrificial Twig)

(13) Rosary

(14) Fire

(15) Materials for Writing

(16) Sacrificial Pit (Kuṇḍa)

(17) Sruvā

(18) Sruk (these two are special ladles)

(19) Stylus[72]

---

72 MAHIDHARA, trans. A Board of Scholars, *The Mantramahodadhi of Mahidhara*, 570.

These requirements are listed to ensure that all components are compatible with the force being evoked, and the goal of the rite dictates what the mood should be.[73] One example of these prerequisites concerning compatibility can be found in the *mālā* beads (referred to as a 'rosary' in the list above), in which different types of beads and different numbers of beads are used for each type of magic. The number of mālā beads is usually 108 but the *Kulārṇava Tantra*,

> Mentions lengths of 15, 25, 27, 30 and 50, which are used for different purposes. For example, *japa* with 30 beads is used to obtain money, while one of fifteen beads is used in black magic.[74]

The *Kulārṇava Tantra* also cites different finger positions for using the mālā within magical rites. "By (using) the thumb (in counting) liberation is attained; the index finger destroys enemies; one should consider the middle finger as granting money; the ring finger (is useful) for rites of pacification, the little finger is said to be the finger (for the rites of) immobilization and attraction."[75] The color and material of the beads are also of importance:

Śāntī – pearl/white
Stambhana– yellow/gold
Uccāṭana – rudraksha, quartz, or red coral (depending on purpose)
Vaśīkaraṇa – red coral
Aakarshan – red coral
Māraṇa – rosary *jeeva potha.*[76]

Another important feature of the Six Acts is that prior to performing a ritual, one must obtain approval from the divine to

[73] These exact correspondences are in Appendix II.
[74] BÜHNEMANN, G., Selecting and Perfecting Mantras in Hindu Tantrism in *Bulletin of the School of Oriental and African Studies*, Vol. 54, No. 2, 302.
[75] Ibid., 302.
[76] SHUBHAKARAN, K. T., *Mystical Formulae: Mantras* (India: Sagar Publications, 2004), pp. 15-16. The term "jeeva potha" does not translate accurately in this context. For most spells in the Liquidation category bones or teeth are usually used.

enact it successfully. This is determined by oneiromancy, a form of augury which uses dreams to predict the future.

> [The practitioner] who wishes to perform the worship of a deity should first consider the future. Having taken a bath, performed the twilight [ritual] and so on, [and] having collected the lotus like feet of Hari, he should lie down on a bed of Kuśa [grass and] pray to the bull-bannered Śiva.
>
> "O Lord, Lord of the God of Gods, bearer of the Trident, who rides a bull! Announce, O Eternal One, the good and the bad, while I am asleep. Salutation to the Unborn, Three-eyed, Tawny, Great Souled One. Salutation to the handsome, omnipresent Lord of Dreams. Tell me the truth in the dream regarding all matters completely. O Great Lord, by your grace, I will accomplish success in the ritual."
>
> Having prayed to Śiva with these mantras, he should sleep calmly. In the morning he should tell the preceptor the dream he had at night. The connoisseur of the mantra should himself reflect on the [significance] of the dream [without the preceptor if he is unavailable].[77]

All of these requirements are complicated further by the Hindu belief in karma, for as one would expect, the use of magic is not exempt from the rule of cosmic law. In the case of Liquidation and other *maleficia*, the karmic blow-back would be high. Therefore, the Six Acts also cites ways to avoid this in the form of offering gifts to the Brahmin, and the more grievous the magical act, the more expensive it becomes to avoid accumulating inauspicious karma.

Not all Tantric magic uses the Six Acts as a foundation, however. There are numerous other forms of magic. Some of these are equally complex, and before even attempting to practice these rituals, one

[77] BÜHNEMANN, G., The Six Rites of Magic in ed. White, D. G, in *Tantra in Practice* (USA: Princeton University Press, 2000), 461.

would have to be able to raise *energy through all three of the nāḍī*, as each one is used for a different purpose:

> The iḍā is applicable for pacification and acquisition of goods, the piṇgalā [for] ritual killing and eradication of an opponent; and the suṣumṇā grants release, following the soul's course.
>
> When one meditates on [the God as] residing in the piṇgalā, one should imagine him to be red; in that case, one can execute acts such as liquidation and eradication.
>
> Concentrating on him as being within the amṛtā (the iḍā), one should meditate on him as being white as snow; then one will be able to realize pacification, acquisition, subjugation, and attraction.[78]

One important distinction in the *Vīṇāśikhatantra* which separates it from other Tantric texts is that it mentions the kandmūla cakra, which corresponds to the mūlādhāra cakra,[79] and that the main power center (granthi "knot") in the navel region contains a lotus in the midst of which is the object of the meditation (in a magical rite).[80] The process is described thus:

> The deity is again located within a subtle particle (kalā) striving upwards within a hollow tube in the pericarp of the lotus ... He rises through the yogīc ducts iḍā, piṇgalā, or suṣumṇā. The iḍā is present in the left part of the body, the piṇgalā in the right, and the suṣumṇā which creates and destroys, which as the text says, is in the middle. Raising the God through the iḍā is applicable for acts of protection, acquisition, and attraction (147a, 149c), through the piṇgalā, for acts of evil consequence, the suṣumṇā affords final release. Within the piṇgalā, the God is red, within the iḍā (amṛtā 149a) he is as white as snow.[81]

---

[78] GOUDRIAAN, T., *The Vīṇāśikhatantra*, 113.

[79] Ibid., 37.

[80] Ibid., pp. 37-38.

[81] Ibid., 38.

It is assumed that the reader will have some basic familiarity with the process of Tantric sādhanā, involving the iḍā, piṅgalā, and suṣumṇā channels within the body. It is through this system that kuṇḍalinī (representing both śakti and prakṛti) rises, channeled through the body of the yogīn. The serpent is, of course, almost exclusively representative of chthonic power within all traditions. Its simulated ascension towards the crown cakra in sādhanā is no less than an enactment of the heirogamous marriage of heaven (usually represented by birds) and earth (usually represented by a serpent). In this instance, the symbolism of the bird is conjoined with that of a snake in the form of a *haṃsa* (goose). Due to the serpentine shape of the bird's long neck, it is utilized as an emblem of the union of the telluric and uranic, in effect being a composite body of a snake coupled with the wings of a bird, which is an obvious analogy to celestial and the terrestrial power combined within a single creature. White describes the process thus:

> The identification of the haṃsa of the cranial vault with the subtlest of minerals, mercury, the suṣumṇā can also double as both a bird and a serpent; thus this channel is identified as well, with the kuṇḍalinī serpent, who, when awakened, pierces its opening at the base of the spinal column "like a key in the lock of a door-panel" to rush upwards to the cranial vault.[82]

In occult practices, the energy is not always raised via the central channel, and the channel that is used is dependent on the desired result of the spell, as indicated by the previous passages quoted from the *Vīṇāśikhatantra*.

***

The *Vīṇāśikhatantra* belongs to a group of early Śaiva Tantras and is an interesting text, even when compared to other Tantric works devoted to the occult. Firstly, it belongs to a period of very early

[82] WHITE, D. G., *The Alchemical Body: Siddha Traditions in Medieval India (*USA: The University of Chicago Press, 1996), 218.

Tantric literature and, secondly, it is regarded as the only surviving text of the "Left Current" (*vāmasrotas*, not to be confused with *vāmamārga*) in Śaiva Tantrism. Vāmasrotas texts are characterized by the rajas guṇa and include concepts such as siddhi. The other feature which makes the text unusual is that it refers to the deity Tumburu as a manifestation of Śiva.[83] Generally, Tumburu has a connection to royalty and is sometimes worshiped for magical purposes, such as in the 11th century Tantric *Śāradātilaka*, but is usually considered to be a Gandharva.[84] Tumburu is described in the *Vīṇāśikhatantra* as,

> A royal manifestation of Śiva who specializes in wielding protective supernatural powers directly applicable in real life, with an emphasis on healing (in this function he may be compared to the "Rois thaumaturges" of medieval France; the function is most prominent in the MMK, less so in the VST; besides, the healing is effected by means of potent herbs. His worship may lead to yogīc siddhis such as flying through the air, but this is not insisted upon.[85]

Though the comparison is unusual, the *Vīṇāśikhatantra* is not the only text to identify Tumburu with Śiva. In the *Yogavasisttha-Ramayana* (Nirvana-prakarana, I. xviii 23-26), we find the following:

> These things are spoken of the eight mātṛkās who were one day out for amusement. They are here characterized as the followers of the left current (vamasrotogata) and related to Rudra who is Tumburu i.e. the Tumburu aspect of Rudra (Tumburum-Rudram). The eight mātṛkās are here made to worship the two Gods Tumburu and Bhairava.[86]

---

[83] GOUDRIAAN, T., *The Vīṇāśikhatantra*, 18.

[84] Ibid., 20.

[85] Ibid., 57.

[86] BAGCHI, P. C., On Some Tantrik Texts Studied in Ancient Kambuja in *The Indian Historical Quarterly*, Vol. VI, No. 1 (India: J.C. Sarkhel, 1930), 103.

Bagchi has a theory concerning the mysterious identification of Tumburu with Śiva. He believes that Tumburu was introduced to Kambuja for establishing the mystic rites of Devaraja and had a connection with the Devaraja cult. Bagchi explains this connection to Śiva by stating that "Devaraja was a phallic representation (lingaraja) of Śiva—and we have already seen that Tumburu was an emanation of Śiva himself."[87]

The *Vīṇāśikhatantra* also contains another unique feature, which is deemed to be essential to practice but is curiously absent from the textual instructions, which suggests it was a technique transmitted directly from the Guru to disciples. This teaching is called 'The Doctrine of Time', and is reproduced here:

The Doctrine of Time

When the Eternal Śiva is realized, the practitioners attain success. But the real nature of Time should be fathomed; from this Real Nature, success is derived.

Hear, O Goddess, the supreme mystery, the embodiment within oneself of the Real Nature of Time. Having obtained knowledge of this, the possessors of mantras easily obtain success.

... For the benefit of the practitioners I shall explain the Haṃsa ("Goose") as it resides within the body in divisible and indivisible form.

The wise men recognize twenty-five categories of reality within the body: feet, organs of excretion and generation, hands and speech as the sense-organs [of activity]; ear, skin, eye, tongue and nose [as the sense-organs of awareness]; sound, concreteness, form, taste and smell [as their objects]; and mind, will ego-consciousness, the Unmanifest [primordial matter], and the Soul (puruṣa).

---

87 BAGCHI, P. C., On Some Tantrik Texts Studied in Ancient Kambuja in *The Indian Historical Quarterly*, Vol. VI, No. 1, 104.

> The Puruṣa, the substrate, and the superstructure, the indivisible Supreme Śiva—the body which consists of the six "covers", the twenty-five categories;
>
> The Fortress, provided with the ten breaths, pervaded by yogīc ducts; this body of three strands (lucidity, activity, and inertness) and inhabited by all sorts of deities;
>
> (this whole system) revolves like a wheel under His presence, just like the complete host of stars, the orbit of planets and celestial bodies,
>
> The whole of which, presided by the Pole Star, revolves although being immovable. In the same way, the Body of God which is identical with the complete host of Bījas.
>
> That which exists within the body has been told, O Goddess. A practiser who is aware of the due "season" and has ascertained the "time" and the "real nature" can begin a ritual act.[88]
>
> *(Further Application of the Secret Doctrine)*
>
> One can perform the rites of pacification and acquisition, of dissension and eradication, of subjugation and attraction if one has the esoteric knowledge of Time.[89]

It is quite clear from the terminology utilized that this teaching was used to homologize the microcosm of the body with that of the external macrocosm. It places the practitioner at the center, where time itself is absent, resulting in the phenomenon which is not referred to explicitly but is known as the 'cessation of breaths', where the illusion of time is stripped away from the subconscious bodily functions themselves. Experience of this state of 'timelessness' provides a direct perception of the transitory nature of time. The Doctrine of Time is not the only hidden teaching either, there is a great deal of secrecy around the construction of the rituals themselves, especially with regard to the creation of mantras.

---

88 GOUDRIAAN, T., *The Vīṇāśikhatantra*, pp. 121-123.

89 Ibid., 124.

The rites presented in this chapter are only brief examples selected from a wide array of magical rituals and therefore are not indicative of all the contents found in the occult aspects of Tantrism. Whether or not they are utilized, or substituted with other forms of preternatural abilities such as siddhi or alchemical concoctions, the complexity of technique is deliberately obfuscated for those who are outside of the Tradition, thus ensuring that these powers did not fall into the hands of others. Furthermore, many of these occult rituals are extremely transgressive, and most certainly not in the manner imagined by contemporary advocates of neo-Tantric 'sacred sex' or Thelemic 'sex magick'. Alchemy, siddha doctrines, and occult rites all present a hidden aspect of Tantrism which is very rarely observed, but ever present, for, in order to view the world as power, one must eventually be able to harness this power and 'ride the tiger' of the Kali Yuga.

APPENDIX I

OCCULT FORMULA

OCCULT FORMULA

APPEASEMENT

A mantra to predict the future via oneiromancy/dreams:

> Om Kshaam Ksheem Kshoom Kshyem Kshowm Ksha: Bhagavathi Sarva Nimithi Prakaashinee Vaagvaadini Ahiphenasya Maasam Dhuvaam Kam Kathaya Kathaya Swapnam Darshaya Darshaya Ta: Ta:[1]

SUBJUGATION

For Political Power

> 65-67. The devotee shall make the Idol of the Lord with the Neem tree (*Margosa*) on an auspicious day. He shall then perform the *Prāṇa Pratiśṭhā* (Installation of Vital Airs) and repeat the mantra in front of it. The deity, meditating on whom the devotee repeats mantra, becomes under his control like a slave.

[1] SHUBHAKARAN, K. T., *Mystical Formulae: Mantras* (India: Sagar Publications, 2004), 234.

The devotee brings water from the river and invokes it with mantra Twenty-seven (27) times. He then washes his face thereby and goes to the court of the King. The person whom he sees and the person by whom he is seen come under his control in an instant.

68. For the sake of getting people like Kings under one's control, one should adore Gaṇeśa with Four Thousand (4,000) Dhattura flowers repeating the mantra. [2]

For Sexual Attraction

Take the pāṃśulikā (ashes?) of a grown woman who died childless and write (a victim's) name (or the first syllable of his/her name) within the bījas of the Four Goddesses; draw a female figure by means of gorocanā and trample upon it with the left foot (for a man with the right foot), one will be able to attract a woman or a man from as far as twelve miles.[3]

For Control of Another

Having made an image of salt, the clever man should speak the mantras over it a hundred times,

And sacrifice [it in parts], beginning with the feet, dividing it into eight hundred parts, in due concentration, during the three crucial points of the day; he will reduce [the victim] to a state of unfailing subjugation.[4]

---

[2] MAHIDHARA, trans. A Board of Scholars, *The Mantramahodadhi of Mahidhara* (India: Sri Satguru Publications, 2014), 39.

[3] GOUDRIAAN, T., *The Vīṇāśikhatantra* (India: Motilal Banarsidass, 1985), 38.

[4] Ibid., 125.

ERRADICATION

To Remove an Enemy

33-35. The Leaf of the Palmyra is shaped like a human being and Vital Airs of the Enemy are instilled therein. It is then smeared with Tīkṣṇataila (Liquor) and inspired with the repetitions of the mantra (8,000) times. Then the devotee cuts it into fifty pieces. Five from the cremation ground are brought and kindled with the twigs of Unmatta tree and homas are performed therein. If the devotee continues to do thus for three days the enemy is either killed or deluded (rendered mad).[5]

ENMITY

To Control or Create Animosity

He should mediate on the moon's full orb within the palm of one's hand, combined with the Five Bījas. Any person whom he causes to behold this hand comes under his power by the mere sight of it, even those who were intent upon his death. Anybody he touches with his hand will henceforth be his slave.

In the same way, he might design the solar orb in his right hand; any people who he touches with it or to whom he shows it will become enemies to each other, even if they were friends.[6]

[5] MAHIDHARA, trans. A Board of Scholars, *The Mantramahodadhi of Mahidhara*, 435.
[6] GOUDRIAAN, T., *The Vīṇāśikhatantra*, 115.

LIQUIDATION (DEATH)

To Slay Another

Having mediated in the same way on the Five Bījas as present in the victim's heart lotus, one should perform worship as before; of the Suṣumṇā …

Then the possessor of mantras should assign the Missile of Destruction [and] Tumburu to the [victim's] head; the experienced yogīn should then surround the victim with [the bījas] of the Goddesses,

And again with that one (the Missile?) who was on the head, with the glow of a flaming fire; having further visualized him in his mind as fainted and out of his senses, lying on the ground,

He should bind him by the Elephant Goad fastened at the heart, and draw him towards himself. Then the performer should lay him on the ground, press him down and cause him to vomit blood.

After that, the group of Five Bījas should be placed in his (the victim's heart). Having extracted in the described way the victim's name (from the *prastāra*), surrounded by the Missile of Destruction,

In this way, bereft of protection, one should recite for eight thousand times [the group of bījas], surrounded by fiery circles;

Thus, by this ritual, in the described method, the victim comes to his end; death, coming at the end (?), will cause him to tremble.[7]

---

[7] GOUDRIAAN, T., *The Vīṇāśikhatantra* , 119.

APPENDIX II
TABLES OF CORRESPONDENCES

TABLES OF CORRESPONDENCES

GENDER OF MANTRIC ELEMENTS

Masculine	A, I, U, E, O, Aṁ, Ka, Ga, Cha, Ja, Ta, Da, Ta, Pa, Bas, Ha, Ha
Feminine	Ā, Ī, Ū, Ai, Au, Ah, Kha, Gha, Chha, Jha, Dha, Tha, Pha, Bha, Da, Sa
Neuter	Ri, Rī, Lṛi, Lṛī, ṅa, ña, Na, Ma, Ya, Ra, La, Va

ELEMENTAL TYPE

Ākāśa (Aether)	A, Ā, I
Air	Ī, U, Ū
Fire	Ri, Rī, Lṛī
Water	E, Ai, O
Earth	Au, Aṁ, Ah

MANTRIC COMPONENTS

Rshi	Author
Chhandas	Meter of Composition
Devatā	Deity of Mantra
Bījā	Seed of Mantra
Śakti	Power of Mantra
Kīlaka	Activating Principle
Viniyoga	Purpose of Mantra

FIVE SHOOTS (PAÑCHA-PALLAVA) OF MANTRA

Namah	Prostration
Svāhā	Offering
Vaushat	Protection
Hūm	Call to Banish
Phat	Breaking Down

STRUCTURE OF MANTRA ACCORDING TO OBJECTIVE[1]

Preceded by	*Closed by*	*Objective*
Oṁ	Namas	Wealth, Enjoyment
Hūṁ	Namas	Eradication of Evildoers
Oṁ	Svāhā	Wealth, Applicable in Sacrifice
Oṁ Raṁ	Oṁ	Awakening of Sleeping Mantra
Oṁ Ram	Phaṭ (in the middle)	Realization of Objectives
Hūṁ Haṁ	Haṁ Hūṁ	Awakening of Mantra
Hūṁ Raṁ Phaṭ	(beginning and middle)	Coercion of Mantra
Oṁ	Oṁ Namas	Complete Siddhi

[1] GOUDRIAAN, T., *The Vīṇāśikhatantra* (India: Motilal Banarsidass, 1985), 46.

SEED MANTRAS & DIRECTIONS OF THE MAHĀVIDYĀS

Deity	*Mantra*	*Direction*
Kālī	Krīm	North
Tārā	Aum	Above
Shoḍaśī	Aim Klīm Sauh	North East
Bhuvaneśvarī	Hrīm	West
Chhinnamastā	Hūm	East
Bhairavī	Hsraim Hsklrīm Hsrauh	Below
Dhūmāvati	Dhūm	South east
Bagalāmukhī	Hlrīm	South
Mātaṅgī	Aim, Hrīm Śrīm Aim Klīm sauh	North West
Kamalā	Śrim	South West

THE SIX ACTS[1]

Rite	*Appeasement*	*Subjugation*	*Immobilisation*	*Enmity*	*Eradication*	*Liquidation*
Devi	Rati	Vāṇī/Sarasvatī	Ramā	Jyeṣṭhā	Durgā	Kālī
Colour/Flower	White	Red	Yellow	Variegated	Dark	Grey
Season	Winter	Spring	Cool Season	Summer	Rainy	Autumn
Time	0 – 4 am	4 – 8 am	8-12 am	12-4 pm	4-8 pm	8 -12 pm
Directiion	North East	North	East	South West	NorthWest	South East
Day	2nd, 3rd, 5th and 7th of the bright half, coinciding with a Wednesday or Thursday	4th, 6th, 9th, and 13th of the bright half, coinciding with a Monday or Thursday	8th and 14th of the dark half, new moon day, and 1st day of the bright half, on a Sunday, Tuesday, or Saturday	8th, 9th, 10th, and 11th of (the bright half) coinciding with a Sunday, Tuesday, or Saturday	8th, 9th, 10th, and 11th of (the bright half), coinciding with a Friday or a Saturday	8th and 14th of the dark half, coinciding with a Saturday
Posture	Lotus	Svastika	Vikaṭa	Cockerel	Diamond	Bhadra
Animal Hide	Cow	Rhinoceros	Elephant	Jackal	Sheep	Buffalo
Element	Water	Fire	Earth	Ether	Wind	Fire
Shape	Half-Moon marked with two lotuse	Triangle with one or several svastika	Square with one or several thunderbolts	Circle	Circle with Six dots	Triangle with one of several svastikas
Breath	Lower part of the nostrils.	Upper part of the nostrils.	Ridge of the nose	Middle of the nostrils	Sideways	Upper of the nostrils
Closing Word	Namaḥ	Svāhā	Vaṣaṭ	Vauṣaṭ	Huṃ	Phaṭ
Arrangement	Granthana	Vidabrha	Saṃpuṭa	Rodhana	Yoga	Pallava

[1] BÜHNEMANN, G., The Six Rites of Magic in ed. White, D. G., *Tantra in Practice* (USA: Princeton University Press, 2000)

DYE/COLOUR

Kuṁkuma	Saffron, Crocus, Sativus
Rochanā	Bright Yellow Pigment
Rakta-Chandana	Red Sandal, Caesalpina Sappam
Jaṭāmāṅsi	Nardostachys
Lāksha	Red Dye
Katstūrī	Musk

MATERIALS FOR MANTRA

Material	*Time Effective*
Palm Leaf	Six Years
Bhūrja/Birch Leaf/Paper	Twelve Years
Copper	Six Years
Silver	Twenty Years
Gold	Effective for life.

SYMBOLISM OF YANTRAS[2]

Symbol	*Interpretation*
Bindu	Supreme Consciousness
Circle	Space, Never-ending Process
Radiating Circle	Expansion, Sun
Square	The Absolute, Earth
Rotated Square	Dynamic Earth Power, Femininity
Over-Lapping Squares	Balance, Preservation
Lines Within a Square	Earth, Static Condition
Rotated Square with Lines	Earth, Dynamic Condition
Over-lapping Triangles on Edge of Square	Earth, Static or Confined State
Square with Outer Loops	Dynamic & Restricted Earth Power
Upward Pointing Triangle	Male, Sun, Creation, Fire, Static
Downward Pointing Triangle	Water, Female, Moon, Dynamic
Right-Facing Triangle	Dynamic Male

[2] RAO, R. S. K., *The Yantra: Text with 32 Plates* (India: Sri Satguru Publications, 1988)

Left-Facing Triangle	Dynamic Female
Bisected Triangle	Equilibrium, Stasis
Interlocking Triangles with One Point Up	Equilibrium, Male-Female Union, Rising Aspiration, Stasis.
Interlocking Triangles	Dynamic, Male-Female Union
Lotus	Divine Manifestation & Expression
Cross	Movement Upwards
Inverted Cross	Movement Downwards
Straight Line	Unhindered Movement
Bindu with Crescent Beneath	Source, Dynamic Sound
Vertical, Horizontal, diagonal lines	Dynamic, Expansion, Points of Compass
Pentagram	Human Being, Magical Elements
8 Pointed Star	Infinity, Endless Cycle
Pentagon	Same as Pentagram
Hexagon	Same as Interlocking Triangles
Right-Facing Svastika	Male, Creative
Left-Facing Svastika	Female, Dynamic, Dissolution

PLANETARY HORĀ FOR CREATING YANTRAS[3]

Planet	*Purpose*
Jupiter	All yantras for good causes, love, affection, hamzad, cure of diseases etc.
Venus & Mercury	For talisman of love affairs, for opposite sex, Mohan, Vashi Karan, and Aakershan, and hamzad etc.
Sun	For love, affection, diseases, power, authority, favor from government, ministers, officials etc.
Saturn	Maran, Uchattan, etc.
Mars	Videshan, Maran, for enemies etc.
Moon	Love, affection, for opposite sex etc.

PLANETARY CORRESPONDENCES[4]

Deva	*Direction*	*Digit*	*Planet*
Sun	East	1	Sun
Bhuvneshwari	North	2	Moon
Ganpati	North East	3	Jupiter
Hanumanji	North	4	Uranus (Negative Sun)
Vishnu	West	5	Mercury
Kartvirya	South West	6	Venus
Kali	South	7	Neptune
Bairon	South West	8	Saturn
Bhairvi	West	9	Mars

3 CHAWDHRI, L. R., *Practicals of Yantras* (India: Sagar Publications, 1998), 8.
4 Ibid., 9.

INDEX

A

B

C

D

I

J

K

L

M

N

O

P

R

S

T

U

V

W

Y

Z

www.ingramcontent.com/pod-product-compliance
Lightning Source LLC
Chambersburg PA
CBHW022015090426
42739CB00006BA/140